To Debbie:
Thanks for being here.
Best wishes!

FROM THE
FARM HOUSE
TO THE
STATE HOUSE

THE LIFE AND TIMES OF
FULLER KIMBRELL

By Fuller Kimbrell

Fuller Kimbrell
10-1-01

T5-AGX-868

For additional copies contact:

Fuller Kimbrell
Tuscaloosa, Alabama
USA

ISBN: 0–9711636–0–X (Case)
      0–9711636–1–8 (Paper)

From the Farm House To The State House
The Life and Times of Fuller Kimbrell
Copyright© 2001 Fuller Kimbrell
Published by Word Way Press, Inc.
Tuscaloosa, Alabama
USA

ACKNOWLEDGMENTS

My thanks to Judy Beavers Sims, my grand niece, who edited the first draft, and for her advice.

My thanks to Dr. Roger J. Handley, my good friend from my home town, Berry, Alabama, for his valuable advice and the final editing.

My thanks to Hellen Long for the many hours she spent on the computer transcribing my tapes.

CONTENTS

FOREWORD

No individual in West Alabama has made a more significant contribution to the public good and the welfare of the people of this area than Fuller Kimbrell in his more than fifty years as a roving ambassador to state and federal authorities in Montgomery and Washington.

Mr. Kimbell's contributions and accomplishments are too many to name them all and his practice of being a part of the team and working privately, rather than to seek recognition for himself, obscures the influence he exerted in all areas of public life. It became and axiom during his period that if you could get Fuller Kimbrell on your side, that the task could be accomplished.

As a state senator, as a state finance director and as a friend of each state administration, beginning with the first Folsom administration in 1947, Kimbrell's footprints can be found in all significant aspects of public life.

In Education, remembering his one room, rural school beginnings, he always supported proposed continual annual appropriations, often leading the move toward increasing budgets. He was among the leaders in promoting the acquisition of lands upon which the University of Alabama at Birmingham was enlarged, the establishment and growth of the junior college and trade school program, and, numerous bond issues, which enabled capital improvements by the various educational institutions.

In Agriculture, remembering his roots as a farm boy, Mr. Kimbrell sought to support agricultural education through the establishment of a farm equipment experimental program and through services as a member of the State Agricultural Board.

In Public Improvements, remembering his youth spent on unpaved, dusty and muddy roads, Mr. Kimbrell through legislation or through his influence, strongly supported the farm-to-market road system, the paving of streets in small cities and towns and the establishment of a more modern state highway system.

In Public Welfare, remembering the poor and needy of West Alabama during the depression of the 30's and even before, Mr. Kimbrell supported the many and varied programs designated to alleviate the pain and suffering of the economically deprived and vigorously supported educational and vocational training and industrial development to meet these needs.

In Public Works and Improvements, Mr. Kimbrell, as a legislator and as finance director, strongly supported the establishment of the Tennessee-Tombigbee Waterway Authority and served on it board for sixteen (16) years. He was an early supporter and advocate of industrial development through the Alabama Development Office and the use of industrial development bonds and was involved in numerous industrial developments in the West Alabama area.

Mr. Kimbrell has been a servant to the people of West Alabama for fifty (50) years. He has freely given of his time, often at personal expense, to so many projects, both big and small, to so many groups and for so many purposes that it can truthfully be said that he has played a significant role in a half-century of progress and growth, not only in West Alabama, but throughout the State of Alabama.

Fullers's friends and long-time observers of the political scene in Alabama have long awaited his literary efforts in recounting all his experiences in this, his memoirs. May he be as adept in the writing of it as he is in the telling of it.

Louis P. Moore, Attorney
Holder, Moore, Lawrence, & Langley, P.C.
Fayette, Alabama 35555

ONE

FAMILY

Most all the Kimbrell family came to Alabama from Georgia. My father's great great uncles came to Fayette County and Walker County as early as 1820. My father's grandfather, Andrew Jackson Kimbrell, who would be my great grandfather, came to Fayette County in 1851.

I heard my father say that my great grandfather, Andrew Jackson, had three brothers who came from Jasper County, Georgia, over on the Oakmulga River. At that time the Kimbrell family had quite a real estate holding all along the Oakmulga River. I understand that land is all under water now because of a dam being built on the Oakmulga River by the Southern Company, which is now owner of Alabama Power Company and several other power companies. One of my father's great uncles settled in Elmore County, one settled in Walker County, and another one settled in Marengo County, and later migrated to Meridian, Mississippi. I visited with some of the Meridian cousins who were in the lumber business. One has a shopping center there.

I remember one of my father's cousins visiting from Elmore County. He was one of my father's distant cousins, named

Archie — a common name in the Kimbrell family. We were sitting by the fire one night, and I was listening to them talk. Archie said, "Asbury," (my father's name was William Asbury Kimbrell), "I'm going to tell you something. I know it won't get back to Elmore County. I was out hunting with an Indian. We stopped to drink at a spring. After drinking the cool clear water, we stood up. The Indian looked at me and said, 'gold under this spring and in there. But if you tell, you and I will both lose our lives. You lose your life, I lose my life.'"

Quite a few of the family migrated into Walker County, and one of them moved on up into Morgan County where there are still a number of Kimbrells. But the Kimbrells who came to Alabama to begin with settled in Fayette County. At one time starting on Highway 18, just over in Walker County and going almost due West, you could go fifteen miles without getting off of land owned by Kimbrell families. No family owned more than 300 acres.

My ancestors were not big land owners. They wanted a good home, a good dog, a good horse, a good gun, and a good garden. They were good providers. All the Kimbrells that I know about believed in having something to eat and believed in growing as much of it as they could. My father and all his brothers boasted that they never bought anything but sugar, flour, and coffee. Not many of them drank coffee. My father believed in providing for the family. He was one of the best providers that I have ever known in the way of growing what we needed at home. We had a large orchard with peach, pear, apple, and plum trees. At one time we had five hundred fruit trees. We dried apples and peaches, and made peach, and pear preserves, and apple jelly and plum jelly. We also had grapevines and made juice and jelly from the grapes. We made fig preserves from the trees in the yard. In addition, we had a year-round garden with a varity of vegetables in season.

Having so many fruit trees created a natural environment for honey bees, so it was not uncommon for my father to have as many as fifty or more bee gums, as we called them back then. The bee gums were made from hollow trees that we found on our farm. My father would take the gums which were about four feet in length and approximately 20 inches in diameter, clean them out inside, and insert crossbars so the bees would have something to fasten the honey to. He would rob (now called harvesting) the bees along in May. As I remember we had honey year-round. To add to this, we usually planted sorghum cane to make syrup, and we had our own syrup mill on the farm, and made our own syrup. We raised chickens, hogs, and cattle, and butchered them for our meat. I still remember how good the ham we cured tasted, especially when Mama cooked it for breakfast on Sunday mornings when we had company.

Since there was no form of refrigeration, quite often we would kill a calf, now referred to as veal, and loan one neighbor a hind quarter, another a fore quarter, and another either a hind or fore quarter. Probably a month later one of these neighbors would kill a calf, and pay us back with like quarters. This would continue among your neighbors until you had received back the three quarters that you had loaned out. By doing this we could have fresh veal more often. Since we had no refrigeration to keep the meat fresh longer, my mother learned to cook and serve the meat in many different ways.

I've said before, the Kimbrell family were small land owners in Alabama. I don't remember that any Kimbrell had a slave. I've never heard of any black people who spelled their name Kimbrell. Evidently, none of my people in Alabama ever had a slave. They were farmers, horse traders, hunters, and fishermen. They were all good providers and had clean homes, not real fine homes, but good nice homes. I remember my father telling about how they hauled lumber all the way up above Jasper to have it planed to build the house my grandfather lived in. But they went right on to the Civil War just the same as if they had a reason to fight. Other than that, they were good citizens and loyal Americans. They loved their state. I've said many times that if my ancestors had been in charge they would have traded with the Yankees and we would not have had the Civil War.

Grandpa Rogers (father of my grandmother, Elizabeth Kimbrell) had five boys and all five fought in the Civil War. One got killed in the war and one died pretty soon after he got back from the Civil War. My grandfather William Marion Kimbrell also fought in the Civil War, as well as two of his brothers Tom and George.

Grandpa Kimbrell had the measles when he was in Mobile, but he survived them. I remember my father telling about him walking all the way from Mobile to the Battle of Murfreesboro, Tennessee. A sad thing was they came within fifty miles of home, but he was not able to go by home, which was two miles north of Berry, Alabama, where his father lived at that time.

My paternal grandfather, William Marion Kimbrell, married Elizabeth Drake Rogers. The Rogers had some connections to the Drakes — Sir Francis Drake. My sister, Mamie Zora, climbed the family tree plumb back to England. She said she got us back to Sir Francis Drake, an English Admiral who later turned pirate. "That was the reason some of the boys were so mean. We took after Sir Francis Drake," she jokingly said. HA!

The Rogers were very humble, very clean people. Their morals were above reproach. Grandma Kimbrell's father, Richard Hampton Rogers was a Methodist preacher. He rode his horse for miles around the county and organized churches. Grandma's brother, John Rogers, was also a Methodist preacher. My great grandfather Rogers first settled in Tuscaloosa County, right near what is now New Lexington. He married a lady named Olive who lived in the area close to what is now Pleasant Hill Baptist Church. He later moved up into the northern part of Fayette County just off of Highway 18 adjoining the Walker County line. He had quite a large farm there. I remember when I was small my older brothers would go to Grandpa Rogers' place and get sacks of apples. He had a fine apple orchard.

My mother, Patience Evergreen Kemp, was born and raised in Tuscaloosa near Jones Mill, which was on Binion Creek and is now a part of Lake Tuscaloosa where Alabama Highway 43 crosses. The Joneses had a grist mill and ground corn for people. My mother's grandfather had a small farm there. She had two uncles who fought in the Civil War. Both of them came back.

I do think my great grandfather Kemp had three slaves at one time, but it is recorded he only had two — a woman and a fourteen year old boy. Great Grandpa Kemp had died earlier. Two of his sons — my grandfather's brothers, John and Tom — later came to Fayette. One was in the blacksmith business, but I don't know what business the other one was in. I just don't know much about them and very little about their family.

When I can first remember, my grandfather was a watch maker and had a jewelry store in Tuscaloosa. I remember Papa taking Mama and us six younger children to visit him when I was six or seven years old. At that time, my father was growing wheat to make our own flour and shorts to feed the little pigs, and he was going to take the wheat to Holt to have it milled. We went down from three miles north of Berry to Northport in the wagon. My mother had fixed a big basket of food containing fried chicken, ham, biscuits, fresh vegetables from our garden, and apples from our orchard. We stopped down at what is Northside now. A turpentine still was located nearby — I remember that very well from the strong odor, and there was a great sheet of rosin spread on the ground. We stopped and put our lunch out on the back of the wagon and ate. We took water, no ice water, just water. I believe there was a well close by where we got some cooler water.

My grandfather lived in Northport just about a block off of what is now Bridge Avenue, in a little brown house. It took us all day to get to his house. We spent two days and nights with him. The first morning my father got up and took the wheat to Holt where there was a flour mill. When he came back, they were having a county-wide singing and dinner on the ground in the basement of the courthouse. We went and I really enjoyed it. There was so much food, and it was so good, I ate too much and made myself sick. The next day my father went to Holt and picked up the flour. The fourth day we came home. I remember quite well, there weren't any bridges except the bridge across North River below Berry, and across the river again somewhere above Samantha. We crossed the river twice on a bridge. But we crossed several branches, and creeks — we waded across. All of us kids would jump off the wagon and wade along behind barefooted. I think it was four days we were gone from home. Of course, there were older brothers back home to take care of things while we were gone.

My grandfather Kemp was a very nice gentleman. My mother's mother died when her youngest brother was born. My mother was only twelve years old. Being the oldest girl at that time and the second oldest child, she acted as mother to all her brothers and sisters. There were eight children — four girls and four boys. Incidentally, two of the boys and all four of the girls lived to be above ninety-five years old, my mother lived to be ninety-nine, and my Grandfather Kemp lived to be ninety-five. He took good care of himself. He was very clean. He never went to a nursing home. He was married again to a very fine lady who was much younger, and they lived at home until he passed away.

But she too, came from a family that were good providers. Grandfather Kemp was a good provider and everything had to be done just right, perhaps because he was a watch maker. I can remember when my father would repair something he would say, "That will do," or "that's about right." But my mother would say, "Well, Pa always said that when you fix a clock about right, then it stops. The clock stops when it's about right." She would tell my father, "It needs to be exactly right."

My mother's family also were devout Christians and church going people. She was twenty-five years old when she married my father; he had eight living children. She took care of her own brothers and sisters until they were old enough to take care of themselves. She was accustomed to doing everything just right in the house and to taking care of children. With all of her duties as a wife and mother, she still made enough time to do community service.

My father was ordained to preach pretty soon after he married my mother. He followed in the footsteps of Grandpa Rogers whose family were people who did a lot of community service, helped with the sick, and organized churches. My father organized a lot of churches and Sunday schools. I went with him several times to help organize Sunday schools at little churches several miles away from home. He also taught school in the Fayette County system. My sister, Zelda, decoupaged his teachers' certificates and gave them to me. I still have them.

As I look back on my younger days, my father was a real inspiration and had a strong influence on our family. Since I can first remember, my father had been most active in building new churches. He was a Baptist preacher at that time. He thought nothing of riding ten to fifteen miles over the weekend to preach or organize another church. What I mean by an inspiration is that he lived what he preached. He taught all of us children, and instilled in us a desire to try to do something for our community and make it better. I guess seeing how eager my father was to organize churches and do community service, and my mother doing the same thing — making sure that we went to church every Sunday and that we sat on the front seat, and seeing that we knew our Sunday school lessons, and taking part in community affairs and helping the needy — taught me the importance of serving my community.

When I started school, my mother saw that each one of us children — from the youngest to the oldest — had studied our lessons and were able to recite. The results were that all of Papa's children made good grades at school, but none of us were valdictorians. My sister, Attie Belle, was salutatorian when she finished high school. Most of the time we were exempted from final exams, but I was always exempted in mathematics, history, and physics. I can't brag about my spelling or English, but I got by.

I can remember my first year in school. You often hear of the one-room school house. I started to school in a one-room school house, but the second year I was in school they made it into a two- room school house. Back then most folks would buy white duck cloth and make great big pick sacks to put cotton in as they picked it. After they got through picking cotton, some of the parents would unravel the seams of the pick sacks, and sew them together to make curtains. A heavy wire was stretched across the middle of the school room to hang the pick sack curtain, thus making a two room school house.

I started in the second grade, as did all my brothers and sisters. The reason was that most of the time we lived right next door to the school house, or two doors from the school house, and the teacher boarded with us. Not only that, but I had older brothers and sisters who would read to us younger children, and help us to write and spell. Also, they helped us with our lessons, and sometimes taught us our lessons at night. My mother only went to school for about six months. But she never failed to see that all of us had learned our lessons, and could recite them, so we could make passing grades at school. I was number eleven in a family of fourteen. Seeing how active my father and mother were in community service instilled in me the importance of doing something to make my community a better place to live, and I felt it would be good for me to do the same when I came of age.

When I finished high school, I left home and went to Indiana to find work. Eventually, I moved back home from Indiana and took over the farm. I saw that the community needed a younger leader. My father was close to seventy years old, or maybe seventy already, and my mother was getting some age on her. They were not able to continue their leadership roles. From the time I was twelve years old, I taught a Sunday school class, and continued to do so until I left home. When I returned home from Indiana, I not only taught a Sunday school class, but I was also the superintendent of Sunday school for a little while, and kind of a leader of the young folks in the community. We had a singing every Sunday night at the little church. It gave us something to do. We had no telephones, and certainly no radios or televisions, so it was something for the young people to do.

After I married Reba, I continued to do that.

I remember hearing my father say to someone one time that Jesus told his disciples, "If anyone among you would be great, let him serve." This was his interpretation of the King James' version of the Holy Bible, St. Matthew 20:27, "And whosoever will be chief among you, let him be your servant." And I thought how diligently and faithfully my father and mother served the community and helped the people.

My father had nine mules and ten boys. When I bought the farm from my father it was still a nine mule farm. The boys were not all at home at the time, and of those at home some were not big enough to plow. I remember one specific time that Marion Harbin's daughter died. Because of her illness Marion (our neighbor) had to lose work during crop time for quite a while. Papa told two of my older brothers, "I want you to go plow today for Marion Harbin. He is behind with his work." It wasn't too far away. They loaded up the plows and hooked up the mules to the wagon. They caught him up with his plowing. We did things like that quite often. Another time we went to another neighbor's place when he had sickness in the family, and helped chop out his cotton. I noticed the benefit that it was to the community and what a pleasure it was to my father and mother to help.

Knowing what an interest my father had always taken in politics influenced me later in life. In 1950, I ran for the State Democratic Executive Committee and was elected. I had enjoyed my experience in politics and had been politically inclined at an early age because my father, Reverend William Asbury Kimbrell, was the first Democratic committeeman for Beat 20 in Fayette County. He was the oldest son. My oldest brother, Arthur, was the next Beat 20 committeman, and his oldest son, Piercie, followed him as committeeman in Beat 20. Now Piercie's oldest son, Byron, is committeeman for Beat 20. Committeemen for Beat 20 in Fayette County have been in my father's family for four generations. Beat committeemen usually serve as returning officers.

Back then when there were no radios, telephones, or television, people who were running for county-wide or state-wide offices would go see the beat committeeman. The candidates would tell my father, or whoever was in office, what their plans were, and what they hoped to accomplish. Quite a number of times, I remember statewide candidates would spend the night at our house — which meant some of us children would sleep on a pallet on the floor, or double up, or have three in a bed. On Sunday morning everybody went to church. After church, people would stand around to visit and talk. I remember quite often I heard my father say, "Candidate So and So spent the night with me Tuesday night or Thursday night (whichever was the case) and he is running for tax assessor or he is running for probate judge, or whatever. He impressed me as being a good, honest and honorable man. I think he will make us a good tax assessor, or probate judge (or whatever)."

One time Ras Jones, who was running for tax assessor, came to our house. He was in his horse drawn buggy. We put his horse up and fed it, then he came in the house and Mama fed him. He spent the night. That was one of the times I remember best about my father saying, "He would make a good tax assessor."

Later, I remember Senator John Bankhead spent the night with us. He was running for U.S. Senate at that time. I also remember when Congressman Will Bankhead, the Speaker of the U. S. House of Representatives, stopped in front of my father's house. He was in a buggy and had a driver. He had some clothes in the back of the buggy. He visited with my father for a while and then went down to spend the night with Ando Simpson and his wife, Ruth (my sister). Congressman Bankhead had been one of our leading representatives for the whole United States. He was the only man from Alabama who was ever chairman of the Rules Committee, although later Carl Elliott served on the Rules Committee.

The only thing candidates campaigning needed then was a place that somebody would feed their horse, a place to sleep occasionally, and a place to get a meal. No money was spent for campaigning. That was the politics then.

As I began to get more experienced, and more acquainted with Alabama, Fayette, Lamar, and Walker Counties, and see the needs of the people, I realized that I really wanted to be of service to my community, my county, my state and my country. I'll tell of those activities later on. I am really proud of what I was able to accomplish as a public servant.

I think back to the leadership of my father and one of his first cousins, Cousin Riley Kimbrell, and Gene Hudson, who was a large farmer in that community. When they decided to build the new school house, which would still be next door to us, but on the other side of our home, I was big enough that I could carry lumber and tote shingles up to the carpenters, and nearly everyone of us boys went there and worked. But the county had not appropriated enough money to build the school house, so the community had to raise some money. My father, Cousin Riley Kimbrell, and Gene Hudson decided to put in $280. I remember my mother said, "Asbury, that is just so much money. I don't know how we can afford it."

My father said, "I can think of no better investment than to help educate our children and our neighbors' children, who our children will be living among and working with the rest of their lives. That makes a better community and a better country for us to live in."

Although I finished high school in June 1927, I did not accept my diploma so I could go back in the fall and play football. I was captain and quarterback of the football team. I completed high school in three years. At that time there were only eleven grades.

When I finished high school in 1927 the Great Depression was just about to begin. So many people had no other opportunity than to grow food and fiber on their farms for survival, because they didn't have an opportunity to go on to college or do anything else. The same was true for me as well as for all my brothers and sisters. There were no jobs. Even if it had been good times, you could only work in the mines, make cross ties to go under the railroads, or get a job clerking in a store, which I did.

Listening to my father's and mother's encouragement to read

has had a lasting effect on me. My father read to us, my older brothers and sisters read to us. We were constantly encouraged to read. My mother would say, "Get your lesson up. Get an education so you won't have to work so hard." It has worked out pretty good because most of us made our living with our tongues — all ten of us boys did. There were two accountants and one barber, and the others were either store clerks or business managers, or salesmen. My four sisters married husbands who were good providers.

The real care and leadership in our community had positive effects on many of the students who attended that two-room school house. Arthur Fowler, the principal of the school, went to Birmingham as head of U. S. Customs. Powell Hamner, another student who attended that school, became sheriff of Walker County. Later, he was a big help in my campaign for the senate. My brother, Orison, who was just older than me, became pastor of the First Baptist Church in Hollywood, Florida — a very large church with 1200 members. My brother, Gordon, was top supervisor for Hill Grocery Company. Henry Hudson, Gene Hudson's son, was a highway patrolman.

Cecil Simpson, another student of that school, was director of the WPA in Walker County and head of the Social Security office in Birmingham, which covered the whole state. He came to the legislature when I was in the senate and asked for copies of the bills affecting Social Security. Of course, one of the ways the clerk of the senate had to make extra money was to charge for copies of those bills. Cecil had no funds to pay for copies, so he asked me to get them for him. I would have my clerk to go upstairs and get copies of whatever bills he wanted. That favor for Cecil Simpson turned out to be a wonderful thing for my friends, and people that called on me for help. I remember one lady who didn't quite have her social security worked out, as she lacked a little being old enough to draw. She was a telephone operator when the operators wore head phones. She developed ear trouble, so she had to retire. She couldn't live on her state retirement. Her daughter came to me and asked me if I could help to get her social security. I called Cecil Simpson and told him her story. Cecil said, "Give me her social security number, her name, and address." After a short while he called me back and said, "Fuller, she will get her check in the mail within the next three days." That worked for several other people who needed a little help to get the benefits they had earned.

Of course, I was also a student of the little two-room schoolhouse. I was later a state senator representing Fayette, Lamar, and Walker Counties—the fourth largest senatorial district in the Alabama. Among the thirty-five senators there were nineteen lawyers, and I was the only one who did not have a college degree. I was also state finance director in Governor "Big Jim" Folsom's second administration, and was elected to the State Democratic Committee for thirty-five years. Also, I was a successful businessman.

Those are the things that I go back and think about. When the opportunity did come to me, I felt like I was willing and able to do a child's part.

TWO

DURING THE DEPRESSION/ DEPRESSION JOBS

I n 1927 the Depression was coming on, there were no jobs and no hope for work except to stay on the farm. In October, my brother, Roy, who worked as the time keeper for Aldridge Mines (owned by A. B. Aldridge, the President of Alabama Power Company) called and told me there was a job at Gorgas in the Southeastern Fuel Mining Company commissary, which was owned by Alabama Power Company. I left home immediately and took the job.

There was a little more to it than that, because the job was really for a delivery boy. Two other clerks who worked in the commissary and I would go out every morning to the mining camps, take orders—mostly for groceries—return to the commissary, and fill the orders. Then I would go make deliveries in the afternoon.

Most of the people we took orders from lived in small houses usually two or three rooms on the side of a hill. The houses were board houses and had no overhead ceiling, and were not sealed. Some had fire places, but most were heated with coal burning heaters. None of the houses had inside plumbing. A hydrant with a spigot out in front of the house was their water supply.

One customer, John Gent, had the contract to furnish motor ties, which the mine car rails were laid on for the cars to go down in the mines to haul the coal out. He worked quite a few people and he had brought in a lot of his kinfolks from around the area. They boarded with him in his house, which was typical of the above houses, only larger. Therefore he bought a lot of groceries. His wife was a strong, healthy lady and did all the cooking. She called in all the orders to be delivered. Mrs. Gent had ordered a big order including lard, which then came in fifty pound cans, and also in four and eight pound buckets. She had ordered a fifty pound can of lard. It had rained all day. Their house was up on a hill. There was no such thing as grass lawns, and most of the houses were on a hill steep enough that all the trash washed off the yard when it rained, anyway. Well, when I went to deliver the lard, I was walking up that red muddy hill to the house — I usually delivered at the back door. Going around to the back door I slid and my feet slipped out from under me, and that fifty pound can of lard I had sitting upon my shoulder and I went down. About a third of the lard poured out on the ground. I scooped up as much as I could, being sure I didn't pick up any red mud. I straightened it up, and took it on to the back door.

"Mrs. Gent. Come to the door," I called. She came to the door and I said, "I fell, and messed up this can of lard something awful. I'll go bring you another one or bring you one tomorrow afternoon." She said, "No, no don't worry about it. We will just use that. It is good enough. Just so you got all the dirt out of it."

I said, "Well, there isn't any dirt in this. I left that part that went in the dirt on the ground." I was really relieved that she took it so nice.

A few days before the lard incident, another interesting incident happened which involved a black lady school teacher. She tried so hard to use real proper English. The road turned a sharp corner around the old store at Gorgas, and you couldn't see a car coming. Coming around one day I ran into a lady – I was in the Chevrolet truck I drove to deliver – and bumped into her car. She pulled off to the side of the road, and I got out and talked to her. It didn't hurt her, or damage her car – it was far enough along that a little damage would not have made that much difference. She was perfectly happy and drove off. The next morning I went by the teacher's to get her order. In her very precise manner of speaking, she asked, "Oh, Mr. Kimbrell, did you and a lady collide behind the old store yesterday?"

I thought a minute, and said, "Yes, I did." I had to think a minute what "collide" meant. I truly enjoyed the job.

An interesting thing was that I slept in the commissary up in the balcony on a stack of mattresses piled four or five mattresses higher than a regular bed. I slept on top of all those mattresses. I didn't know until later that they put me there because they were worried about thieves breaking into the commissary. With the depression coming on, other mines were not working regularly. Of course, the Southeast Fuel Co. owned by Alabama Power Company, and the Aldridge Mines owned by A. B. Aldridge, the President of Alabama Power Company, worked steadily producing coal to operate the steam plant. The power company used its coal and that of Aldridge Mine.

One time one of the clerks, Grady Perry, was waiting on some ladies, and he pulled out boxes from underneath the shelves and saw where someone had bored holes all around so all they had to do was knock that section out and come into the Commissary. That night they set it up so that I would come in after I ate supper and go up to bed — except I wouldn't go to bed.

The sheriff and one other fellow were sitting up in the balcony with double-barrelled, sawed-off shotguns thinking the person would knock the hole out and come into the commissary that night. They stayed until about 1:00 A. M. and decided no one was coming so they went on home, and I was left alone.

I sat up for quite a while, and after they had been gone about an hour, I heard something break and make a lot of noise downstairs. I grabbed my shotgun ready to shoot at whatever put his head up through the hole and I found out it was a cat that had knocked a box off the counter, I was so excited I would have shot whoever stuck his head up without even talking to him. I put my gun aside and went to bed. Nobody broke in that night. The store manager had the carpenter come in the next day and fix the hole.

I enjoyed working at the commissary. The mine foreman, Lloyd Garrison, took me down into the mines one Sunday morning. I enjoyed the cooler temperature, but it wasn't a place I would like to work. They didn't work on Sunday except to clean up. That was the only time I ever went down into a mine.

To go to Gorgas from Berry, you caught the train and rode to America Junction, which was about sixty miles from home, just beyond Parrish on the Southern Railroad that ran from

Birmingham to Columbus, Mississippi. It was too far to go home every week, but I went home about once a month. Woodie Woods, who drove a taxi and picked up passengers at the Gorgas Power Plant, came up by the Southeastern Commissary, then through the adjoining town of Good Springs, and took his passengers to the train. I could ride for about fifty cents one way. If I remember right, the train fare from America Junction to Berry round trip was less than a dollar.

Before I went home the first time, I believe it was a month until I got a pay day. My salary was ninety dollars a month, and — coming right off the farm — that was really a lot of money. I didn't have to pay rent, and I took my meals with Mr. and Mrs. Craig, a clerk in the store and his wife, for thirty dollars a month. That left me sixty dollars. The second month I was there Mr. and Mrs. Craig and I went to Jasper to Hayes, a real fine men's store, and I bought myself a new suit, an overcoat, new shoes, shirt and tie.

When I went home, I was really dressed. Papa commented, "Fuller, you are so dressed up. The girls are going to skin their noses peeping around the corner at you."

When I went home, I rode the train, which arrived in Berry about ten o'clock Sunday morning. I walked two and a half miles home to my mother's and father's house from the Berry railroad station, getting there a little after ten. Then I could get to church in time for preaching which started at eleven.

Mama always had a good Sunday dinner. We would eat and visit, then I would walk back to the depot in time to catch the four o'clock afternoon train going back to America Junction and return to Gorgas by six o'clock that evening. Usually, I would get back to the depot early hoping Reba Shook, my high school sweetheart and later my wife, would be there to visit with me, and she always was.

An interesting thing: The first Sunday after I started to work at Gorgas, I went to the Good Springs Baptist Church, having been a Baptist all my life, and the son of a Baptist preacher. When I walked in, a very gracious lady, Mrs. Price, saw that I was a stranger and came to me and said, "We have people about your age in class right over here," and took me over. I introduced myself and sat down on the second bench.

All of a sudden they realized they didn't have a Sunday school teacher. One of the young ladies that I became very fascinated with later said, "Maybe the visitor will teach the Sunday school class."

Everyone said, "Yes, come on and teach it."

I said, "Well, I haven't studied the lesson, but I will try." So I got up and taught the Sunday school class. From then on, when I didn't go home on Sunday, I would always go back to church there. I taught the Sunday school class quite often, but not regularly.

I remember the first Sunday night after preaching when I started home the lady who invited me to teach the Sunday school class was standing near the door, and I said, "I would like to walk you home." She smiled and said, "That will be fine." So I walked her home. That was the start of a close, lasting relationship with Miss Larue Boyer. Larue and her husband, Addison Brobst, now live in Jasper. Occasionally, I take them out to lunch.

With the depression, things were getting bad. The coal company had been selling some coal other than to the power company, but they lost those contracts. Then they decided to sell the commissary to Lee Rogers' Tire Company in Birmingham, which had bought several other coal companies' commissaries. They immediately laid off almost all of the employees. I went home July 4th, 1929 and when I returned on the 5th, I was told that I wouldn't have a job after that week. I went back home, helped my father and brothers finish the crop, and stayed at home to help gather it.

While I was home helping my father and brothers finish and gather the crop, everytime I could get enough money I would go back to Good Springs to see Larue. Her sister Adelaid's boy friend, Fred Odom, and his father were cutting timber on their land on Loss Creek. Fred arranged for us to do some scaling of logs and rafting them for Taylor Lumber Company fifteen or twenty miles down the Warrior River. I lived with them, and we would go down through the hills to back water in his old Dodge car with small tires and high wheels. He would scale logs from one track and I would scale logs from another. The company hired loggers to bring the logs to the river where we were scaling and then rolling the logs into the river. People were out with poles and they would nail the logs together with big spikes. A little tow boat would pull the rafts down to Taylor's Lumber Company.

I scaled logs for thirty or forty days that fall. That let me be close to my girl friend, Larue. We would scale logs all day. At night, Larue and I would attend some activity in the school or the community. The job played out when bad weather came.

I went back home and, after we got the crop gathered, my brother-in-law, Ando Simpson, gave me a job driving a truck at a dollar and a half a day. Ando was county commissioner and had been for a long time (in fact, he was elected five terms), and was married to my older sister, Ruth.

Beginning January 1, 1930, there was not going to be any road work until spring because the county had no money. In fact, they were already paying the help with script instead of cash. Script was a piece of paper saying they would pay you when they got the money. Local businesses would take script in payment and give you back the balance in cash. Just before the holidays, Ando arranged for me to buy a new suit of clothes, shirt, tie and shoes from Hodges Department store in Fayette, which was the most outstanding department store in West Alabama in a small town. So I did and paid with script. They gave me back thirty dollars in cash, the balance of the script.

I decided I would go to Chicago. My brother, Hubert, had gone to Chicago earlier, married a girl from Valpraiso, Indiana, and was living there. January 6, 1930, I went to Berry depot and bought a ticket for twenty-three dollars and caught the train to Chicago. The next morning when I arrived in Chicago, I got off at the Illinois-Central Railroad depot. I looked around and saw all those trains going overhead. I saw all the cars and people, and I was scared to death. I went to the depot agent and said, "I'm a country boy from Alabama. This is not for me, and I don't have enough money to buy a ticket back home. And I don't want to go back home."

"Have you got five dollars?" he asked.

"Yes," I said.

He said, "Give me the five dollars. If I were you, I would go to LaPorte, Indiana. That is the finest city in the middle west." I gave him five dollars. He gave me back two dollars and some change and a ticket to LaPorte, and said, "Get on that train right there. It's starting to leave now." I jumped on the train.

I landed in LaPorte January 7, 1930. When I got off the train at LaPorte I didn't know what to do. I had one little suit case. I saw a man that looked like a railroad yardman, I spoke to him and said, "I'm a country boy from Alabama. I don't have enough money to go back home, and I don't want to go back home, I want to see if I can find a job."

He said, "Right down that street two blocks is the YMCA, and they will put you up for a week without any cost. But if you do have any money they will charge you a dollar a day."

"I don't have much, less than five dollars," I said.

"Go on down there," he said.

I went, got a room upstairs and slept. The next morning when I came down to the lobby, they had donuts, milk, and coffee. I drank some milk and ate a donut.

LaPorte was a city with a population of about 17,000, about the size of Tuscaloosa at that time. They compared themselves to Tuscaloosa, because the University of Alabama in Tuscaloosa had just come into fame with its champion football team. In fact, quite often they would compare Alabama's football team with Notre Dame's — the most famous football team in the world—and they talked about how they wished there could be a game with Alabama.

I went to Front Street, looking for work, and the first place I came to was a drug store that looked like the Central Drug Store that used to be in Fayette. I had been to Fayette a few times. I walked in, a tall, elderly man was standing in the front; he looked at me and asked, "Can I do something for you?"

"Yes, I'm a country boy from down in Alabama. I don't have any experience, and I don't have enough money to go back home, and I don't want to go back home. I want to get a job and try to make something out of myself," I told him.

He looked toward the back at another tall fellow, his brother, and said, "Son we own this drug store, and we are not trying to do any business. We keep it open for our friends."

I looked around and saw there were people at three card tables. Some were playing dominoes, some checkers, and some playing cards.

He said, "They come in here, smoke their pipes, sit around and talk, play cards, or whatever. We keep it open for them. My son is a chief engineer at U.S. Slicing Machine Manufacturing Co., which is quite a large factory in LaPorte, and my brother's daughter is married to a surgeon. They are both doing well, and I tell you son we are not trying to make any money. We are just trying to be here for our customers and friends. But I tell you one thing, if we needed anybody you would have a job." I thanked him and walked out.

Next door was a meat market. I went in and remember very well meeting Otto Tinkey, the manager. Otto was a German, and he talked the part. I made about the same speech to him and he asked, "When can you go to work?"

"Right now," I answered.

"Go on to the back, and I'll get you an apron," he said.

I went to the back; he put an apron on me, and started me slicing bacon. They didn't have bacon that was pre-packaged back then. They had the slabs, to slice and put on ten-inch galvanized trays about the width of an ordinary slab of bacon. As you sliced you would stack it like it comes in packages at the store now. You would lay a piece of waxed paper on top and start slicing again, leaving the lean part showing just like it is now. I did that the rest of that day and the next day.

I stayed at the YMCA all that week, but before that week was out I found right close to the market an apartment for fourteen dollars a month, furnished and everything in it. So I rented it, but I told the man he would have to wait until I got paid before I could pay him. He looked at me, grinned, and said, "I know folks are having a hard time now." I'll always remember him, Mr. Decker. He was an undertaker and owned and operated a funeral home.

The third day I worked at the meat market, Mr. Tinkey put me to weighing lard. Back then you never heard of Crisco or cooking oil. Lard came in fifty pound wooden buckets instead of the metal cans down in Alabama that I was used to. I used a wooden paddle, put two pounds in little cardboard containers, laid a piece of waxed paper on top of it, and dropped it in a barrel. They were having a special Friday and Saturday: two pounds of lard for a quarter.

Friday morning, Mr. Tinkey asked if I had ever clerked anywhere. I told him I had worked in the commissary at Gorgas, and he said, "We are going to bring you up front and let you try waiting on the trade Friday." He gave me a meat block and showed me how to cut pork chops from pork loins. "You are going to stop and wait on the trade, and later this afternoon we will have more help up here," he said.

I didn't do too good cutting pork chops. I would leave a few small slivers of bone because I didn't know to hit hard enough to cut the bone in one lick, but I learned later. Tinkey said, "On Saturday, we will be so busy with all these specials you won't need to cut meat—just wait on trade all day Saturday." He gave me sixteen dollars for that week's work.

On Monday, when I came back in he said, "Now I ought not to tell you this, but you led the sales Friday and Saturday." There were about seven or eight butchers and clerks. He said, "We are going to give you that butcher block over there, and Eddy Winsloski, the chief meat cutter, will teach you and help you learn to cut meat. But you will have to stop and wait on the trade." So I would stop cutting meat and wipe my hands on my apron or a rag to wait on the trade. It was not my ambition to cut meat by any means. But—really—I enjoyed it.

After about three weeks, in January 1930, I decided I would try to find a different job of some kind. I used my lunch hour to look for a job, and after the second try I went into Hardeman's Furniture Store, which was owned by Montgomery Ward. I understand they had 140 furniture stores throughout the Midwest. I put in my application, and they told me that I could come to work the next Monday morning if I wanted to, and they would pay me thirty dollars a week, which was more than the twenty-two dollars a week I was making at the butcher shop.

I went back to the meat market and told Mr. Tinkey, that I had found a job that would be more to my liking, and if he did not mind I would go take it. He said, "That's fine, and added we are happy with you here."

Monday morning, I reported to Hardeman's which was a reasonably large store. I hadn't been there a half a day, when the bookkeeper, a little blond-haired Polish girl, called me over and said, "Dixie, the customers come in the front door." I knew what she meant, because I was standing back in the middle of the furniture store. I walked to the front of the store and it wasn't but a minute until a man came in with his wife and daughter. I greeted them, and we talked, but they stayed longer than the usual customer stayed. I realized right away that they were fascinated by my southern accent, so I decided I would try to capitalize on it without them knowing. I did alright and enjoyed it.

The third week, the manager called me over and said, "Well, Kimbrell, the Chicago office called this morning about your sales report. It was very impressive. In fact, you led the sales. Next Monday morning, they want you to report to Michigan City to their store. They are going to run three weeks of sales. You will be in Michigan City three weeks. Then you will move to another Hardeman Furniture store and will probably be moving from store to store for an unlimited time."

I was shocked, but I didn't comment. I felt complimented,

but the more I thought about it the less I liked it. I had already found a real nice furnished apartment for fourteen dollars a month just two blocks from the main street. And both stores — the meat market and the furniture store — were on the main street of town. After thinking about it for a couple of days, I went back to the meat market and told Mr. Tinkey what had happened. He asked me if I wanted to come back to work, and I said, "Yes, I do." So Monday morning I went back to work at the meat market. He gave me a three dollar raise which increased my salary to twenty-five dollars a week.

I continued to work at the meat market for a while, but was still dissatisfied. I went to LaPorte Motor Company, the Ford automobile dealer, and put in my application. They had a job in the parts department and would pay me two dollars and fifty cents more a week than I was making, which would be twenty-seven dollars and fifty cents.

Again, I went back to the meat market and told Mr. Tinkey I was going to take the job at Ford Automobile Dealer and thanked him for letting me work. He said, "All right. We have enjoyed having you work for us, don't blame you if you are not happy cutting meat."

"No, I didn't say that. It is just not my ambition, but I don't dislike it," I said.

"Well go on down there and try it, and if it is not what you hoped it will be come back and talk to us. I'm not telling you we will hold your job, but we will be glad to talk to you if you come back," he said.

I had worked for LaPorte Motor Company for three or four

months when J. J. Moore, the President of LaPorte Business College, and his wife came in. They had heard about me and wanted to know if I would be interested in going to the business college located only two blocks from my apartment. They asked me what I would be interested in, and I told them bookkeeping and business courses. They told me I could pay tuition by the month; the first payment would be twenty-four dollars with twenty-four dollars due each month thereafter for nine months making a total of $240. It was a twelve months course. I said, "Let me see what I can work out."

I had developed the habit of eating at least one meal a day at the Bay Tree Cafeteria which was a block from my apartment. That night, I purposely waited until later to eat. After my meal, I motioned for the manager to come over to my table and asked him to sit down. I told him about the president of the business college coming to see if I would be interested in going to school. I said that I was interested and asked him if I could work at the cafeteria for my meals every morning from whatever to seven o'clock and from six to nine o'clock every night. He said that he could let me do that. He asked if I could come in at five o'clock in the mornings, and work an hour at lunch.

"Yes, I think I can," I said.

When I went to work the next morning, I told the owner and President of LaPorte Motor Company, Mr. Woods, that I was going to business college. I explained that I only had a high school education and hoped to qualify myself for something better in life, and I needed to go to classes from eight o'clock in the morning to four o'clock in the afternoon.

"Let me think about it a little bit," he said.

Later he called me in the office, and I told him the cafeteria was going to let me work for my meals. He said, "You know bad weather is coming on, and since we are located on Lincoln Highway — the busiest highway in Indiana — we have automobile storage for people traveling through. We don't open the garage on Saturday and Sunday, and you could work all day those days. Right now, we alternate those days with other employees, but if you want to you can work both Saturday and Sunday. On other days you come in the mornings at seven o'clock and work until eight o'clock and then you could come in the afternoons at four o'clock and work until six." He said he would pay sixteen dollars a week.

"I'm going to try it," I said. I registered at the business college and started the classes, just about the time it began to get cold.

When spring came, people stopped storing their cars inside the garage at night. Mr. Woods came to me and said, "We don't really need anybody on Saturday and Sunday anymore." I told him I was doing well in my business classes, and I needed to keep going, but I also needed to work.

"See if you can work out something else," he said.

I went back to the meat market and told Mr. Tinkey what happened. Mr. Tinkey said, "Yes we will work with you. Come on back." When I told him what the motor company was paying me, he said, "We can do that too." I went back to work at the meat market.

After about seven and a half months, Mr. Moore called me and another student, Ruth Gardner, in and said, "You both have finished your twelve months courses. Ms. Gardner, you paid your tuition to start with, but Mr. Kimbrell, you still owe two months' tuition. We could give you your diploma, but we don't usually do that until we have all the money."

"I can't get up forty-eight dollars right now, but I can continue to pay twenty-four dollars a month easier because I will be working and making a better salary," I said.

"All right. "If you promise to pay, I will give you and Ruth your diplomas, and we will make your pictures and put them on the wall because you were the two people who finished the courses in the shortest length of time," Mr. Moore said. So I got my diploma.

Since Ruth and I were leaving, Mr. Moore decided to have a spelling bee, Ruth being captain of one team and I the other team. We each chose students until we had the entire school on one side of the classroom or the other. Unbelievably, we were the two last standing, having missed no words until the last word which was "arson." I missed it, Ruth spelled it making her team the winner.

Going through my scrapbooks while putting together information for my book, I came across my diploma from LaPorte Business College in LaPorte, Indiana, dated October 31, 1931. I wondered if there was still a LaPorte Business College. I picked up the telephone and got information for LaPorte, Indiana and asked for LaPorte Business College, and they gave me a number. I dialed, the number had been changed, but I got the new number. The school had been moved to Michigan City, Indiana. When the receptionist answered, I told her who I was, and she said, "Wait a minute. Let me get the campus manager." The campus manager answered, and told me they had three campuses now — one in Michigan City, another one in Indiana, and one in Illinois.

"Spell your name for me?" he asked. I spelled it and he said, "Hold just a minute."

I heard him calling to someone, and then heard a lady's voice over the phone. He asked her, "Do you remember when we were going through an old list of students a while back, and we came across the name Fuller Kimbrell? You said you read that name in a newspaper in Montgomery, Alabama, when you were coming through there. Well, he is on the phone now."

I visited with them over the phone a little bit. They invited me to come to see them, which I promised to do, but haven't yet. They asked if I would send them a resume, and I did later. They sent me their college catalog, and an invitation to come to the college. Later, one of the administrators called and said they had made my resume available for the students there. While I was talking to them on the telephone, I asked them if they remembered Ruth Gardner, and they said they didn't know anything about her.

Afterwards, my curiosity was still active, and I got information for LaPorte again and ask for Ruth Gardner, although I didn't expect her to be listed as that. They said they didn't have a Ruth Gardner, so I told the operator to just give me a Gardner, and she gave me two.

The first Gardner I called, a man answered and said he didn't know anything about her. The next call I made a lady answered and I asked her if she knew anything about Ruth Gardner. I told her about me going to LaPorte Business College, and that I had dated her a few times while we were going to school.

She said, "It wouldn't be any of my relatives because we did not move to LaPorte until 1960. Would you like for me to try to find her?" she asked.

"I sure would," I answered.

She said she would be happy to.

I usually go to coffee every morning with a bunch of old folk, and one morning I was just getting back when the telephone rang. Mrs. Gardner, her first name was Carolyn, said, "Mr. Kimbrell, I made fourteen calls, and haven't had any luck. I'm sorry, but I'll try a little more. I have left messages a couple of places."

A few minutes later the phone rang, and it was Carolyn. She said, "Mr. Kimbrell, you're in business. Not only have I found her, but I have her address, and her telephone number. Her husband passed away a few years ago; she is eighty-five years old, and she lives alone." She gave me Ruth's number and address.

I called the number she gave me and a lady answered. I asked, "Ruth Gardner used to be?"

"Yes," she answered.

"Does the name Fuller Kimbrell mean anything to you?" I asked.

"Not really," she answered.

I asked, "Do you remember a country boy from Alabama who went to LaPorte Business College with you, and we got our diplomas at the same time because we had finished early? One time this country boy came out to your father's dairy, and you and I sat on the front porch in the swing and ate cake and drank sweet milk?"

"Yes, I remember that," she said.

"That's me. I'm writing a book, and going through my scrapbooks I came across my diploma, and I wondered if anybody I knew from the school was still around," I said.

She said, "I have no connection with anybody at the school. I live in Portage, a little town located fifteen miles west of LaPorte. I have one son who is a federal judge, and his office is in Gary, Indiana. I still drive, and am in good health."

"I'm going to come see you sometime," I said.

"Come ahead," she said.

At this time, I have not gone yet, but I have talked to her a few times on the telephone and we enjoy visiting with each other.

I went back to the meat market and Mr. Tinkey asked, "That means you want to work full time?"

"Yes," I replied.

In the meantime, I met the adopted son of the owner of the meat market. I think his name was Hugh. When he came in he would always stop to visit with me, and we would talk about Alabama and other things. He did not know where his parents were. After about a month, Hugh and his brother came in and took me into the back and said, "We are building a new store in Elkhart, Indiana. And since you are single, would you like to go as assistant manager? You don't have the experience to be manager now, but we feel further experience will qualify you later. Would you be willing to do that."

"Yes," I answered.

A few weeks later, they came back and said, "The store is going up fine, and we want you to go on over in that direction and maybe stay at Mishawaka, Indiana, which is about half way between Elkhart and South Bend. We have two stores in South Bend, one is large with fourteen butchers employed, and in order to give you a little additional experience in a different store, you can work there. Why don't you go over on the weekend and see if you can find an apartment in Mishawaka?"

At his request, Sunday I caught the train to Mishawaka. When I arrived, I walked down the street from the depot, and I just didn't know what to do, but I saw a sign that read, "Two Bedroom Apartment for Rent, Inquire at Brown Furniture Store Across the Street." I walked across the street and looked in the store window and saw someone in the back. I knocked on the door, and a man answered. I asked if he was Mr. Brown. He said, "Yes." I told him I had noticed the sign "Apartment for Rent", and he asked if I was interested. I said, "Yes, but I don't need a two bedroom apartment," and asked him how much. He said $35 a month, and asked if I would like to see it. We looked at the apartment, and I told him I thought I would take it and asked if he would hold it until next Sunday.

"Yes, I probably can't rent it anyway. Times are hard," he said. He agreed to hold it for me.

I went back to the market and told Mr. Tinkey that I had gone to Mishawaka at the request of Mr. Tittle to work in the big store at South Bend. Mr. Tinkey said he would notify Mr. Tittle at the office in Gary, Indiana. Two days later, they came down, and we went to the back room. He asked, "Why don't you take that, and in the meantime I'll notify the manager of the store in South Bend that we are sending you down to work. Later you are going over to the new store we are planning to open in Elkhart, Indiana, but in the meantime get established. Since Mishawaka is half-way between Elkhart and South Bend, it won't be too inconvenient for the time being." At that time there were buses and streetcars running in both directions that you could catch easy enough either to South Bend or Elkhart.

The next Sunday, I went to Mishawaka and reported for work Monday morning at the meat market in South Bend. After about three weeks, the manager came in and said, "Kimbrell, things have changed. This Depression is getting rough. It's taking hold of every business in town and every business in the United States. Our business has dropped off, and Mr. Tittle has just said he is not too sure if he will open the store in Elkhart, even though plans are well under way. We will have to cut you back to three days a week." I told him alright. I didn't know what I was going to do, but I could make it on three days a week.

One night, I was visiting with Mr. Brown and noticed a cafeteria a short distance away. He said, "Let's walk up the street, I want to show you something." We walked up the street where he had a big nice cafeteria fully equipped with kitchen and tables downstairs. Upstairs was a real nice restaurant which seated all total about 150 to 175. He asked, "Why don't you take this and operate it?" When I had rented the apartment from Mr. Brown,

I had told him that I had worked my way through business college working part-time in a meat market and a cafeteria.

I said, "Mr. Brown, I don't have but $300 hundred dollars, which is all I've been able to save in the year and a half since I've been up here from Alabama."

He said, "I'm a real good friend of Albert Pick Borth Co. They sell restaurant and hotel equipment. Let me get him to come out here and see what we can work out."

Mr. Pick was there the next morning and he, Mr. Brown, and I went to the cafeteria and worked out that I could open the following Sunday. I put my $300 in it, and Mr. Pick suggested a list of groceries and meats to buy to start with. Mr. Brown remembered the names of the cooks (both the meat and vegetable), who had worked there previously, and ask them to come and talk to me. They did, and we worked out for them to come in Saturday to get organized and tell me what kind of meat and groceries to buy. I bought the groceries they suggested and the grocery store delivered them.

Sunday morning, we opened up. I had advertised in the South Bend newspaper, and they had announced it on the radio, but there was no television then. I had a big business on Sunday, and it went over well. The food was fine and everybody seemed to be so happy. Everything went well for six weeks. I was doing about $275 a day in sales, which was outstanding because you could get a full meal for thirty-five cents—not more than fifty cents, and the best steak was less than seventy-five cents including potato, coffee and everything else to go with it.

By the Fall of 1931, depression was being talked about

everywhere, You would hear that banks were closing. Or people were afraid the banks would close, so they drew their money out, and the banks did have to close. After operating the cafeteria about six weeks, everything was fine, and I was so happy with what I was doing and felt like I was on the way to success. Then Ball Band Rubber Co., maker of rubber boots and tires and other rubber products, lost its Russian contract and had to close down, leaving 6,000 people out of jobs. Mishawaka was a town of about 17,000 to 18,000 people. My business dropped down to about $175 a day. I could still make it but not well enough to brag about.

That continued on about two or three weeks and then the Dodge-Bendix plant that made parts for the Dodge automobile shut down, and 4000 more people were out of a job. After a week my business dropped down to thirty-five or forty-five dollars a day, and I just couldn't make it. I went down and told Mr. Brown, "I've just gone as long as I can. If I go any longer, I won't be able to pay the grocery bills and other bills."

He said, "I understand. My business has been falling off too. Not only that, but people are not paying me. They can't. They don't even have money to live on. I will call Mr. Pick and get him to come out. I think he will pick up the things he sold you that you haven't paid for. You have taken such good care my equipment, in fact, you've cleaned it up, and my investment is as good as it was before, and you've paid me $175 rent for two months which I wouldn't have gotten." Mr. Pick came out, and we boxed up and shipped back to Chicago the things he had sold me that I had not yet paid for. I closed the cafeteria.

I went back to the meat market, and they gave me three days a week. Thursday morning I went in to work and worked three days. I could still pay that $35 a month rent on the apartment, as I could ride the bus to and from work. After two weeks, the manager called me back and said, "Kimbrell, the store at Elkhart is not going to open, and I don't know how much longer any of the stores of Tittle & Sons will stay open. But I can still give you two days a week."

"I don't know if I can make it," I said. I worked two more weeks and found that I could not make it. There were no jobs at all. Nobody would even talk to you about hiring. If you went anywhere and asked for a job you were told they had just laid someone off.

The Depression was really beginning to bear down on everybody. I wired Ando and asked him to send me twenty-five dollars to come home. I was just that broke. He sent me a check for the exact amount. I sent one of my suitcases by train, and caught the bus to Birmingham. Back then telegrams came to the depot. Since Berry was a small town, the depot agent told everybody, "Fuller Kimbrell had wired for money to come home on." It was no surprise when I stepped off the train and was greeted by an extra large crowd.

After I had been home a while, I corresponded with the folks back in Indiana. They told me that Joe Tittle & Sons had to take bankruptcy about three months after I left. They went out of business along with thousands of other businesses all over the United States.

THREE

HOME FROM INDIANA

I rode the bus from Mishawaka to Birmingham, caught the train from Birmingham to Berry, and arrived in Berry on what we always called the "seven o'clock" train. Berry was a small town, with no entertainment for young folks, except to meet the train and wait until the mail was put up at the post office. I was met at the train by Ando and Ruth, and Reba, whom they had asked to ride with them to bring me home. Ando and Ruth took me home and took Reba back to Berry. My family had been expecting me ever since I had wired for money to come home.

Times were getting worse. Thousands of banks were closing. Bankruptcy was the greatest it had ever been in the history of the United States. But people on the farms were hoping they could produce enough to eat and survive, which was not the case in the industrial cities. Every day you would read in the newspaper about people committing suicide, in bread lines, dying from starvation, particularly in the larger cities in the east.

In Alabama the effects of the Depression were just as bad — if not worse — than in Indiana, with the exception of small farmers, who were not hurt as bad as the people in industrial sections of the United States, because they were accustomed to growing what they needed to survive and required very little money. The only problem was what little they did have to sell, the merchants had no money to pay for. People with farms the size of my father's grew almost everything they needed. About all they needed to buy was sugar, flour, and coffee.

I had not been home long until I realized there was no hope of getting a job, because no one was hiring. I decided to stay on the farm that year and help my father make a crop. Times continued to get worse. I went to the bank and borrowed $200 to buy fertilizer and other supplies that we needed in order to farm. Of course it was mule farming. It was not a good crop year. Cotton went down to five or six cents a pound, which meant twenty or thirty dollars for a bale of cotton. It took eight or ten bales of cotton to pay off the $200 I had borrowed at the bank. But fortunately I made enough to pay the interest, and renewed the note until the next fall. That satisfied the banker.

The year 1932 was election year. Hoover had been president for three years, and from the time he took office the economy had been on the downbeat all three years, including 1932, and continued to be. Roosevelt was nominated on the Democrat ticket. In his campaign, he didn't say how he was going to do it, but he claimed that he would set up a program that would turn the economy around. That was the first year I voted in any election. You had to go to Fayette — the county seat — to register and pay $1.50 poll tax. I worked to earn $3.00, borrowed a car, and picked up Reba Shook, my future my wife. We went to Fayette, registered, and I paid the poll tax for both of us. We voted for Franklin Delano Roosevelt on the Democrat ticket. I still have the poll tax receipts and the registration receipt. I have continued to vote Democrat in every election since. I have always been a loyal democrat, and have been awarded the honor of being called a "Yellow Dog Democrat," and have certificates and plaques to prove it.

Roosevelt was elected and went into office in March, 1933. He immediately called Congress into session and in a hundred days he had things moving. In this hundred days Roosevelt — FDR, as he is known to this day — did more to change the United States than anyone ever in the history of the United States before or probably since. For instance, some of the programs he put into effect were unemployment compensation, a public works program I will talk about later, which consisted of enlisting young boys into CCC Camps and training them for sixteen months. After finishing their training they were awarded federal grants to attend college.

Included in the hundred days were public works, rural electrification, farm support programs, minimum wage and hour law, and guarantee of collective bargaining for labor. If you could realize the effect it had on the people, it would be mind boggling. The young folk today can't understand how hard times were during 1929-34 before Roosevelt went into office. During that time it was almost impossible to get paid in cash for your day's work.

Roosevelt closed the banks and set up insurance so that people who had money in the banks would have insurance on their accounts starting at $5000 then, but today it is a $100,000 guarantee. Almost immediately people began to work for pay.

Roosevelt set up the Public Works Program. Congressman William Bankhead, who was the Speaker of the U. S. House of Representatives from Alabama, added into the Roosevelt programs the highway department. This included all the United States and has become since then one of the biggest things in federal government, resulting in federal participation for building roads. Since then they have added gasoline tax to support it.

But in the Public Works Program, federal matching funds were extended to cities and counties to pave and widen streets, to improve sewer systems, to build bridges, to build public buildings, and to repair courthouses and some schools. Also under this program, the Vocational Agriculture schools were started. The schools offered courses to train young boys to be farmers.

The Rural Electrification Program also meant telephones as well. The program was set up so that the federal government loaned money for a long period of time to telephone companies and electric power companies at two and a half percent to expand their telephone equipment, including putting lines out into the rural areas. I remember reading that less than five percent of the people living in rural areas of the United States, practically none in the South, had telephones at that time. But now, I understand that above ninety-five percent of the people in rural areas have electricity and telephones.

Roosevelt set up work programs of various kinds, such as WPA and CWA. There was no big money to be had, but people were willing to work for fifty cents or a dollar a day.

Mr. Theron Cannon, owner of Theron Cannon & Co. in Berry, hired me to assist farmers in preparing terraces, so their land would meet the approval of the Federal Land Bank, and they could qualify for a loan. Of course, in the Roosevelt programs there were so many things that turned out good, one being the Roosevelt program accommodated supply merchants like Mr. Cannon all over the United States. For instance, Mr. Sam Simpson, who owned a large farm was one of Theron Cannon's largest debtors. His son happened to be the head of the WPA program that first started out in Alabama. Walker County being a mining town meant that they were qualified and much more in need of the Roosevelt program, as it was commonly called, than most any section of Alabama, because the mines had been closed down and the people who worked in the mines were really in bread lines. Among the many things that resulted from the WPA program, one was the development of the Winston County forest, which was designated as the Bankhead National Forest. They decided to use people out of work in Walker County and various places in the United States, particularly in Alabama, to build roads, streets, bridges, and install culverts, to give these people work. Most people only got fifty cents a day, but they got $1.50 a day if they had a mule.

Sam Simpson worked out with his son to buy a lot of mules and hire them out to the WPA in Walker County. Clell Ray, the mule dealer and also a partner with the Theron Cannon Company, went to St. Louis and bought a carload of mules — twenty mules — for Mr. Sam Simpson. The WPA program paid for the mules for Sam Simpson, and also paid for the collars, hames, and full harnesses. This was before there was a lot of power equipment to work on the county roads. The purpose was not to do it with a small number of employees, but to give as many people as possible work. Mr. Simpson brought all twenty mules down to the side of Theron Cannon's store, and I put the collars, hames, and full harnesses on every one of the mules in one day. He took them to Walker County and got $1.50 per mule per day. Back then, you could buy a pair of mules for about $300, unless it was a pair of real big fine ones. He sent them all to Walker County. I sold him axes, shovels, hoes, rakes, and picks. I also sold him big plows to plow the land, and everything else needed in building the roads. I even sold him slip scrapes, pieces of equipment pulled by a mule or a pair of mules, used for many years to move dirt to fill in low places in roads. With a slip scrape you could pick up about a fourth of a yard of dirt and the mules would drag it down to where it was needed, lift it up, and dump it to help level out the land. Working with the slip scrapes enabled the government to work a lot more people because they didn't have a motor grader in every area.

After they slip scraped the dirt down the road 100 feet, or 100 or 200 yards, these extra hands would come along with their shovels, hoes, and rakes and level and smooth it down. One of the things that made the WPA program so beneficial to the people was that it gave employment and gave the people enough money to buy the bare necessities of life — which really boiled down to food.

The WPA program also leased a lot of equipment from

various people. Later, after I got into the farm machinery business, I leased to WPA a lot of equipment. But J. D. Pittman, the dealer for the Caterpillar Tractor Equipment Company in Birmingham, just leased motor graders and small crawler tractors, as they were called back then, to build roads all over the state. Even out where they were using mules, they would have a motor grader to shape up the land, clean out the ditches, and finish up the roads.

Since I'm known as a Yellow Dog Democrat, I hesitate to say this, but one congressman told me that the programs Roosevelt set up received very few Republican votes. For instance, he told me that social security, which was one of the most beneficial laws that Congress has ever passed, was passed in 1936 without a single Republican vote. I shudder to think what would happen in the United States today if we did not have social security. One thing I need to say is that Roosevelt's opposition had gotten to the press, which was controlled by what we call nowadays "the establishment," and his popularity had gone down to almost zero by the end of the hundred days. But he got these programs through in spite of what was going to happen later. The benefits were there and they knew they couldn't stop them, and he used his power as president to make them as effective as possible.

Back then there were very few automobiles, but everybody was assessed a road tax. You could either pay a dollar and a half or work four days. My father's first cousin, Riley Kimbrell, who was a road foreman and county surveyor, told me that since we owned a good steady pair of mules, I could plow a day and a half for him. He wanted to change the road down the hill towards his home. The public road washed out every time it came a big rain, and he was going to slope it down the side of the hill to control the flow of the water. I plowed a day and a half instead of working four days for my road tax.

People walked everywhere they went, rode horseback, or travelled by horse or mule drawn vehicles. I've said several times if you had a nice, good-looking pair of mules and an almost new wagon, you tied your mules up close to the church on Sunday. But if you had an old wagon and thin worn-out looking mules — as a lot of people did — you tied them up farther away from the church so folks couldn't see them.

My parents were devout Christians, and they lived the part. They attended Sunday school and church every Sunday, and all church functions. After my return home, I went to church more often than I did in Indiana.

We didn't take our mules to church since we were within walking distance. But it wasn't always the best thing to live so close, because the preacher and kinfolks stopped by for Sunday dinner most of the time. Of course, there were no refrigerators, but we did have an icebox. If you had company for dinner you caught a chicken, dressed it, and cooked it after you got home from church. How many people stopped by after church determined how many chickens you killed and cooked.

My father always killed several hogs each winter and cured the meat. My mother would save a ham or two for the summer protracted meetings — now known as revivals. Usually the preacher would stay with us because we lived close to the church. On Sunday mornings, if we had company, Mother would have ham. Otherwise, we had what we called bacon, which people now call white meat. It was cured pork sides. Quite often my mother would roll the slices in meal and fry them, and that was really good. We grew hogs much fatter then, and cooked out the fat so we would have the grease, which was called lard, to cook and season with. You never heard of cooking oil or Crisco. You cooked with lard all the time.

By fall of 1933 times began to look better. I made another crop, but it was not the best of crops. My father had just barely kept his farm during that time and had taken a mortgage on it. One of the programs Roosevelt set up was the farmers' loan program—the Federal Land Bank. In this program, Roosevelt also amended the Farm Extension Service, which provided every county with have a county agent. To get a farm loan, one of the first requirements was to have the land terraced so it wouldn't wash so badly. Farmers had small mules and were unable to build terraces, and the land had begun to erode. Top soil was washing off. So the county agent told the people that they should terrace their land.

In the summer of 1933, I went to Fayette and stayed with one of my mother's first cousins for two nights and took a course in terracing. I had studied this a little in high school in the Vocational Agriculture Department. The Vocational Agriculture Department had also been strengthened under the Roosevelt program.

Theron Cannon, one of the biggest farmers' supply merchants in Fayette County, and certainly the biggest in eastern Fayette County, held mortgages on farms to the extent he could hardly survive. Mr. Cannon asked the county agent about the terracing program, and the agent told Mr. Cannon that I had taken the course. Mr. and Mrs. Cannon came to see me at my father's home, where I was still living, one Saturday afternoon and wanted to know if I could lay terraces to fit the new Land Bank requirements. I told him that I could do that before I took the course, but I had learned a lot from the terracing course I took in Fayette. He asked me, "Would you like to go to work and lay off terraces for me?"

"Yes," I answered.

Mr. Cannon said, "I'll pay you forty dollars a month if you will come to work. Part of the Federal Land Bank Program is to furnish the county with two big machines and men to operate them to build the terraces. But I need you to lay off the terraces."

I traded with him and went to work the first Monday morning November 1, 1933. I lived three miles from Berry and walked to work, but Mr. Cannon had one of his clerks drive me to the farm where I was going to lay off terraces. He had a big farm north of Berry that he wanted terraced first.

Mr. Cannon had not said anything to me about clerking in his store. He had only told me to lay off the terraces. But it was raining, and farmers had begun gathering their crops. They were coming into the store along with other people, so I didn't ask any questions, I just went to clerking in the store when he asked me to.

In the store were piles of overalls, which was the uniform all the men wore to work, regardless of what kind of work they did — they didn't have blue jeans back then — and piles of shirts and work shoes. Since there were no customers in the store to wait on, I decided to put them in line. I sorted out the sizes, and put each size in a stack. When I had them all stacked neatly, I started straightening out the shoes. The stock numbers were all mixed up on the shelves against a wall ten feet high, and I had to get upon a ladder to get them off the top shelves. You found size seven of a stock number in one place, and five or six feet down on another shelf there would be another one. You looked for hours sometimes because you knew you had the shoe, but just couldn't find it. So I put them in line.

When I came down, Mr. Cannon was waiting on a customer, and I heard him ask, "J. D., who lined up all those overalls like that?"

"Well, Fuller did," J. D. replied.

About two hours later Mr. Cannon came over and said, "Fuller, I've been in business since I was a boy, my daddy was in business, and we have never had anybody do anything like that. Where did you learn that?"

"I don't know if I even learned it. I just thought it was awful that you couldn't find anything," I said.

"Well, that's sure a good idea," he said.

Two or three days later, there was a lot of freight to unload in the back of the warehouse — feed, fertilizer, seed oats, flour by the carload, and sugar by the big truck loads. One of the clerks said, "Fuller, come on. We need you in the back."

J. D. Waldon, who was a partner, walked over and said, "Fuller, you stay right here in front. They can unload that freight and stuff in the back. Customers come in the door right there."

I didn't go to the back, and very seldom did I have to help unload any of the freight. But there is one thing I do remember that I helped with several times. We sold barbed wire, which is used in building fences. Back then you did not have the four-wheel carts to transfer merchandise. You only had breakdown carts. You would stack three rolls of barbed wire on them. Just about the time you got started, the barbed wire would roll off on the floor, and you had to put it back up on the cart again.

We also sold metal roofing, which came in carloads, and you would have lengths from five feet to twelve feet. We had to unload them according to lengths. We put the twelve foot on the bottom, then eleven foot, then the ten foot, eight foot and on up to the five foot. You could stack that five foot on the cart by laying it down and just roll it by holding the steel, then you would get the six foot, seven foot, and eight foot the same way. But by the time you got down to the eleven and twelve foot you'd get one end and another clerk was at the other end. It would start flopping in the middle. You were bent over, and that would really put a kink in your back.

When the weather cleared up, I went back out to survey farms. It sounds like very little money now, but most of the farmers had a $1500, $2000, or $2500 mortgage they got from the Federal Land Bank. When the Federal Land Bank appraiser came to check and appraise the farm, I would go with him a lot of times to make sure they had the outlet to the terraces. Sometimes I would check the field rows and help get those straight. This was in the winter of 1933 and 1934.

By the end of the next year, the terraces I had laid off were approved, and Mr. Cannon received $25,000 from the farmers who had received Federal Land Bank loans. That was a life saver for the Theron Cannon Co. of Berry, because, like the individual farmer, they had used up all their resources, since the farmers were not able to pay for the supplies they had bought on credit to make a crop.

The next year I laid off enough terraces so that farmers were able to get $30,000 in approved loans. And loans paid off by the farmers put back into Mr. Cannon's business a total of $55,000 for the two years—which was an enormous amount of money back in those days.

My father's nine mule farm consisted of 300 acres with approximately 200 acres in cultivation. Though there were ten of us boys to start with, all had left except me. Mamie Zora, my youngest sister, was also still at home. The Federal Land Bank regulation was that a man over sixty-five years old was not eligible for a Land Bank loan. My father said if I would sign the loan and help pay it off, he would give me the farm, but he and my mother would continue to live there. I agreed to it. The land was approved for $3500, and I signed the mortgage since the loan was made to me instead of my father. Mr. Shepherd, the owner of the bank, was my father's unofficial attorney, and did what little attorney work he needed, so it was easy for him to make the deed. My father deeded the farm over to me.

In the Spring of 1934, times begin to look better. Cotton looked like it was going to bring ten or twelve cents a pound, and I decided I needed another mule. I had one mule that was crippled, and I really needed an extra mule. I wanted to trade the crippled mule for a pair. The mule dealer, Clell Ray, who was partners with Theron Cannon, shipped in a carload of mules from Missouri, including a pair of big mules. I looked at them, and he said, "I'll take $500 for the pair." He offered me $125 for my crippled mule — which meant that I would have to get a loan for $375. My father had a first cousin who was kind of a horse trader. He came by, and I said, "Cousin Harry go look at those mules Clell Ray has, and tell me what you think about them."

After a little while he came back and said, "Fuller, that's a fine pair of mules. You can't go wrong with them."

"Yes, but Cousin Harry, I've got to make a mortgage for $375 to get them," I said.

He said, "Son, let me ask you something. If you have a pair of mules and they are worth $500 and you owe $500, are you any worse off than a man that doesn't have a pair of mules?"

"I guess not," I answered.

"If I have a house and lot that I owe $1000 on and it's worth $1000, am I any worse off than a man that doesn't have a house and lot?" he asked.

"No," I answered.

I went out the door, bought that pair of mules, signed the mortgage, and bought close to $100 worth of farm equipment, including a plow, a disk harrow, a section harrow, and other items that I needed on the farm. It turned out that I made more cotton and corn than was ever made on the farm. Also, I fertilized a little better.

Although I continued to work at the store, I hired two farm hands and had four sharecroppers. From thirty-nine acres I gathered forty-two bales of cotton, and every time I could get twelve cents a pound I would sell that cotton. I paid for the pair of mules and the farm machinery that year and had thirteen dollars left.

Theron Cannon, the owner and manager of the store, did business a funny way—he never paid you! You never drew a payday. Back then, there was no social security or withholding tax to pay, so if you needed any money, you would get one, two, or three dollars out of the cash register and get another clerk to charge it to you. That's the way you got your money. If you had two dollars in your pocket over the weekend, you were in pretty good shape. I worked there three years and two months and got paid when I quit. I had less than thirty dollars coming.

I had started to work in November, 1933, for forty dollars, and in two months, after I did all these things I just told about, J. D. Waldon took a liking to me, I thought. He raised me to fifty dollars. I worked until November, 1936, for fifty dollars a month, and for about a year and a half, I walked three miles twice a day. I would be down at the store by seven o'clock in the morning, and sometimes I would stay until seven o'clock at night. I wore my overalls and shirt and plow shoes, but I was young and didn't think it was hard on me. I thought when people talked about being tired, they were just making conversation because I didn't get tired. I continued to farm and made a good crop the next year.

Every Sunday, I would walk down a muddy road to see Reba Shook. There wasn't such a thing as a paved road in Berry and only about two blocks of paved sidewalks. The first time I saw

Reba was at a Chautauqua tent show. She was sitting with John Robert Miller, a boy I had known for a while, and his date, Flora Mae Freeman. I walked around to the side of the tent and motioned for him to come out. I asked, "Who is the beautiful little blond sitting with you and Flora Mae?"

"Reba Shook," he answered.

"Ask her if I can walk her home after the show?" I said. He returned to his seat and I saw him asking her, then he looked over at me and nodded his head, yes. Then she looked at me and nodded yes. So I walked her home. I was so excited when we got within twenty feet of her front door steps, I turned around and said, "Good night. I hope to see you again." And I walked on back home.

Reba was in grammar school when I started to high school, and I saw her at a ballgame later. When she started to high school she became a cheerleader. I continued to go see her, and all the time I was in Indiana I had written to her. We had never said anything about getting married, but in January, 1934, I said, "Well I got a raise, and it looks like my job is secure. If you want to get married, we will either get married the second Saturday or the third in February."

"Let's just make it the second," she said. I've told that several times, and it is actually the truth. Although she used to fuss at me a little for telling it.

Reba Shook was originally from Dennis, a small town in Tishomingo County, Mississippi. Mr. J. C. Shepherd was the president and owner of the bank in Berry, and his wife was a member of the Christian Church — later changed to the Church of Christ. Mr. Shepherd had built Alabama Christian College almost entirely from his own funds. The grades were primary through the eleventh grade. Mr. Shepherd selected as president of Alabama Christian College a man named Mr. Baker, who was a Christian Church preacher and, also, a school teacher from the area of Belmont, Mississippi. He was also to be pastor of the Christian Church in Berry. Mr. Baker remembered that Reba's father, J. W. Shook — better known as Jim — was a school teacher, a member of the Christian Church, and a finish carpenter. He called and asked Mr. Shook if he would come teach in the school. He would see that he got carpenter work during the summer when school was out. Mr. Shook agreed to come and teach. This happened when Reba was about seven or eight years old. She went to Alabama Christian College for a few years, but the school did not survive. Fayette County bought the College, and it became Berry High School in the fall of 1922.

I started high school in the fall of 1924 and finished in 1927 while Reba was still a freshman in high school. She would come to the ballgames, and I would meet her. During the summer, I would go to Berry to see her, and we went to church on Sunday nights, visiting the Baptist, Church of Christ, and Methodist churches. The only dates we had were about once a week, but not every week. We continued to court, and two years later she started to high school. She was selected head cheerleader, and I was captain and quarterback of the football team, so we got to see each other quite often.

When I was in Indiana, I corresponded with her at least once or twice a month, and when I came back to my parent's home in

Berry, Alabama I continued to court her as I did when I worked at the commissary in Gorgas. During those hard-farming two years, I saw her only once or maybe twice a week on Saturday and Sunday nights, and we had about the same habits that we did when we were in school — go to church on Sunday nights.

Sometimes there would be a party in Berry at Tom Carrot Flats'. In his house was a large room where all the young folks would gather. There would be a string band, and we danced and had a good time, though we never stayed out late. I would walk her home and walk the three miles back to my home.

When I started working at Cannon's, sometimes she would come uptown, and I would meet her at the drugstore. We would have a Coca Cola, which I was not able to afford when I was only farming, because hardly anybody had a nickel, the price of a Coca Cola.

Reba had one sister, Audra, who married Loyd Strickland and lived in Parrish. She had five brothers. The oldest, Adrian, had left home married and was working in Birmingham for Stockham Valve & Pipe Fitting Company. The other four boys, Ray, Trevor, Norman, and Floyd were not married and were still living at home working like their father. During the hard times, they worked where they could find jobs painting or carpentry and what ever work they could get in order to earn enough money to survive. Reba's father never taught school after Alabama Christian College closed and became Berry High School. He was a finish carpenter, but there were no big jobs.

As I continued to work in Cannon's store, I begin to feel more confident. J. D. Waldon did all the buying of cotton and merchandise, including buying o'possum, coon, and fox hides. But in the spring I noticed he was unable to do all he had been doing because he had developed cancer. I began to take over some of his duties, although I was not told to do so. We sold dry goods—ladies' waists (blouses), some skirts, overalls, khaki breeches, work shirts, and Arrow dress shirts. Overalls sold for $1.35 a pair, and work shirts sold for $1.25. We did not have what we call blue jeans today, that sell from seventeen to over fifty dollars a pair. I don't remember that we handled any dress shirts except white shirts, and that was Arrow shirts, always white, which we sold for $2.95, just as nice as what we pay $30 for today.

In early fall of 1936, Roy Sewell, a nice energetic, personable, young man, started a men's clothing manufacturing business— Sewell Manufacturing Company—in Bremen, Georgia. He was his own salesman and stopped by to sell Mr. Cannon men's suits. After he made his sales pitch, Mr. Cannon said he guessed he would not add the suits to his line since almost everything was sold on credit. Roy Sewell said, "Why don't you let me send you six dozen suits and if you don't sell them, I'll pick them up."

While Mr. Cannon was giving it some thought, I said, "Mr. Cannon, let him send them. I believe I can sell them easy enough."

"Okay," he said.

We didn't return a single suit. I sold the whole six dozen. At that time blue and brown gabardine and serge were most popular materials and were what Roy Sewell sent to us to sell, with a few suits made of material called basket weave. The serge cost $8.25, and a three piece suit sold for $24.95. The basket weave cost $6.75 and sold for $17.50. I could have bought over 100 of Roy's basket weave material suits for the $700 I paid for one suit in the Spring of 1998.

Mr. Waldon began to turn the buying over to me. When fall came, he taught me to grade and buy cotton. Before the cotton season was over that first fall, I was buying most of the cotton. One of Mr. Cannon's brothers said, "Fuller, I've never known Theron or J. D. to risk anyone doing anything like this." I told him that I appreciated what he said, and thanked him. Not only did I do all the buying, but I also priced all the merchandise in the store. I began to feel more confident that my job was secure. Although it was just fifty dollars a month, I had no gas bill, no water bill, no electric bill, no car payments, and no telephone bill. Of course this was before the Roosevelt programs became a reality.

I continued to walk three miles twice a day since we were still living on the farm with my parents. Reba was an expert seamstress, and her mother was an expert seamstress. In fact, her mother did a lot of sewing for people to subsidize the family income, and she made all of Reba's dresses and the boys' shirts. When the dry goods salesmen came by with all the pretty prints of fine looking cloth, I would get them to cut off three yards. Reba only weighed 105 pounds, and three yards could be bought for fifty cents at retail price. But a lot of times the salesmen would just cut off three yards and give it to me, and I would take it home. Reba was the best dressed girl in the community at no cost hardly. She would have a new dress for less than you can buy a Coca Cola today.

I continued to walk to work all that year and until the next March or April. I walked the three miles twice a day for about a year and a half. I also continued to farm. Reba and I would get up early Sunday morning and walk over the farm. I would advise the two hired hands and four share-croppers about what to plant in different fields, the amount of fertilizer to put out, and the kind of seeds to use. I would check the mules to see that they were being taken care of. I would also see if the help needed tools or anything.

As mentioned earlier, I didn't get a payday until I quit Cannon's. But since I could charge merchandise out to myself, I paid the hired hands almost entirely with merchandise. I would get groceries and clothes right out of the store and only had to take very little money out. They all used tobacco and snuff that I could get from the store too.

I remember one time I bought a new Remington 22 gauge single barrel rifle for $3.00 or $4.00. About once a month I would go down to where one of the hired hands and his son-in-law lived together in the same house, and I'd take my new rifle along. We would walk over the crops and talk farming and talk about what they needed. I would take my little account book down and have a settlement with him. One time we went out to the front of the house and shot hickory nuts off the tree. Then, everything was agreed to.

That fall, after the sharecroppers made a crop they didn't have enough cotton to pay what they owed. They disputed the fact that they owed it, but they had made a crop of corn also and were fixing to move to another farm down south of Berry. I wouldn't let them move the corn until they paid the thirty-five dollars that I showed they owed me. They said they didn't feel like it was right and came down to talk about it. I said, "Well you just find anybody you want to and go over the books together."

They picked the mayor of Berry, Honorable Fred Berry, and he was a good old fellow who wore overalls around town which almost everybody did at that time. They went out by the side of the store and sat down on a pile of scrap lumber. In a minute they sent for me to come out. So I went out, and one of them asked, "You remember that time you came out to the house on Sunday morning with your rifle to settle up with us?"

I thought Lord have mercy, if I had been in court that would sure be a bad statement. But we agreed, and after talking a little bit everything was satisfactory. They agreed to just move on off and leave the corn which was alright with me. Of course, you could only get about thirty-five cents a bushel for corn.

The mayor came in, and I asked, "Brother Berry, what do I owe you?"

He said, "I need a new pair of overalls. How about just giving me a pair of overalls?" he asked. I went, picked him up a pair his size and charged the $1.35 to myself. So I had gotten an arbitrator and lawyer for $1.35.

It continued on, and by fall of 1936, my farming got better. I had accumulated some cows. My mules were all doing well, and they were outstanding mules. My farm machinery was in better shape. That fall I had two cribs of corn, four or five milk cows to sell, and several big fat hogs to kill, cure or sell. Reba and I were doing well, although I was still making just fifty dollars a month. My brother, Gordon, who had been in Birmingham with Hill Grocery Co. for quite a long while, came down to have Sunday dinner with us. While sitting around visiting, he told me that he was making twenty-seven dollars a week and got his groceries at a discount. Later, Hill Grocery Co. made everybody pay full retail price, but then he got a discount. Every once in awhile they would come by and hand him a five or ten dollar bill because he was doing a good job. He was real happy with his work.

November 1, 1936, I said nothing, not to Reba or anybody. But on the way to work Monday morning, I decided I wasn't going to work for fifty dollars a month any longer. When I got to work, I called Mr. Waldon. He was still there, but he would come to the store and just sit all day. We went back into the warehouse. I told him I felt that I could not work any more for fifty dollars a month. But I realized that was all they paid anybody, and I was going to resign Saturday night.

Thursday morning Curt Cannon, Theron Cannon's brother, said, "Fuller, let's take our wives to the picture show at Fayette tonight. I understand there is a good one on."

"All right," I said.

I had bought a 1932 Chevrolet, and it was in good shape. I went home a little early and picked up Reba. On the way back home from the movie, Reba and Mrs. Cannon sat in the back seat. Curt said, "Fuller, Theron needs you pretty bad from now through Christmas. Everybody is coming in paying their bills and having a little money left and trading with us, and you have been looking after the buying, and are a little better acquainted with the books than any of the other clerks. "What would you stay on for until the first of January?" he asked.

"Well, for seventy-five dollars a month," I said.

"I don't know whether he will do that or not, but I'll tell him," he said.

I never heard any more about it, but Saturday afternoon about the time I was ready to leave J. D. called me back into the warehouse again and said, "Curt said you would stay until January for seventy-five dollars."

"Yes, I'm not unhappy. I just think I can do better. I'm not getting any younger," I said.

"All right, just come on back to work Monday morning," he said.

I went on back to work Monday morning. I worked on through Christmas, and things went along well. The crops turned out pretty good, collections were good, and we had a good fall business. Putting everything off until the last week, J. D. called me to the back and said, "Fuller, Theron doesn't think he can pay you seventy-five dollars a month. We have other clerks that we pay only fifty dollars a month."

"I don't blame you a bit in the world. I believe I can do better. In fact, I'm not willing to stay for seventy-five dollars, but I would stay for eighty dollars a month," I told him.

"I'm sure he won't let me do that," J. D. said. I thanked him and went on home.

I happened to remember a man named Fred Johnson—

everybody called him Sox Johnson — a fellow I knew who lived in Berry. He would pick up dry cleaning in Berry and take it to Tuscaloosa on Monday. He would get to Tuscaloosa fairly early, wait until they finished it and bring it back to Berry that night. I got up real early, drove down to Berry, and I asked, "Sox, you going to Tuscaloosa today?"

"Yeah, I just got loaded up," Sox answered.

"You got a front seat I can ride in?" I asked.

"Yeah, I'd like to have you ride with me," he answered. So I rode down with him, down the dirt roads — still dirt roads — to Tuscaloosa.

When we got to Tuscaloosa, I was just looking around and really had not even thought of any kind of job because I was doing so well farming. I decided I might buy a tractor. I'd been reading magazines like "Southern Agriculture," "Progressive Farmer," and "Country Gentleman," pretty regularly and thought I might do better than I was doing just farming.

I walked down to the International Harvester place, and just as I got there, coming out the door was Barney Dunn, whom I had played football with. I played end at first; he was a tackler and played right beside me. I had known him a long time. His daddy traded at Theron Cannon's, and Barney traded there too. He had married a girl when they finished high school in Berry. They both finished high school one year later than me. Barney said, "Hey Fuller," and turned to the man standing beside him and said, "Ralph here is your man." Then he walked on off.

The man, Ralph Hackney, was the owner and operator of Tuscaloosa Truck & Tractor Company. He said, "Come on in

Fuller. Fuller what?"

"Fuller Kimbrell," I answered.

"Come on in. What Barney was talking about is we just agreed to open an International Harvester Truck & Tractor agency in Fayette, and we need somebody to run it. What he was saying is that you are the man I was looking for," Mr. Hackney said. "Are you interested?" he asked.

"Yes, I guess so," I answered.

"When can you come back?" he asked.

"I think I can come back next Monday." I told him I could ride with Sox Johnson who brought the cleaning from Berry to Tuscaloosa.

"Write me a letter and tell me something about yourself. Come back next Monday," he said.

Next Monday, I rode again with Sox. I had told him on the way home from Tuscaloosa that I had agreed to come back to Tuscaloosa the next Monday, and I'd like to ride with him. He said, "I'll just save that seat for you."

When I got to the Tractor Company, Mr. Hackney said, "Come on in. You ready to go to work?"

"Yes, I guess so. Did you read my letter?" I asked.

"No, I haven't even opened it, but I have you a new International pickup here, and the territory manager (they called them blockmen), Mr. Perkins (who was originally from Cullman, a very nice country kind of fellow), is ready to go back to Berry and work all this week advising you and telling you the plans," Mr. Hackney said.

It was quite a new thing with me because all the major

machinery companies like John Deere, International, and Allis Chambers financed their own equipment. But since Alabama's "one cash crop" was cotton, harvested and sold in the fall, farmers were required to pay one-third down, then the company would finance the other two-thirds over a two-year period at six percent. Trucks, pickups, and larger trucks could be financed by the month, or they could be financed on the Farm Plan.

Perkins followed me back home. In Berry, there was a little boarding house operated by a widow woman named Nannie Olive. I got him a room there and I went on home. One little old restaurant in Berry, that was all there was, but he managed to make out alright.

It rained all the week. Reba and I picked him up and went to Fayette to the movie one night, but he usually just stayed in his room at the boarding house. Most of the day he would pretend he was selling me the equipment he thought might be used — and I thought might be used — in the surrounding areas.

Of course, at that time sawmilling, what we called "peckerwood" sawmilling, was the big thing, and International Harvester Company had several sizes of power units that were good for sawmilling, grist mills, and wood working equipment. You could meet almost any requirement in that area.

Friday morning Perkins left and went back home. That afternoon and Saturday morning I sold a truck and a power unit to pull a grist mill and something else. Anyway, my commission for the first week's work was thirty-six dollars. The next week, I sold a used tractor and other equipment. Counting those three weeks it turned out to be a real good month. At the end of the month, Mr. Hackney gave me a check for $188. It was my commission for three weeks.

I stopped at Cannon's store, as I did many afternoons, on the way home. I had a good relations with them, I liked them and they seem to appreciate me. Mr. Cannon asked, "How are you Fuller?"

"Fine," I answered.

"Why don't you come on back and visit?" Mr. Cannon asked me. We went back to a little side room he called his office and sat down. "How is it going?" he asked.

"Pretty good. I'm enjoying it, I guess, Mr. Cannon," I answered.

"You know what?" he asked. I hired two people for that seventy-five dollars I was paying you, one for thirty-five dollars and one for forty dollars," he said.

"Well that's fine Mr. Cannon. I'm sure glad you bettered yourself," I said.

He had a bad habit of spitting. He spat, and said, "I didn't say I bettered myself." You want to come back for the seventy-five or eighty dollars you talked about?" he asked.

I pulled the $188 check out of my shirt pocket and showed it to him. "That's what I made for the last three weeks," I said.

"I knew you would make it. I knew you would make it," he said.

FOUR

FARM MACHINERY BUSINESS

Since sawmilling was becoming one of the principal sources of income in this section of the state, I decided to concentrate on selling power units for sawmills. I also sold several power units for grist mills. When I sold a power unit or tractor, the buyer would almost immediately tell me of someone else who had been talking about buying one. I got my leads from people I sold to. Of course, if I sold a man a power unit it was a good sales pitch to tell the next prospect how satisfied the other man was because he was able to harvest his timber, which gave him an added income.

My success in selling was good from the very beginning. Every month my income was tripled or quadrupled what I had been making for the last three years, and after a couple of months — along in March 1937 — the sun began to shine and people started talking about farm machinery. Not too many people were ready to buy a tractor. In fact, the first year I think I sold only two or three to cultivate with. But I sold several tractors with heavy disk harrows to prepare land, and it was a wonderful thing for farmers. For instance, if it was a rainy spring they couldn't start plowing early. Now they could put a light on the tractors and make up for the lost time. Tractors didn't come with lights then, but they could hang a lantern out front and run until midnight, sometimes all night, with the disk harrow preparing their land. A lot of them would come behind with the section harrows, smooth the land and be ready to plant corn almost immediately. Of course I concentrated on selling horse drawn disk harrows, walking cultivators, and one or two riding cultivators that could be pulled by mules. John Deere and International concentrated on heavier tractors to prepare land, because they had not perfected a tractor power lift to be used with cultivators and planters. All in all, I continued to sell farm equipment during the entire farm season. But when crops were laid by along in July, people went back to sawmilling, so I kept pushing sawmill equipment and even sold some sawmills that were manufactured in Corinth, Mississippi, known as the Corinth Sawmill. The tractor company had never sold any sawmills before, but I came up with the idea while talking to people about power units.

During that time International Harvester Co. had a sales meeting in early March in Birmingham. I went to the meeting and learned a lot about the equipment I had not been able to learn myself. After that, at night, I read sales manuals on various equipment, because often farmers and sawmillers would ask questions that I couldn't answer. The next time I called on them I would try to be ready to answer their questions. Sometimes I would come home, read about some equipment, and go back to see the man who had asked about it the next day. Or I might call the sales manager in Tuscaloosa, Mr. Sewell from Florence,

Alabama, who was surely a nice fellow and had been selling equipment for many years. A couple of times he came up, and we went to call on farmers.

Mr. Hackney continued to look for a building in Fayette to put in a shop and farm machinery business, but was unsuccessful. About July 1, he told International Harvester that he wouldn't locate in Fayette. The company contacted Charlie Vick, a businessman and retired school teacher who lived in Fayette. He took the agency, bought land by the railroad in Fayette, built a building, and asked me if I would go to work for him. I did and worked for eleven months. All in all, I worked a year and a half selling International Harvester equipment, including the time I worked out of Tuscaloosa and the time I worked for Mr. Vick in Fayette. I continued to live in Berry on the farm, and continued to farm and my farming was still good.

I started to work for Mr. Vick July 1, 1937, when he first opened up. we went to Birmingham and brought back two new pickups. I still lived in Berry, and on the way to Fayette Saturday morning I stopped at a service station, and one of the fellows asked, "Fuller, don't you know George Simmons?"

"Yes, he used to live on my farm," I answered.

"Well, he is at the bank right now getting money to go to Winfield to buy a Chevrolet pickup," he said.

I was in that new International pickup, so I went to the bank and waited, and when he came out I said, "Get in George."

He looked at me and asked, "Why?"

"Put your bicycle in the back, and let's go get your wife, Bessie and the boys," I said.

We rode about four miles up the road north of Berry, and on the way he said, "This is a nice truck."

"Yes, I want to sell you this instead of you having to go to Winfield to buy one," I said.

"Let's see what Bessie says," he said.

After we picked up Bessie and their boys, they drove me to Fayette. Then he gave me a check on the Bank of Berry for the truck.

Mr. Vick let me drive the other new pickup, and about three days later I heard of a fellow who had gotten an insurance check. Somebody told me he was going to buy a pickup truck. I went by his house, picked him up, and took him to the mill. His boy was there and could drive, and he asked, "You want to sell me this pickup?"

"Yes," I answered.

"Well, I think this is what I like," he said, and gave me a check.

Another time Mr. Vick and I went back to Birmingham and brought back a pickup, and I sold it to a Maddox boy who lived down below Berry. The International Harvester truck representative was in Fayette, and had been waiting until I got there. I called him on the phone from Berry, and I told him I was coming over on the train, because the pickup was giving a little trouble.

"We will meet the train," he said, and asked "What in the world is wrong with that new pickup?" That was the way he talked. He was bad to worry about anything that might cost an extra dollar, not to criticize him, because he was a good fellow, all in all.

When I got off the train he asked, "Fuller, what happened to that pickup?"

I pulled out the check for $725, and I said, "This is a list of things it needs."

"You mean you got that for the new pickup? he asked. "Come on. Let's go. I'll buy your dinner," he said. We went down to the Pan Am, a small cafe in Fayette, and he bought my lunch and the salesman's lunch. Then you could get a meat, two vegetables, bread, dessert, and drink for thirty-five cents, so he could afford to buy our lunch. He made about $250 on the pickup sale.

Mr. Vick hired Zack Sanders, the "brag" salesman for the Chevrolet dealers in Fayette, who also sold for the Ford dealer. Mr. Vick had already hired a young fellow named Hop Frye. Later he and his son became the International Harvester dealers at Ashland, Alabama in Clay County, and Mr. Vick also sold. But in four months, I sold more equipment going home to Berry from Fayette than all three of them. Another reason that I out-sold them, aside from being a good salesman, was that people around Berry kept telling me of prospects which developed into sales.

Folks began to feel a little better since Roosevelt had taken office and cotton had gone from five or six cents to twelve cents a pound. Things worked out well and I continued to work for Mr. Vick for eleven months.

I had only one problem working for Mr. Vick. He and I just could not agree. He agreed to pay me a percentage of profit on each sale, which was thirty-five percent of the profit, but he would do his best to increase the expense of the sale or delivery of equipment more than it really was, and I felt that was not right. Finally, about ten months later, every time we sat down to settle up he would sit there and study and say, "That's a lot of money to have to pay." My commission was still running over $200 a month, even after I started working for him.

One day he charged several dollars more than the actual expense of delivering and setting up the equipment, and I said, "Mr. Vick, I've argued with you two or three times about trying to reduce my commission. I don't want anything except what is right. This is the last time I'm going to argue with you. If you can't figure it on the exact cost of the sale and equipment, I'm just not going to go through this anymore."

Three weeks later when we sat down to have a settlement, sure enough, he had added on to the expense of the sale again. I didn't say a word when he gave me the check. I simply pitched the keys to the pickup I was traveling in on his desk and said, "It's been nice knowing you."

I took my brief case up to Fowler's service station owned by Fletcher Fowler, who was a good friend of my family. When I walked out of the station, Wayne Pinion was sitting in a pickup truck and I got in with him. Wayne said, "Mr. Caine Butler wants to talk to you." Caine Butler had the John Deere Tractor Agency in a little shack like building. We drove around to see Caine, and he asked, "What kind of deal did you have with Mr. Vick?" I told him I got thirty-five percent of the profit from sales I made. "You want to go to work selling John Deere for the same thing?"

he asked me.

"Yes," I answered.

"Furthermore, Daddy owns the Ford automobile dealership, and the manager is Zeb Rowland. I've talked to them, and they will pay you a commission on cars and trucks," Caine said.

I went in to see Zeb Rowland, and he said, "Since Caine is going to hire you, and you are going to work for us, too, let's just put you in a new automobile."

I went home that night in a new Ford automobile. I bought it, but when I got to Berry, I pulled into the Gulf service station Joe Everette was operating and told him I was going to start selling John Deere equipment and Ford cars and trucks. J. D. Waldon's son, Jack, was there, and Joe said, "Fuller is selling Fords, and you are talking about buying a truck. Why don't you buy from him?"

"I'm ready to buy Mr. Fuller," Jack said.

I asked him, "Do you want to go to Fayette and get it now?"

"Yes," he answered.

I called the Ford place and told him the boy wanted a truck. He was going to start hauling logs. They had what he wanted, and I told them to get it ready we were coming over to get it. I was feeling pretty good, I bought a new car, and on the way home, I sold a Ford truck.

Next morning we went to church. A little while after we got home from church, a car pulled up in the yard. I looked out, and it was Mr. and Mrs. Vick. They came and sat on the porch. We visited and then Mr. Vick and I walked outside. I showed him my hogs, and took him to the barn. He said, "Fuller, maybe

I wasn't being quite fair. If you will come on back, I'll take your word for the settlement every time."

"Mr. Vick, I've already taken a job with the John Deere folks, Butler Tractor and Implement Company, and in addition, I'm going to work for the Ford dealer. I've already sold a Ford truck and made the commission on nearly a $700 sale. I guess I'll just stay with them," I said.

"Well, I wish I had been a little more careful about the way I treated you," Mr. Vick said.

"I appreciate you saying that. I don't have any ill will against you. We will always be friends," I said.

"All right," he said. He called Mrs. Vick; they got in the car, and left.

Monday morning I went back to Fayette in my new car and surveyed the situation at the John Deere Agency. First, I noticed they were in a metal building about 60'X 80' with a dirt floor, and when it rained water stood in it, and there were planks to walk on. Furthermore, they had three shop-worn tractors. In fact, almost everything they had in inventory was shop-worn, which meant it had been there for at least a year or more. All three tractors were John Deere Model B with steel wheels. Then people began to talk about tractors on rubber, but they still were not convinced that rubber was better than steel. I didn't get discouraged. Caine Butler and I got out the very first day, and we drove to Millport, toward Columbus, Mississippi, and found a lady named Ms. Lizzie Hitt. Ms. Hitt had two nephews who were quite some characters. She had promised to buy them a tractor to prepare their land. We talked to her and figured around and around but couldn't make a trade with her. Uncle Meek, my father's brother and quite an individual, was with us, and we drove back to Millport for lunch. I told Uncle Meek and Caine Butler, "Take your time eating, I am going back to Ms. Hitt's and sell that tractor." I went back, and sure enough, I traded with Ms. Lizzie, got a check for the tractor, and we came on back to Fayette.

Two days later, we went down to see Brother Lucius Clemons, a Baptist preacher who lived on the edge of Tuscaloosa County. He had traded with me when I worked at Theron Cannon's, and knew that my father was a Baptist preacher. In fact, he had spent the night with us a time or two. We sold him another one of those shop-worn tractors. Then we found out that Jeff Lawrence, who lived up on New River above Fayette, was interested in a tractor. So we loaded one up with a disk harrow and went to see him, demonstrating the tractor in some sage grass fields. He decided he wanted the tractor. We sold him the other shop-worn tractor, which was on steel, and the harrow. We were rid of all three.

John Deere Company announced a sales meeting in Memphis, Tennessee, so Caine and I drove to Memphis and spent the night. The next morning we went to an all-day sales meeting. Unknowingly to any of the dealers, the reason John Deere had the sales meeting was to announce that they were coming out with a new style tractor. They were a few months ahead of International Harvester with a new model tractor. I had hesitated trying to sell the old John Deere tractor with two cylinders, since I was convinced that International Harvester had good equipment—and they did, I thought—far superior to John Deere's. I had to bite my tongue trying to sell the three old tractors that were in stock, even though they were still cheap.

But when we saw the new model John Deere tractor, and Mr. Maddox went through and pointed out all the advantages of it and how it had so many less moving parts, everybody was convinced that it was far superior to anything on the market. They had added a self-starter. Mr. Maddox was the sales manager for the whole St. Louis division, which included about eleven states. Fayette's dealership was from the Memphis branch, where the sales meeting was. We came back home that night, and Jim Dyer, a fellow who traded with me at Theron Cannon's, came in, and I showed him a folder on the new tractor. He looked at it and took it home.

We waited two or three days, went down to his house and sold him a new, bigger tractor. We got more new tractors and put them in stock. John Deere had a movie made. We rented the movie theater and invited people from all around the Fayette County area to come. They showed on the movie screen all the equipment and cultivators and demonstrated what they were capable of doing. As a result of the movie, I sold five or six John Deere tractors with disk harrows. Things were really looking good. This happened around July 1, 1938.

Things kept getting better. We didn't sell any tractors to cultivate with, but sold several tractors to prepare land. The price of cotton was higher, and farmers had a better attitude. Sawmilling was really good. In fact, I sold quite a few power units while I still worked for International Harvester. John Deere had a power unit, too, that was very popular with sawmillers. It was cheaper and sold for only $700. I sold several.

When I first began to talk and trade with Mr. Butler and to work with him, I didn't know that Caine had a drinking problem. He and Crick, his brother-in-law, who was in the coal business, shared a bookkeeper, Wayne Pinion, and each paid him fifteen dollars a week. When Caine got his money he never put it in the bank, and when John Deere came to collect — which was every sixty or ninety days — they took inventory. He would give them a check for whatever had been sold. He would still get five percent cash discount. Like International Harvester, they financed their own equipment without recourse to the dealer. But there was never any money in the bank, so Caine would go to see his daddy, who owned Allen Lumber Company. Mr. Butler would give him a check for the amount he owed.

We had a good spring and sold a lot of power units for sawmilling purposes. In fact, I worked out with Corinth Mill Company that manufactured small sawmills to allow me to sell their sawmills. I sold several to people to cut their own timber. They could get in the sawmill business for $1200 to $1500, and I sold several sawmills with the power units to go with them.

One time we stopped at a cattle auction sale barn. Back then farmers brought their cattle to the barn to sell. We stopped at this place in Russellville, and there were a couple of hundred cattle, cows, and a lot of hogs. They were selling like hot cakes, so we decided on the way back to Fayette that it would be good for us to put in a sale barn.

We moved all of the equipment out of that little old building.

There were no restrictions then about getting permits to do such things, although we were right in town. We were only one block off the main street in Fayette. Caine went out to call on the Newmans, Mr. Grady Newman, and swapped him a power unit for lumber to build a sale barn. They took the power unit to Mr. Newman and a few days later they brought in great big, wide twelve inch planks. We got busy and boarded it up around there and opened up the sale barn.

The first two sales were pretty good. I knew Mr. Cannon had a lot of fine heifers, so I traded with him at two and a half cents a pound. When we brought them in, though, they only brought two cents a pound. We lasted in the cattle business about three months. We decided that it wasn't for us, because we didn't have time to go out and encourage the farmers to bring their cattle to our barn. They had more buyers at other cattle sale barns, like Russellville, Tuscaloosa, Eutaw, and Livingston. Columbus was very popular, too. Of course folks brought in mules, too, and hogs. The opportunity to get a better price for their cattle was at Columbus or Russellville, so we just closed down after losing $700. I've told quite often that I gave $1.50 for a hickory bent stick made into a real nice little neat walking stick, which I purchased from a farmer who came to every sale selling hickory walking sticks. I still have it. When I show it to people, I tell them it cost me $700.

We continued along and every two or three months when the John Deere people would come in to settle with Butler Tractor and Implement Company, they would have to go back to Mr. Butler. In October 1938, John Deere came in to settle and went down to see Mr. Butler. Mr. Butler said, "Well I'm going to pay you off, and you go down and pick up whatever equipment still belongs to John Deere."

I went down to see him, and we were sitting there talking. He said, "Son, I don't want to give up that John Deere business. I've got a pretty nice farm, and I enjoy farming. I like it, and it's got possibilities. Tell you what let's do. We will go inventory, and for whatever inventory there is, I'll type up a little letter for that amount. When you pay me that much money, you will own half-interest in the company. If you want to do that."

"Mr. Butler, the company owes me $288 commission. I sure need it," I told him.

"I'll pay you that out of my pocket, and it won't have to be added to the deal," Mr. Butler said.

We went up and inventoried. It inventoried $2200, and almost all of it was shop-worn equipment, plus $400 in accounts receivable. I don't remember how much of the $400 we collected. We had collected $3.65 that day, and it was all the money we had. That was the 7th day of October, 1938.

In the deal, Mr. Butler said, "I will have Caine come back to the farm and manage the dairy. We are milking cows now. You will manage and operate the business by yourself, and change the name to B&K Tractor & Implement Company. I realized this was a lifetime opportunity. I really went to work. Farmers' confidence and opportunities had improved along with the economy. My success in selling and profits had improved, as well as my confidence.

January 1, 1939, I walked into Allen Lumber Company and

said, "Mr. Butler, I'm ready to pay you the $2200." He said, "Son I knew you were doing good, but I don't need that money. The bank has just been down here, and they have 466 acres of land right down just south of town. The old Bankhead place. Let's just go let the B & K Tractor & Implement Company buy that farm."

"Okay," I said.

We went and looked at the farm, then went back to the bank and made out a note and mortgage. I signed it, and Caine Butler signed it. I decided I would move from Berry over there instead of driving that twenty-six miles twice a day. By that time I was traveling in a pickup truck instead of my car. I would leave the car at home for Reba.

I decided to build a house. Reba's brother, Ray Shook and her father were expert carpenters. So I traded with them to build the house. Reba had a lot of talent and could sketch and draw pictures and had developed into quite an artist later on. So she drew off a floor plan, and they came over and started building on the first day of February. I traded power units for lumber, and a tractor for cypress shingles on Luxapillia River in Lamar County.

There was a great big fine spring on top of the hill on the farm where we built the house. It had the finest "freestone" water—commonly called back then because it was free of minerals—you've ever tasted. I built a great big concrete trough, and put a screen over it so animals couldn't get in it, and ran a one inch water line down the hill into the new house. The pressure was sufficient and we had running water in the bathroom and kitchen. We had plenty of free water.

I planted fruit trees, and cleared the surrounding land. I traded a power unit for lumber to build a big crib, which we filled with corn, traded a tractor and power unit to build a fence around the area, and built a nice big western-type barn. I had built a really nice house. It was a fine liveable home. It was the talk of the county about how I had progressed down on the farm.

We moved into our new home the first day of May, 1939. I paid for the house while it was being built. It cost $2345 out of the tractor company's pocket.

The farm had grown up in weeds and bushes. I had a couple of families who were sharecroppers on my farm at Berry, and I would bring them over to cut down bushes and clear the land. I got busy, built a fence, plowed up the land, and planted corn. It was all going to be planted in corn and hay. I would go out and get customers to whom I had sold tractors, but not a cultivator or planter, so far. They were just preparing their land. I would take them to the farm and show them what pretty rows and what a fine stand of corn we had. I sold nearly everyone that I had sold a tractor to a cultivator and planter by planting time, which enabled them to plant corn and cotton and use their cultivators that season.

At first, I had a problem selling two-row equipment. But later, farmers saw they could cultivate with a two-row as well or better than they could with a one-row tractor.

As I've said, Caine and I had developed a very close friendship. When he came by occasionally, I would report to him what I had done, what was going on, and what things looked like. Caine and I continued to farm, and gathered a good corn crop. As I have said, I would bring farmers in to show them what perfect rows we had and what a good stand of corn we had, which was getting them ready for the next season.

We decided that since Caine was out and going to farm anyway, we would rent Mr. Butler's farm, which was located in Fayette, where Brewer Campus is now. Mr. Butler owned all that land and the surrounding area. So we decided instead of planting corn there we would plant oats. We would then plant Lespadesia in the spring and harvest hay. We fertilized the oats and got a grain drill, which was unheard of in this section of the country. We planted about 100 acres of oats, from which we got both a good yield and a good price. In the spring, we would use the grain drill to fertilize the oat crop and plant Lespadesia seed. Along in August we would harvest the Lespadesia and have the finest hay. We got two crops off the land and both were very profitable. All this was done under the name of B & K Tractor & Implement Company. We made good money farming.

The second year, the idea came to me that if I bought seed oats that were certified by Auburn Extension Service I could get about fifty cents a bushel more for my oats than I could otherwise. I got the oats certified, had them sacked neatly, and sold Sumter Farm & Stock Company at Geiger, Alabama 100 bushels of oats for plant seed, getting $1.35 a bushel when oats were bringing only eighty-five cents a bushel otherwise. I sold nearly all the oats we had that year for seed and made an extra 50 cents a bushel. In the meantime, I developed a very close relationship with Sumter Farm & Stock Company. They had a 17,000 acre farm, about half of it in pasture, and grew a lot of hay and corn. I sold them several tractors, a mower, and balers to bale their hay. The second year we planted the oats and had Lespadesia coming in.

One Sunday I was sitting looking at the Farm & Implement News, a magazine that catered to farm equipment. I saw an ad about the New Holland Machinery Company in New Holland, Pennsylvania — a Dutch company. The ad was for an automatic baler that could bale hay. Monday morning when I got to the office, it was time to cut and bale our hay. All we had was a little old baler you had to feed by hand. It was dangerous and run by a little gasoline engine. Baling hay in the summertime was the hottest and hardest work in the world, because it had to be done in August when the weather was the hottest. I called New Holland Machinery Company in New Holland, Pennsylvania, and told them I had seen their ad in the magazine. I asked if the baler would do everything they claimed. He said, "Yes, we will ship you one, and if it doesn't do the job you can ship it back at our expense. We will ship it with bill of lading attached." I told him all right.

In four or five days, I had a New Holland baler. We baled almost 11,000 bales of our own hay with it. It was the first automatic hay baler in the South.

John Lee (later one of my nieces married his son) and I developed a real close relationship. I had sold him a tractor, and I knew that he had a lot of hay down in the Johnson grass country, which was all over middle Alabama in the Black Belt and Mississippi. I told him I was almost through baling and wanted him to come watch us bale the last day with our baler. He came up, bought the baler, and gave me my money back for it—and a little more than I had paid for it—right then. We sent it down to him, and he baled his hay crop. I talked to him later and found out he used it for over ten years. From that we developed a real good relationship with New Holland Machinery Company. In one year I sold thirty-three automatic balers, which was enormous for those times.

Another very profitable sideline came from selling disk harrows. When I worked for International Harvester, they had a bush and bog harrow, which was a large heavy disk harrow with only the front section. Most of the farmers used it only to prepare land. Instead of using a plow, they would use the disk harrow, and then drag the section harrow over the land before they planted.

John Deere did not have a heavy harrow like that. I was very well-connected with the Caterpillar Tractor Co. in Birmingham, which was Pittman Tractor Company at that time. They told me about Rome Plow Company in Cedar Town, Georgia. In December, 1939, I drove to Cedar Town to see the Rome Plow people. Although I sold for John Deere Tractor Agency, it worked out that I could buy disk harrows from the Rome Plow plant. Reba was with me and we found a place where they made extra good cheese. We brought a lot of cheese back— since it was during the Christmas Holidays—to give out to special customers, to the bankers and others. It turned out to be a very profitable trip.

Later farmers began to buy more and more plows. One time I called the Rome Plow Company and told them I needed twelve harrows. The salesman said they had them, but they didn't have any disks. So I told him, "Well, you just ship them over here broken down, or I will send for them, 'cause I have the disks."

"What!" he said.

"Yes, I have the disks," I repeated. I don't know how I came to have that many disks. I sent a dump truck over to Cedar Town, Georgia, and they loaded frames, bearings, and everything in that dump truck. We brought them back and spilled them out — like unloading a load of gravel — in the shop and put them together.

The trip that Reba and I made to Cedar Town, Georgia, to call on Rome Plow Company in regards to the heavy disk harrow, turned out to be a very profitable trip, because people were not using many plows at the time, but used a heavy disk harrow to prepare the land. They were able during those times to supply me with most all the disk harrows I wanted, which made it possible for me make a lot of sales I would not have been able to make, and to sell a tractors to go along with the heavy disk harrows. I remember one time when Caine Butler and I went to Gorgas community near Tuscaloosa, a very profitable farming community and made 38 sales. I would say that at least a third of those sales were heavy disk harrows, some with the tractor to go with them, but most of the people already had a tractor.

FIVE

FARM MACHINERY BUSINESS EXPANDED BEGINNING OF POLITICAL CAREER

I first started selling International Harvester trucks and tractors for Tuscaloosa Truck and Tractor Company, owned by Ralph Hackney. I called on Mr. Hugh Harkins, a very successful farmer who owned quite a large cotton and corn farm west of Fayette on the Luxapilliar River, and sold him two tractors. One was a large tractor to prepare his land and one was a small tractor to cultivate with. A sale like that was kind of unheard of in Tuscaloosa then. When I called on him to sell this equipment, his son, Bruce, and his wife were there. Bruce was the vocational agriculture teacher in Cuba in Sumter County. He was moving back to Fayette and planned to run for superintendent of education. I developed a quick friendship with him that day and told him I was traveling all over Fayette County and would be glad to help him and have him go with me sometimes to call on customers. Since I had been working almost two years selling farm equipment, I was getting to be well-known all over the county. He said he would appreciate it. When it was time to run for superintendent of education, he resigned from his job in Cuba and came back to Fayette, and traveled with me often. He was elected superintendent of education, and he and his wife moved back to Fayette.

When President Roosevelt's Farm and Defense program expanded and became effective all over the United States, Bruce Harkins — as superintendent of education, took advantage of the program and built a canning plant in Fayette. Since they needed something to can, they rented a farm and hired people to work. People were willing to work for almost any wage. They were in dire need, as they had been without money for several years.

I had cleared and cultivated the land on the farm I owned and built a home there. It was in good shape, so I rented him a hundred acres at ten dollars per acre for two years. Sometimes he would have as many as forty people working on the farm. They did a great job cleaning the area and kept every sprig of grass and weeds out of the vegetables. They canned thousands of cans of vegetables to be used for the war effort, and even shipped some to the cities where people were still in the bread lines. Not only did I rent him the land, but I also rented two tractors to the government to be used to prepare the land, plant, and cultivate the vegetables to be canned.

A funny thing was when I bid to rent the tractors, I was the only bidder. He wanted one-row tractors, and I rented him two at $5.50 per hour. According to the contract they would be used fourteen hours a day because the country was on daylight saving time. When I sent the first invoice, they had only used one tractor five days and one three days. I thought I wasn't doing too good, but I sent the invoice in for those number of hours at $5.50 per hour. They sent it back with a note to "read your contract." I looked at it and read it over, but I couldn't find anything wrong.

I took the contract to my lawyer, Alex Smith, and asked, "Tell me what I need to read in this contract that I haven't read?"

Mr. Smith read the contract and said, "Fuller, you are supposed to bill them for fourteen hours a day every day except when the tractors are broken down for over four hours at a time."

Instead of billing them for less than $100, I should have billed them for nearly $3000 and finally did so for the first month. It was a sixty day contract and was renewed for another sixty days. I got twice the value of my equipment out of those two sixty day contracts.

I also furnished equipment for another farm in Gadsden about the same size; I rented them two tractors. After thirty days they wanted a larger tractor, so I sent them one and got the price of my equipment back. At the end of the sixty day contract, a fellow in Gadsden underbid me on the equipment to be used for gardening the next year. I lost the contract, but they bought my equipment, and I didn't have to bring it back.

Another successful enterprise we got into that didn't interfere with my selling equipment was trading cattle. One time Caine and I went over to Tupelo, Mississippi to the State Fair. Johnson Dairy in Tupelo had the finest Jersey cattle in the South. We bought a fine young Jersey bull. We traded tractors and equipment for some fine heifers and bred them to that fine Jersey bull. We could get five to ten dollars more for a springer heifer (a cow that is ready to drop a calf pretty soon and will be a milk cow). Often a calf would be born before we sold the heifer, and it would always be the prettiest calf you'd ever want to see. That made it easier to sell. We continued to do that and we also traded in corn. We grew a lot of corn. We expanded our farm into corn and oats.

The government offered for sale in carload lots surplus wheat. We traded in some hogs and got into a separate little business with Bruce Harkins. I offered to swap him my interest in that little business for his interest in the pigs, and he traded with me. So I had nearly 300 real small pigs. I bought a carload of wheat and mixed it with corn to feed the pigs.

Early one Monday morning, Reba and I went to Memphis to the stockyard. I told the fellow showing me around what I wanted, and he took me over to the pig lot. I pointed to a pig and asked what it weighed. He told me about ninety pounds.

"How long will it take you to pick 100 pigs about the same size and send them to me in Fayette, Alabama?" I asked.

He said, "I'll be in your yard with them Thursday morning by the time you get up." He sent me a truckload containing 105 pigs, and if they had weighed fifteen pounds more they would have averaged each pig weighing ninety pounds. We fed those pigs and in sixty days the top hog—as it was classified in those days— dressed out about 180 to 200 pounds.

During the war, meat packing houses could not ship very much meat to local markets, but a farmer could sell anything he produced without a permit or permission of any kind. We went to Walker County, to Jasper and the surrounding area, which was more of an industrial and mining area with less farming. We called on a lot of the small grocery stores and worked out with managers and owners for them to buy our meat. We would take them a butchered pig one week, and they told us to bring them another one next week. We started butchering those hogs in about sixty days, and we killed anywhere from ten to twenty-three a day. We would throw them in the back of the truck and deliver them. We'd get paid for them on the spot.

We were making a real good profit with hogs. We went to Selma to an auction sale and bought thirty-eight feeder steers. We paid $1830 for them and made $400 profit. But we made $1000 on our hog operation in a shorter time.

When we butchered hogs, we cooked the fat for lard and had several fifty pound cans of lard. One day Mr. Jenkins — a fellow I knew real well — and Bone Tilley, the man I sold my first power unit to, came into my office at B & K Tractor & Implement Co. I knew he was bad to drink, but he wasn't drinking then. I asked, "What you got in your pocket?"

"I found some lard at Williams' Grocery Store, and I bought two pounds. That's all he would sell me," Jenkins said.

"What will you give me for a fifty pound can of lard?" I asked him.

He exclaimed, "God, you got a fifty pound can of lard!"

"Yes," I answered.

"I got to have that," Jenkins said. What will you take?" he asked.

"I guess twenty-five dollars," I said.

"I'll take it," he said.

I told him to go to the bank and get the cash. I wasn't going to take a check. Meanwhile, I sent to the farm to get the lard. A fellow had given me a fifth of wildcat whiskey, and while they were still there I held it up and said, "I'll bet you would like to have this."

"By God, we got to have that," Bone Tilley said.

"No, I'm not going to let you have that," I said.

About an hour later they came back and from the way they sounded I could tell they had been drinking. Jenkins gave me twenty-five dollars for the can of lard and handed me another ten dollars and said, "We'll give you that for the fifth."

"No, I'm not going to sell you that fifth of whiskey. A fellow gave it to me," I said.

"Yeah, we've got to have that," Bone Tilley said.

"All right, give me six dollars. I'm not going to charge ten dollars for it. Get in your car and I will bring it to the car," I said. I wrapped it in newspaper and put it in a paper sack and laid it in their car. By the time they got up the road, I got scared. I thought, "Lord, have mercy. Here I've sold lard that may be illegal and wildcat whiskey I know is illegal. If they get stopped up the road by the law and are asked where they got the lard, they would say 'Fuller Kimbrell.' 'And where did you get the wildcat whiskey?' 'From Fuller Kimbrell.'" I was really worried for a few hours until I knew they had time to get home.

Fayette did not have a country club, so a group of business leaders were called together to organize and build one. They found a suitable piece of land west of town. I was in the organizational meeting and told them Caine and I would give a tractor and mower, provided we would have a membership. The people who donated were to have a first year's membership. I think dues were to be about twenty-five dollars per month, as they were planning to build a nine hole golf course. Back then, the county commissioners could do more work than they can do today and were not restricted from private work. But that was not thought of as private, or it was debatable. The county commissioner had agreed to do quite a bit of excavating—and more—provided we would buy the gas and furnish the equipment operators. It worked out Caine and I had our membership. We furnished a John Deere Model M one-row tractor that had been used several years for mowing. It was not good for mowing greens on the golf course though, because they did that with a little hand mower for a long time.

Mr. Butler's oldest son, Joe Neal, who was the Sinclair gas and oil distributor for Fayette and Lamar Counties, developed a brain tumor and was taking so many pain killers he had almost become an addict. Mr. Butler called me in one morning and said, "Fuller, Joe is not able to run the Sinclair Agency anymore, and it's working on me like the tractor business did. How about you taking it over and running it?"

It was early fall in 1939, and I knew I would not be working all that hard in the equipment business during bad weather. So I said, "All right." We inventoried and I gave Mr. Butler $1800 for the agency, and I took it over and begin to straighten it out.

The first year I made $5500 profit, but I just didn't like it. If I could have toughed it out until recent years it would have really been fine. It has changed names twice, but is still not one of the most popular brands. I got a chance to sell it a little later and got $5100 for it, making about $3300 in the deal plus operating profit.

At that time we would take checks from service stations located all over Fayette and Lamar Counties. Service stations would take checks for gas, and when our truckers would go out to deliver gas he would take checks. We had more bad checks returned than I have had during all my life before or since. They were small checks for five and ten dollars. Times were still hard and money was not back in good supply. That was one reason I wanted to get out of the oil business. Besides, I was really sold on the farm machinery business, and I needed to put more attention to that.

John Deere had several parent branches: one in Baltimore, Maryland, one in St. Louis, one in Atlanta, one in Chicago, and several in the west. The possibility of getting equipment out of Atlanta was much greater than getting it out of Nashville or Memphis.

Dealerships were established in most of the larger counties, particularly in the farming areas in Alabama. The Extension service was real cooperative, and every county had a county agent who had farming experience. They were very eager for us to come and demonstrate to farmers how to build the terraces required by Roosevelt's farm program. Quite often at farm meetings, the county agent would ask me to come and talk about farming, and quite often he would bring people to our farm to show them our farm operation. This happened particularly when we were using the grain drill, which was brand new for our area, to plant oats and also when we put out fertilizer.

As I said, dealerships were established all over the state. J.

B. Wilson, a farm equipment manager at Auburn University, came up with the idea of organizing the farm machinery dealers. We met at the Whitley Hotel in Montgomery and organized the Alabama Farm Equipment Association and elected him secretary. He served as secretary for several years until he retired from Auburn. They picked four board members. An International Harvester dealer from Mobile was the first president, and I was on the Board of Directors they selected the first year. I became president the third year after the organization was formed. The Board would meet in different cities, and it gave me a chance to swap equipment with them or find out what they had they didn't need and what I had I wanted to swap for something else. If you had a piece of equipment, you didn't want to sell it to another dealer. You wanted to swap for something you could sell and make that additional profit.

Alabama Farm Equipment Dealers Association Board met once a quarter, so we decided to have regular farm equipment conventions. At that time, it was easy to get representatives from John Deere or International Harvester for speakers. And Auburn was always willing to furnish a speaker, because they were beginning to get as excited about power equipment as the farmers and dealers were. Of course, none of the speakers charged. The convention was a wonderful place to swap ideas. It was especially fine since business management was a new experience for me. I would talk to the other dealers who had more education and whom I felt were more qualified to operate a business than I.

I talked with them about how they managed their parts

departments and shops, and always swapped ideas with other dealers as to what they allowed for trade-ins, especially tractors that had steel wheels. After 1944-45 you didn't sell farmers tractors on steel anymore. The ones you had sold you took back in trade and changed to rubber. To buy new wheels from companies like John Deere or International Harvester, a lot of times you would just buy rims and send them to the shop. They would cut the rim off, weld a rubber tire rim on, and you would change it to rubber. We did that on three of the tractors that were in the Butler Tractor and Implement Company stock when I first went to work for them.

Farmers began to have money again. They had money to buy equipment and became more and more confident in power equipment. After that I would go every few days and visit, particularly in the Tennessee Valley. I would go to Decatur and Huntsville, visit the dealers and trade bigger tractors for smaller ones, as I did in Earl, Arkansas.

A company in Illinois had developed an easy-flow fertilizer spreader used for wheat, oats, and pastures. One summer I bought a truckload of fertilizer spreaders. By that time many farmers had begun to plant oats and even planted soybeans with the grain drill. But soybeans were planted only for hay and had to be harvested before they got so ripe they would shatter. They made wonderful hay, particularly for people who had dairies. The beans in the hay would really make fine feed for dairy cows and for fattening young steers.

During the war, John Deere offered surplus peanut pickers, and I bought four. It happened Max Branyon from Fayette was a captain in the Army at the helicopter field in Enterprise. He called and wanted to know if we had a hay baler, mower, and tractor we could sell him. Caine and I jumped in the car and went to Enterprise to see him. When we got there we told him we had a peanut picker too. In fact, we had taken the hay baler, mower, and tractor when we went because he said he would buy it for the Army. I went back and sent the peanut picker, but Caine stayed in Enterprise and rode the truck back the next day.

On the way back, I stopped at the John Deere Dealer and swapped him a peanut picker. In fact, I think we had four peanut pickers, and I swapped him two for some kind of equipment — I don't remember what kind it was. At that time John Deere had not come out with automatic balers — maybe it was a tractor. But anyway, I traded with him. Later I called the dealer in Montgomery, and he told me of a dealer in Dothan, Alabama that would like to have the peanut picker. I sold it to him at retail price even though the prices on some things were frozen. But if you bought a clean piece of equipment from somebody you could add any kind of profit the buyer was willing to pay. If you bought it shipped from the factory, you had to sell it at dealer's price, plus your freight and handling, but we shipped one to a dealer and sold it at retail price.

In the early 1940's John Deere decided to give a few key dealers an extra discount on carloads of horse drawn equipment, so I bought a carload. John Deere had the finest corn planter in the world and still does as far as I know. It was horse drawn and later they were made to be used with tractors. They also had the one- and two-row horse drawn planters. In our area around Fayette and north and west of Fayette, everyone used a one-row planter. I bought over 100 of those planters at one time. R. F. Odom & Sons in Millport was one of my dealers and Will Crump in Tuscaloosa County was another dealer. I sold them several planters. John Deere gave fall payments on equipment. Of course, I gave those fellows fall payments, too, because I didn't have to pay for it until fall. Along about then, I made Paul Guin, who owned Guin Hardware in Guin, Alabama, a horse drawn farm equipment dealer.

After I sold Paul Guin's horse drawn equipment and made him a subdealer, he decided maybe he could sell tractors. He went to Nashville and worked out with them to be a power equipment dealer, too. I had spent thousands of dollars to build one of the nicest new buildings in north Alabama and carried a large inventory of repair parts for all the equipment we sold for tractors and other farm machinery and horse drawn equipment. But he never stocked anything as a dealer was supposed to. He would sell somebody a tractor for a hundred dollars over cost and let them go pick it up at Nashville. They would give him a check for it and knock me out of a sale. He did that a couple of times.

Finally one morning, I found out he had sold a tractor to a fellow in Sulligent, and I called Mr. Baldridge, the branch manager at Nashville, and told him I wanted to invite him to the auction sale. Mr. Baldridge asked, "What do you mean?"

I said, "Paul Guin just sold another tractor for $50 or $100 above cost and let the man go up to Nashville and pick it up, and here I've spent thousands of dollars building the finest building in North Alabama, and carrying a heavy inventory. I can't compete with a man who has no investment at all."

He said, "I'll take care of that right now," and he did. They canceled Paul Guin's contract immediately.

The Tuscaloosa store developed several customers with large farms. One very profitable customer was Sumter Farm and Stock Company, in Sumter County. Sumter Farm and Stock Company owned and operated Yellow Front Stores in most small towns in West Alabama and down as far as Mobile. I developed a close relationship with the President, Mr. O. J. Henley. He would meet me or go with me to the farm in Sumter County. He had International Harvester equipment when I first met him, but right away he got rid of all the International tractors and bought John Deeres. They produced registered white faced cattle, had a lot of feeder cattle, and grew a lot of hay and corn. Their business was not just tractors, but balers, corn pickers, mowers, and whatever it took— even hammermills to grind the feed and a mixer to mix the feed. They also bought a carload of wheat one time.

In order to promote farm machinery and get as much attention as possible, my son, Donald, who was old enough to be in the 4-H Club, and I went to Sumter Farm and bought two fine calves. Mr. Farquhar was the beef cattle farm manager, so I got him to help me pick calves he thought would be winners. He asked me to give him a few days to go through the herd.

About a week later, he called and asked, "Why don't you come down here? I have some calves I want to show you. You can bring your pickup. No, let me deliver them if you decide you want them."

I bought the two calves and Donald fed and cared for them. He won the Fayette County championship and the championship in Birmingham with his steer. He took both of them to Birmingham and let his first cousin, Harold Dean Simpson, show one of them, and Harold Dean came in with second prize at the State Fair in Birmingham. I have several pictures of Donald and Harold Dean with the calves. Later, I had Donald show a Jersey calf at the County Fair in Fayette, and he won a blue ribbon.

I had another interesting customer, Walker McKee, in Marengo County. His father-in-law had the Tom Christian General Store in Tuscaloosa. I remember one time I sold him a tractor and had lunch with him. Senator John Bankhead, also, was having lunch with him the same day. The Senator had sent Walker McKee's daughter a Shetland pony, and we were out in the yard looking at it. I had a nice letter from Senator Bankhead after he went back to Washington. I wish I had kept it.

A couple of other interesting things that developed into sales: Caine and I were going to Memphis to a meeting, and we left on Sunday morning. A fellow by the name of Knight, who lived in Detroit, Alabama, in Lamar County, sent word that he wanted to buy a tractor. We decided to stop by and see him on the way to Memphis. It wasn't much out of the way, so we went by his house. His wife said he had gone to church. We went to the church and he had already gone in. We asked a man that was walking in if he would tell Mr. Knight that Fuller Kimbrell was outside and wanted to see him. Mr. Knight came out and we told him we were on the way to Memphis and we thought we could get him a tractor. He wanted a Model B, he said, "Just go on and get it, and since it's Sunday we won't settle down to a price. But I do want the tractor."

We got him a tractor. As I best remember, we had it sent to him. Later I talked to him over the phone, sent him a bill, and he sent me a check.

Another interesting customer at Sulligent was Lee Crump, a U.S. Marshal for north Alabama. His son, Paul, came to my house one morning about three o'clock, and said, "Daddy's coming home this week, and if you will be over there in the morning I think he will buy me a tractor and some other equipment."

"All right," I said, and went back to sleep.

I got up early and drove over. Sure enough they were out in the barnyard. Russell, his other son, was out in the barn with him. I didn't tell Marshall Crump that Paul had talked to me. Finally, Marshal Crump spoke up and said, "The boys say they want a tractor."

"Yes I heard you needed one. You have a lot of hay. Maybe you will buy a baler and a mower," I said.

"Yes, I guess we have to have it," he said.

We sat down, and I sold him a tractor and a mower, a hay baler, and a rake, and financed it by the month. He paid so much down and so much a month, as U. S. Marshals didn't make any thing like the money they make now. But it was a good salary for those days.

Another thing I remember so well: I was on my way to Dallas

County to see a farmer at Orville, Alabama, who bought a tractor and New Holland baler from me, and I was hoping I could collect for it. It was "D Day" and I heard over the radio President Roosevelt asked that everyone go to church or have silent prayer at eleven o'clock that morning. It just so happened I was passing by the Baptist Church in Greensboro, Alabama, and I pulled over to the side, got out and went into the church. Already there were several people in the church and several more were coming in. But I didn't know any of them, and nobody was saying a word. I sat there about thirty minutes and whispered a prayer.

About 1942 the Ford Motor Company began to sell their tractors, which turned out to be strong competition. The Ford tractor was good for lighter, sandy soil — not heavy soil, and they only produced one size. But Ford had something that was very convenient, as all their equipment fastened with a three-point hitch that was operated by a hydraulic lift. They advertised that it had down pressure as well as up pressure. If you came to a hard place in the ground when you were plowing, it would keep plowing the same depth as it would if you were plowing in soft ground. If it came to soft ground, it would hold the plow up instead of running deep as for hard ground — and it was pretty well true.

The Ford Distributor representative came to the Ford automobile dealer in Fayette. By that time, I had moved my business out of the little metal building that I described before and into another building next door to Allen Lumber Company. Mr. Butler called and said, "Fuller, Ford Motor Company folks are here." I remember one was Mr. Carpenter, but don't remember the other person's name. "They want to put the Ford Tractor business in with the Ford Automobile dealer, but I told them it would be better to let B & K Tractor Company have it."

"Yes," I said. We talked and I showed them the building I was in and signed up with them.

We sent trucks and picked up a couple of tractors, some parts, and whatever else they recommended. We did pretty good. It wasn't any problem. Equipment was still scarce, and we could sell anything we got in the way of tractors and equipment that could be used in this area.

It rocked along. We were doing pretty good. We had John Deere on one side of the building and Ford tractors and equipment on the other side. John Deere didn't like it a bit because they had tried to put some John Deere dealers in with the Ford automobile dealers and Ford wouldn't let them. The John Deere sales manager, Mr. White, called and said they were going to demonstrate a light disk plow at Athens, Alabama and wanted me see it. I knew what was up before I got there. I went and noticed that the plow was a little too light for that heavy red soil in the Tennessee Valley. They finally sent a part down to a machine shop to put a crease in the metal part that was bending, and it worked well. That gave it strength to work the heavy red Alabama soil. We sold several later for the small tractors to be used in our lighter soil here.

But what they really wanted to talk to me about was that they were not going to let me keep the Ford dealership. I wasn't worried about it because they had trouble in the smaller communities having a dealer that sold much equipment before, and I knew I was doing a good job for them. I wasn't worried about them taking the dealership from me because they didn't have anybody they wanted to give it to. Finally Mr. White said, "Fuller, I just don't understand why you want to do that."

I said, "Mr. White, I've explained to you that if I didn't take it Caine's daddy would put it in with the Ford dealer, and we would have rough competition. I used every word I have in my vocabulary to explain it."

"You've explained it all right," Mr. White said.

They didn't make me give up the Ford dealership. But about six months later two representatives from Ford came in one morning and looked around a little bit. They said, "Mr. Kimbrell, you are either not a Ford dealer, or you are not a John Deere dealer."

I was pretty cocky then, and I said, "Well, no decision to make there. I'm not a Ford Dealer." They didn't answer, just stood around and talked a little while and walked out. I thought, "Maybe I've hit the jackpot; I may have bluffed them." Two days later, I had sold Brown Lumber Company seventeen tractors. The first Ford tractors had eight inch wheels, and the new ones that had just come out had ten inch wheels and tires. Mr. Loper, President of Brown Lumber Company, came in and asked, "Fuller, can you get me wheels and tires for all seventeen of my tractors, and come change them out for me?" I told him I would be glad to do it. I called the Memphis Branch and told them I needed thirty-four wheels for those seventeen tractors.

The person who answered the phone said, "Mr. Kimbrell,

you are not a Ford dealer anymore."

"They came by and talked to me about it, but they didn't say that," I said.

"You gave a firm answer," he said.

I said, "This man has seventeen tractors. Can you sell me those wheels?"

"We have a dealer in Sulligent, Alabama selling them. Get him to send for them, and we will sell them to him," he said.

"I have a fellow here right now that has a bearing out of one of his front wheels," I said.

"We can't ship you that, even," he said.

It happened I knew Mr. Gibson, the distributor out of Atlanta, who had relatives around Fayette, I called him and said, "Jack, I need 34 ten-inch wheels to change out Brown Lumber Company's wheels. If you have them I can send my truck tomorrow to pick them up."

"Hold a minute, and let me check," he said. In a minute he came back and told me they had them.

I asked, "Can I send a truck and pick them up tomorrow?"

"Sure," he answered.

I was the Firestone distributor for this section, so I called Firestone in Birmingham to confirm they had the ten-inch tires in stock and sent someone to pick up the tires. I had several in stock, but picked up enough from Firestone to finish the order. That, however, was the end of my Ford dealership.

The trade with the Butlers for the purchase of Caine's half of the B & K Tractor and Implement Company, and selling my half of the farm happened in March 1945. At that time we had already acquired the Tuscaloosa dealership from the Atlanta Branch, and later that year I added the Columbus dealership, which was out of the Memphis Branch. That was really a good arrangement. As I stated before, you could sell almost anything you had. Prices of farm products had increased. Prices of livestock had increased a like amount, and I was really bullish and would take anything either branch offered me. It was a very favorable arrangement because John Deere would give two seasons with no interest. If you sold for cash, you still got your five percent discount. I took anything they would ship to me. The only cash outlay was the freight. As it turned out, quite often John Deere would recommend to other dealers, "Call Fuller Kimbrell for he might have the piece of equipment you are in dire need of."

In mid 1945 the sawmill business continued. I had an opportunity to expand sawmill operations through an offer made by Minneapolis-Moline Manufacturing Company. There were no big sawmills, and the log trucking business was not very popular. The logs were hauled on bobtailed trucks in very small loads. It was still the most profitable thing to do to buy a small sawmill, put it on your own land, and buy your neighbor's timber.

The representative for Minneapolis-Moline Manufacturing Company came by told me his company had power units in three or four sizes. As I said earlier, John Deere only had one size power unit that would pull a small sawmill, but it would not handle planers or other things like that. Neither did they have a small motor that would pull a feed mill to grind feed for livestock or gristmill or things of that nature. But Minneapolis-Moline did have several sizes.

I signed the dealership with Minneapolis-Moline. They had a storage place at Tupelo, Mississippi, which gave me the same arrangements as John Deere except it didn't run by seasons. It would run ninety days, and if you had not sold they would give you another ninety days — no interest. There was no cost but the freight. I put two or three of their power units in stock by sending my truck over to Tupelo to pick them up, and they sold extra well. Of course, you still had to get a permit to do that, but that was no problem because I had good relations. The OPA Board in Fayette realized the importance of cutting lumber for the war effort.

Later on, things begin to look so good that when the Minneapolis-Moline representative came to see me I bought two carloads of power units. I then had three different sizes, but most of them were the big power units that could handle the large size sawmill and planing mill. They came in just as the price ceiling went off. Minneapolis-Moline billed them to me, and I had the invoice. They came in on a freight car two days later. The two cars had thirty-six power units. I unloaded one power unit off that afternoon.

The sawmillers and farmers had money. They reached in their shirt pockets and pulled out hundred dollar bills to pay for equipment. The next morning before anybody came, I had notified most people that the power units would be in on certain days if they wanted them. The next morning before any of the people I had notified got there, I had a telegram from

Minneapolis-Moline stating the price had increased fifteen percent. Of course then they were much cheaper than now, but that telegram made me $4400. I showed the telegram to the customers and said, "I have no choice. The price has gone up fifteen percent." But they were able to sell at their price all the lumber they could cut, so they didn't complain at all. I sold thirty-one of the power units off the railroad cars and only put four in my store. I doubt if they stayed over a week or ten days. As I said before, sawmillers would just reach in their shirt pockets and pull out the money to pay for them. That was a wonderful situation.

Later I bought other equipment from Minneapolis-Moline. They had a wonderful feed mill which I bought a few of for people that had small dairies. The company representative that called on me passed away, and I lost my contact with them. But by then John Deere equipment was coming in better.

Times continued to be good. Bruce Harkins, owner of Harkins Lumber Company, bought land and built a building, and moved out of the place where Allen Lumber Company was. That gave me more room and a certain advantage. Times got better, so I decided to go all out and build a real nice building. I built a 100' X 100' concrete block building with a 100' glass front. It had a nice office, built-in vault, and plenty of floor space. The shop was 50' X 100' and the showroom and parts department was 50' X 100' with another building on the side 50' X 100' and had an equal amount of storage room behind it. It was written about in the John Deere folders, and I was the talk of all the dealers out of Memphis and Nashville concerning what a wonderful building I had built.

The building was located a block and a half from the two banks in Fayette, one block from City Hall, and a block and a half from the courthouse. It was a most favorable location right on two highways. Since I had the three dealerships, word begin to get out all over the farming area—which was five or six counties—that Fuller Kimbrell in Fayette might have what they needed. With a minimum sales expense, I moved all the equipment I could get.

My schedule was to go to Tuscaloosa one day a week and come back the next day and go to Aliceville, maybe, or to Columbus. I tried to make arrangements to go to each of the dealerships at least one day a week, and the other days I would stay in Fayette. I paid all the bills out of the account in the Citizens Bank in Fayette, although I had bank accounts in Tuscaloosa and Columbus. I still paid all the bills and transferred the money to the Citizens Bank.

As time went on, it seemed apparent that if I would go to the branches in Memphis, Nashville, and Atlanta, I would always see something they had and manage to get it. Many times I drove my truck because I figured if I had my truck up there they would load a tractor or something on it for me to bring back. And they usually did. It developed into a wonderful situation.

I began to add other lines, such as the New Holland baler. I would fly up and catch a taxi out to the New Holland plant and get equipment. One time I was just about to get sued because I had sold a New Holland baler to a man in the Black Belt in Hale County, and I just couldn't get it. So I flew up to New Holland

and told the secretary in the reception office located in front of the factory, "I've got a taxi waiting and I want to catch the plane to go back to Fayette tonight."

She ran to the back and told the manager who was also the sales manager, Mr. Morgan, a big Dutchman with a loud coarse voice, and he came out and asked, "Oh, Mr. Kimbrell, you mean you got a taxi waiting for you?"

"Yes, and I'm about to get sued. I sold a baler. I've just got to have one baler," I said.

He said, "I'll tell you what. Railroad cars are so scarce we don't dare put just one baler on a car, but if you send your truck we will load it. Let me check a minute." When he came back he said, "You know we can load out a carload for you today and we can load out another carload for you next week if you want it."

"I want them," I said. They were shipped right away, and I sold all eight balers at once.

Caine Butler had bought a brand new truck, and he came by the office that morning. "Caine, how would like to go to New Holland, Pennsylvania?" I asked.

"What you got in mind?" he asked.

"You have a new truck?" I asked. Then I told him that they would not ship only one baler, but they would load it on a truck. I said, "I'll tell you what I'll do. I'll go with you, and we will share the driving. I'll take care of all expenses and give you $100."

"When you want to leave?" Caine asked.

"Soon as we can pack a bag," I said.

"I'll be back time you are," he said.

We took off and drove as far as Knoxville that night, and the next morning went on in to New Holland. They loaded the baler.

Coming back, I drove right through the city limits and came back down Highway 1. They didn't have interstates and very few four lane roads then. I drove right through Washington, D.C. with that baler sticking out about a foot and a half on one side of that truck. Back then you just couldn't get a hotel room, so we came on down to Richmond to spend the night and couldn't find a hotel. It was a big problem, because we also couldn't find a place to park the truck. So we drove through Atlanta and all through the night.

Finally, we got to Tuscaloosa the next morning about seven o'clock. I had driven all the way from New Holland, because Caine was in no condition to drive. I kept the baler on his truck and delivered it to the man in Hale County who was about to sue me because I had not made delivery. In addition to getting full price for those eight hay balers, I had bought a carload of twine. That was back when the first automatic balers baled hay with twine instead of wire. So I required them to buy about fifty balls of twine to bale their hay—which they needed anyway, and I had a nice profit on that too. With that day's work, I made $5200, a nice profit.

In 1945, after I bought Mr. Butler's interest in the business and moved to town, I joined the Lions Club and was active in all the drives. During the war there were many drives such as the Red Cross, Community drive, etc. I participated in all of the drives. I became fairly well acquainted with almost all the business people in town, and was a member and attended the local Baptist Church. I continued to call on farmers, and many began to buy power equipment. They believed I was really the top farmer in the country — particularly with power farming and with livestock, as well — although I had sold my interest in the farm.

Early in 1946, before reapportionment, Fayette County only had a senator every twelve years. It was Fayette's time to elect a senator for the twelfth senatorial district: Fayette, Lamar, and Walker Counties. The probate judge, J. C. McGough, and three or four businessmen of Fayette came to see me at the office and told me they wanted me to run for senator, since it was Fayette County's time. I was really shocked and surprised at them asking me. I had never given it any thought, and I didn't know if I could get elected or not. One of the fellows spoke up and asked if I used to work in Walker County. I told him I had worked at the power plant in the commissary, and he asked if I had any friends left there. I told him I did. I had the top. The probate judge, Lloyd Garrison, who was superintendent of the mines when I worked there, was my best friend. And another close friend was the sheriff, Powell Hamner, who had been the manager of the other commissary at the power company. Not only that, but he was from Fayette County, and I went to school with him in the first and second grade. Almost every summer, someone would teach a singing school at Bethabara Baptist Church that we both attended. Also, in those days, the grapevine was our jump rope, and I remember very well he could lay a grapevine on the top of his head — back up and run jump it.

The fellow said, "We want you to run."

I said, "Let me think about it. My wife and I have planned to go to Hollywood, Florida to visit my brother, Orison, who is the pastor of the First Baptist Church there. I'll think about it until I get back. We will be gone a week."

We drove to Hollywood, Florida, spent two or three days going down and an extra day coming back. During those times it was almost impossible to get a hotel room. We were able to manage it by taking a room with two beds, and Basil, my brother, who we picked up in Monroeville, Alabama went down with us, and had to share a room with us. Basil snored really loud, and when we started back, Reba said she just as soon stay in the car as she didn't think she could stand his snoring another night. The first night we stopped at a hotel in Orlando, and sure enough, they offered us a room for three people with two beds. I laid a $10 bill on the clerks's desk, and said, "Tonight is my wedding night and I want a separate room."

An elderly fellow standing behind the clerk laughed and said, "You will get it." I learned later, the clerk, a young fellow, was newly wed. It worked out okay.

When I pulled in the yard at home, a car pulled in behind me with most of the same people in it that had asked me to run. They asked, "What's your answer?"

"I've been eating oranges and grapefruits right off the tree and haven't thought much about it," I said.

"We want you to do it," they said.

"All right, I'll let you know in the morning," I said. I didn't know what to do, Reba was not all that strong on politics. But the next morning when they came over, I agreed to run.

Before I announced I was going to run for the senate, I decided I had better go up to Jasper and talk to Probate Judge Lloyd Garrison and to Sheriff Powell Hamner. I went to Lloyd's office first and told him that a group of men in Fayette were insisting that I run for senator. He said, "Let me call Powell. Isn't Powell from down around your community?"

"Yes. I went to school with him. In fact, Powell married my brother-in-law's niece," I answered.

He called Powell, and Powell said, "Yes, Fuller has a good family name in Fayette County, and is well thought of and highly respected. He ought to get a lot of votes. His family has one of the cleanest records of any family in the county."

Judge Garrison spoke up and said, "We'll just take care of Walker County for you." One of the things that's most interesting just as Judge Garrison got through speaking, in walked an elderly fellow wearing ragged overalls. The Judge said, "Mr. Drummond, I want you to meet our next senator. This is Fuller Kimbrell. He just said he has decided to run, and they are insisting he run for state senator for Fayette, Walker, and Lamar Counties, and it's Fayette County's time. We want you to support him."

"If you boys want him, he's my man," Mr. Drummond said. He was the father of the Drummond brothers who own Drummond Coal Company, one of the largest coal mining companies in the South today.

I campaigned in Walker County only about four half-days and carried it by a big majority. I didn't know anything about politicking and didn't know you were supposed to see and talk to the people like you do now. Of course, we had no television.

Two days later, I went to see the Lamar County probate judge, Mr. Johnson, who also owned the bank. I told him they had asked me to run and I had agreed to. He said, "You look all right to me. I understand you've sold a lot of farmers tractors around Lamar County. Are any of them mad at you or suing you?"

"No, these cold days they are sitting by the fire when they would be out feeding their mules," I said.

He laughed about what I said, and said, "I'll support you."

Later the group that asked me to run had second thoughts. Since I was in the farm machinery business, they thought that I might be interested in getting tractors exempt from the gasoline tax. They came to see me and said, "We want a promise out of you that you will not support taking the tax off the fuel used on the farm."

"Well, I'm not promising that," I said.

Funny thing about it was it wasn't too late to get an opponent. So they got Jim Ayres, the owner and editor of the Fayette weekly newspaper, "The Fayette Banner," to run against me and supported him. He led me in Fayette County by a small lead, but I won by a big majority in Lamar and Walker Counties.

All the things I did for District Twelve when I was senator were never printed in the Fayette Banner because my opponent would not put it in the paper. I found out later J.C. McGough, the probate judge, knew I was gaining popularity and being accepted by people all over the county. He was afraid if I was elected senator, later I might decide to run for probate judge. Of course, I never gave that a thought. I enjoyed farming and being in the farm machinery business too well. The Republicans had no primary, so once I won in the May primary I had nothing to worry about in November.

When we got to Montgomery, I did not know that Governor Folsom had run for governor in 1942 and was defeated because the Extension Service had fought him, and I didn't know all that much about the race in 1946. In 1946 there were three people running for governor – Handy Ellis, the lieutenant governor from Shelby County, Joe Poole, the commissioner of agriculture, from Butler County, and Big Jim Folsom from Cullman. During the campaign, Ellis and Poole never thought that Governor Folsom would be in the run off. They figured the Extension Service and Farm Bureau would keep him out of the run-off again with the rural people. In the runoff, Joe Poole was eliminated leaving Lieutenant Governor Handy Ellis and "Big Jim" Folsom.

While campaigning, Handy Ellis said Joe Poole would not make a good governor, and Joe Poole said Handy Ellis would not be a good governor. When Big Jim got on that stump facing the biggest crowd that any candidate for governor had ever had at any rally, he reminded them of that and brought the house down. He would say, "Joe Poole says Handy Ellis is not fit to be governor, and Handy Ellis says Joe Poole is not fit to be governor. I think they are both right."

In the runoff, the Extension Service and Farm Bureau, which

had both backed Joe Poole, got so upset with Handy Ellis that they decided to turn their support to Jim. Governor Folsom won over Handy Ellis by a nice majority, but he had not forgotten that the Extension Service and Farm Bureau had not supported him in either campaign. The Extension Service and Farm Bureau folks thought since they had switched their support from Poole to Folsom they would have a big say as to who would serve in the cabinet. In fact, they were sure Joe Poole was going to be director of finance. When Governor Folsom took office the second Monday in January, Joe Poole was left out. As a result, Joe Poole and Senator Bruce Henderson of Wilcox County, along with the Extension Service and Farm Bureau, organized the strongest opposition that any governor of Alabama has ever faced or that I have ever known or read about.

After the November 1946 election, Governor Folsom was preparing for the organizational session. He called all the members of the legislature to come to Cullman to find out what their wishes were, and what they hoped to do for their districts, and to see if they would endorse his program. He called for Miles Dobbs, the representative of Fayette County, and me to come, and we drove over together. Later I met with the representatives from Walker County, Chester Black and McDaniel, and the representative from Lamar County, Mr. Hankins.

Governor Folsom first asked Representative Dobbs what he wanted. Mr. Dobbs said, "If you will pave the roads from Fayette to Townley, it will give a short route to Birmingham for the people in Fayette County."

Governor Folsom asked, "Mr. Dobbs, if I pave that road will you vote for the Speaker?"

"Yes," Mr. Dobbs answered.

The Governor said, "Let's shake hands. For Speaker, I want you to vote for Bill Beck, the representative from DeKalb County."

Then the governor turned to me and asked, "Senator Kimbrell, what do you want?"

I said, "Governor, I didn't vote for you. In fact, I put money in Lieutenant Governor Handy Ellis' campaign, but only because my attorney was his county campaign manager. I went to quite a few of your rallies, and listened to your speeches where you announced your program to the people at every rally, and the people voted by an overwhelming majority for you. You carried all three counties I'm elected to represent as state senator in Montgomery. You don't have to ask me, or worry about me, or make any promises. I'll be trying to help you put your program over because the people voted for you."

"I sure appreciate it," Governor Folsom said.

When we got to Montgomery, Mr. Dobbs decided not to vote for Bill Beck. Instead he voted for Doc Martin, who was part of the opposition, not really strong, but he turned out to be a real good friend. In fact, Doc Martin's request got the first appointment Governor Folsom made — he appointed Frank Lee, the sheriff of Greene County to replace Frank's father, although Frank was elected later. He was still serving when Governor Folsom was elected again in 1954.

There were four vacancies on the Auburn Board of Trustees.

Governor Folsom figured if he could fill the vacancies with people of his choice he probably could fire Director P. O. Davis and Assistant Director, Jimmy Lawson, of the Alabama Extension Service, or at least change the philosophy to insure that they would not be out trying to defeat somebody running for statewide or local office again. In the organizational session, the first thing he did was to appoint four Auburn Trustees. The well-organized opposition, led by Senator Bruce Henderson, knew it was coming, so they had already gotten the Supreme Court to rule that you could not pass legislation or confirm trustees and various other things that required the approval of the senate in the organizational session.

As soon as the organizational session was over, Governor Folsom called us back for a special session. Of course, since I had promised to support Governor Folsom's program, I was sympathetic to his philosophy. Since I was in the farm machinery business, I was also supportive of Auburn and their agriculture program.

Rankin Fite, the senator representing Marion, Franklin, and Colbert Counties, and I were desk mates. We picked out seats next to each other in the senate chamber. We also agreed to room together part of the time when we were in Montgomery — which we did. We stayed at the Jeff Davis Hotel in Montgomery. We had a corner room with two single beds and an entrance hall with large closets, so we roomed together most of the time. The four years we served, we pooled rides. He had a Henry J, a new car made by Henry J. Kaiser, and I drove a Studebaker since I had the Studebaker dealership, and sold them. He lived north of Fayette in Hamilton. One week he would pick me up in Fayette in his Henry J., and the next week his wife would bring him to Fayette and we would ride down in my Studebaker. It turned out that we became the best of friends. Not many days passed that we didn't talk to each other over the telephone. Even after the four years were over, we continued to be best friends, and remained so until his death.

When we got to the special session, Ward McFarland from Tuscaloosa had been appointed highway director. He came to Rankin and me and said, "If you will go along with the Governor and vote to confirm his appointees to the Auburn Board of Trustees you won't be sorry. Because I'm going to be sympathetic to West Alabama which has not been treated fairly by the state government before." IT IS STILL TRUE TODAY due to the antiquated 1901 Constitution.

Rankin and I looked at each other and we both spoke up right away and said, "We will do it." We talked about it on the way home at the end of the organizational session.

The conversation with Ward McFarland turned out to be one of the closest political bonds I have ever experienced, as well as the most beneficial thing I could have done for my senatorial district. It developed, gradually, into thousands and even millions of dollars worth of programs, roads, streets, etc., and more essential civic service.

The legislature usually met on Tuesdays and adjourned on Thursday mornings. We went to Montgomery on Tuesday mornings for the regular sessions and came back home Thursday afternoons. But Governor Folsom had a habit of calling special sessions when he wanted to, and sometimes he would bring us back on Monday. One time the senate adjourned a special session within thirty minutes after we got there. But Folsom knew they were going to do it, so he had an identical call on his desk and called us back the next morning, and we didn't get to go home. As I remember this was the biggest fight that has ever been in the State Legislature. In fact, I repeated to some of my friends the other day, "Governor Fob James' battle in trying to get Auburn Trustees confirmed now is dwarfed by the effort made in the first Folsom administration."

SIX

WORK DURING WAR TIME

My business continued to get better. December 7, 1941, the Japanese attacked Pearl Harbor, which meant all out war. President Roosevelt immediately declared a moratorium on automobiles and various machinery that could not be used in the war effort. Farm equipment was made a priority. Fortunately I had put in my inventory twenty-eight farm tractors. I felt that I would be able to sell that many in the upcoming season of 1942. These tractors were parked out in the street in front of Kimbrell Tractor & Implement Co. My neighbor, Harvey Cannon, who operated a general store across the street, said to me, "Seeing all those tractors parked out on the street, Fuller, you either know something or you are crazy."

"I'm crazy. I don't know anything," I said. Which I didn't. This turned out to be very profitable.

Farmers were becoming more confident with power farming, and it became much easier to discuss tractors and tractor cultivating with them. In the winter I would go out and talk to farmers who had ten, fifteen, or twenty acre fields. If it could be seen from the road, I would stop and talk to them. We would walk around the barns and look at their mules and livestock. I remember one time I went to see a doctor who had the reputation of being conservative. It was a cold, rainy day and looked like it might change to sleet or snow. I said, "Doctor Branyon, you take a day like this and you have your mules eating up your corn in the crib. If you had a tractor, you could sell that corn and not have to go out in the cold and wade through the mud to feed those mules. You could wait until later in the season to get out to prepare your land. Your farming would be much easier, and you could have your corn to sell."

"Yes, but how about the manure?" he asked. He was just that conservative. Later on he decided to sell his mules and bought a tractor and cultivator. Pretty soon afterward his age prohibited him from farming. He sold the whole outfit, and the fellow he sold to became a very good customer.

The Office of Price Administration (OPA) was created by the federal government to control distribution of equipment and various products used in the production of food and fiber necessary for the livelihood of people, as well as the war effort. To buy many things, you had to get a permit. I was selected by Fayette County's probate judge and superintendent of education to serve on the OPA Board. The OPA Board approved the sales of farm machinery to farmers, which included pickup trucks, tractors, gasoline, and also power units for sawmill purposes, since a lot of heavy timber used to build barracks for the army and training was being shipped overseas. In addition, to buy many food items, such as meal, lard, sugar, and coffee required stamps commonly called ration stamps. It was common practice for people to swap stamps to take care of their needs, more especially gasoline stamps.

At the John Deere store in Tuscaloosa my partner, Caine Butler, and I would quite often go across the street to the Modern Cafe, a little cafe that had really good food. Usually behind the counter was a little young lady whose husband was off in the service. She had red hair, weighed about 105 or 106 pounds, and was very nice looking. She was very clever, had a wonderful personality, and was a good waitress. One day she said, "I'm going home for the weekend. I understand that farm machinery dealers have extra gasoline ration stamps. I sure wish I had a stamp that would get me five gallons of gas. Once I get home in Memphis, I'm going to ride the bus." So I just pulled out of my pocket a ration stamp for five gallons of gas and gave it to her without thinking anything about it.

The next day, while Caine and I had gone to lunch, a fellow came into our business and asked, "Where is Fuller Kimbrell, the owner of this business?" The fellow said, "He gave my girl friend some ration stamps for gasoline. I want to know what his idea for doing it was. If he is trying to get close to her, he is in trouble."

Claude Galloway, who lived in Fayette and was a mechanic there, said he sat there and waited a minute. Then he said to the fellow, "He will be back in thirty minutes, if you want to wait for him. I don't think you will be happy that you waited. If I were you I would drop this question, and move on out right now." Claude told me the fellow walked on out. I never heard from the man again. I saw the girl two weeks later, when I came back on the weekend to Tuscaloosa to work. She was still behind the counter at the cafe. I never mentioned it and she didn't either.

Times continued to get better, and I needed some help. Caine had done well in the dairy business and had settled down. One day he came in, and I asked, "Caine, don't you want to come back and go to work with me? I need more help, and it looks like the army is going to take all the young folks and might get me. But we will have priority for a while because we are doing so much farming and growing beef cattle and hogs."

"Yes, if that's what you want," he said. He turned his dairy business over to somebody else for a while and later sold the cows.

We began to push farming and grow feed, which was more important than growing cotton—the cotton picker had not been invented yet in 1942. With the war effort, not only were young men drafted into the armed services, but they went to work at the defense plants. Even the women went all over the country to work in the powder plants and other defense plants. The pay was so much better than it was anywhere else.

I was in a position to get power units and sawmills that could be sold to small farmers, who would put them down right by a defense plant being built. I remember one in Aberdeen, Mississippi: a farmer came in, and I sold him a power unit and a sawmill. I delivered it to him, and he sawed lumber from his own timber, which was used in building a powder plant nearby.

Times began to look better. One day I was visiting in Tuscaloosa and had called on a farmer nearby, when I noticed the John Deere Tractor place was not active at all. I came back and said to Caine, "Let's go to Atlanta and see if we can get the

Tuscaloosa John Deere dealership." It represented a large area, and the Atlanta branch was a much larger branch than the Nashville branch we were working out of.

In the meantime — before we went to Atlanta — I went to see the dealer in Tuscaloosa to ask if we could buy the dealership. He said, "Yes, you can have everything in here for $1500." They bought scrap iron and had a parts department, traveled and called on dealers in the area, and sold them parts for automobiles and trucks — which was better for them also.

We went to Atlanta to see the branch manager, C. S. Masterton, who was a nephew of the president of John Deere Plow Company, Charles Deere Wyman. He didn't have to worry if he made a mistake or not. And his assistant, Charley Hassell, was a very clever and talented fellow in the farm machinery business.

While we sat in his office visiting, I told them what we wanted, and Charley Hassell took out a pack of Bull Durham tobacco and rolled a cigarette. I said, "Mr. Hassell, seeing you roll that cigarette reminds me of something that happened to Caine and me. A fellow came by our place selling various items, and one of the items was W. M. Rogers Silverware. He laid it out on the table as we were both interested in buying a set of silverware for our wives. We looked at it, and I said, "That sure is pretty."

Caine said, "Yes, that's fine. Isn't it?"

And the old fellow — a country kind of a fellow with a chew of tobacco in his mouth — spit his tobacco into the corner on the concrete floor and said, "Yes, that will get it when snuff fails."

We all looked at each other and laughed and Mr. Masterton looked over at Charley and said, "Charley, they just got the dealership." That turned out to be really good for us, because the Atlanta branch was a parent branch which served several state branches—North Carolina, South Carolina, Georgia, Florida, and Montgomery, Alabama, which represented the south half of Alabama, starting at Tuscaloosa. Our Fayette dealership was out of a branch that just served part of Tennessee and North Alabama, so having the Tuscaloosa dealership gave us a tremendous advantage because the Atlanta branch had a much larger inventory available.

We came back from Atlanta and went to Tuscaloosa. We rented two buildings and shipped in a lot of equipment, and opened the dealership. We got the lumber yard in Fayette to build bins to hold parts. In fact, Harkins Lumber Company, owned by Bruce Harkins, who had bought the company from Caine and me, built the bins for us. When we moved the $1500 worth of inventory into the bins, it cataloged out to be $3500 worth. The buildings, which were in good condition, were in a good location, except there was no outside storage space for equipment. But they did have a large railroad concrete loading dock.

The dealership in Tuscaloosa turned out to be a really successful and very profitable machinery business, although the war was still going on and equipment was scarce. You didn't have to go out and try to sell what you could get, because somebody was in there looking at what you had or what they hoped they could find.

I developed good relations with the loafers, so to speak, around Tuscaloosa. I didn't have comfortable chairs or a place for them to sit, but I brought in some wooden nail kegs, and put them around in the store. Men would come in and sit on the nail kegs and we would talk. We'd go across the street to the little Modern Cafe and have coffee or lunch, and I enjoyed it very much. Sometimes I would go to Tuscaloosa one morning, spend the night because the road was a dirt road, and hard to drive at night, and come back late the next evening.

Back then you did not trade in much equipment. There were no used tractors to trade in. If we traded for anything, it was usually for cattle, hogs, corn or syrup. If we traded at Tuscaloosa, we would then take it to the farm in Fayette. The Tuscaloosa dealership turned out to be one of the grandest moves we had made at that time, since Atlanta was the parent branch. John Deere had several parent branches: one in Baltimore, Maryland; one in St. Louis; one in Atlanta; one in Chicago; and several in the West. The possibility of getting equipment out of Atlanta was much greater than getting it out of Nashville or Memphis.

Pretty soon—with the war going on—machinery began to be harder to get. I found out that if you went and sat down with the branch manager and told him how bad you needed a tractor, power unit, or whatever you needed, you would come a lot nearer getting it than if you called a salesman or somebody else. Charley Hassell, the assistant manager, was already impressed with us. When I went to Atlanta he would meet me, and say, "Come on in." He would make every effort to get the equipment I needed, as well as some other equipment. It turned out that when machinery got more and more scarce, John Deere would ship to the branch managers some items that might not have been sold in their territory before. It was really profitable for us.

We would go to Atlanta quite often, and always have lunch with Mr. Masterson, the branch manager, and Mr. Hassell, the assistant branch manager. That gave us a great opportunity to get whatever tractors and equipment they had available. I was bullish all the time, and Caine let me charge ahead full steam. Of course, I was careful to discuss my ideas with him, and we took everything they offered. We swapped with other dealers in Mississippi, north Alabama, and other places quite often, trading for equipment that we didn't need in our area, but they needed in theirs. Since we had Fayette and Tuscaloosa, it gave us a real advantage as we began to do business in the Black Belt— around Hale, Perry, Marengo, and Greene Counties. I sold quite a few power units in Greene County.

Joe Baldridge was a branch manager at Nashville and was a deep water Baptist—like me. I met him up at Tennessee Valley on the Tennessee River and fished with him a time or two. One time, Reba and I went up and spent Saturday night with him and his wife, and went with them to church Sunday morning. It turned out to be real advantageous, because when I called for a piece of equipment, I usually talked to Mr. Baldridge, since the head man could get you something better than a blockman or salesman could.

We continued to work with those two dealerships, and it really worked out well. This was a real advantage. If one branch office did not have a piece of equipment for us maybe one of the other branch offices would. If Nashville did not have it, maybe Atlanta or one of their state branches might.

As the war progressed and the defense became more and more dominant in the U. S., equipment became more and more scarce. A lot of the farmers would work at defense jobs in the winter and come back to their farms in the summer, which gave them money that they would not have had otherwise. A lot of them used it to buy equipment. The banks had more money, and it was easier to finance equipment for the farmers because the bank and John Deere Plow Company knew that they could go to work in the winter and make money to make their payments. If their crops did not turn out good, they could work two or three months in a defense plant and make their payments.

In fall, 1939, John Deere decided to give a factory trip. We all — from east and middle Tennessee and north Alabama — met in Nashville, got on the train, went to Chicago and spent the night. Arrangements had been made to visit one of International Harvester Company's plants in Chicago. But the next night we caught the train and went to Moline, Illinois where almost all of John Deere's equipment for tractors and horse-drawn equipment was manufactured. Horse-drawn equipment was still a major part of business, particularly where the farms were small, like in Fayette, Lamar, and Marion Counties. We went through the plant that manufactured horse-drawn cultivators, riding cultivators drawn by horses, planters of various kinds, such as riding and walking planters. Wooden wagons were still the thing, because a lot of people still had mules. The farmers, particularly in the fields of northwest Alabama, still would not get rid of their mules until they got used to farming with power equipment.

John Deere divided the dealers into groups of seven or eight and had a guide to take each group through the plants. The group that I was assigned to was especially interested in watching the manufacturing of wooden wagons. We didn't have the rubber tire wagons. We got to the place where they were boring the holes for the spokes in the hubs for wagon wheels. The boring bit went round and round, but when they lifted it up, the holes were 1-1/4 X 1-3/4 inside. That hole was the prettiest smoothest rectangular hole you've ever seen. One old fellow with a great long handlebar mustache had a chew of tobacco in his mouth. He spit over on the pile of shavings and said, "I want to see that again." We turned back and watched them bore holes in the whole hub, which had fourteen spokes. When it was completed, the fellow spit over in the shavings again and said, "It's a damn lie; they can't do it."

It was a very interesting trip. From there we spent two days going through the various plants and caught a train to Waterloo, Iowa, where John Deere manufactured tractors, and spent a full day going through the plant. We watched them do the casting and everything pertaining to manufacturing a tractor, and even went out in a field and watched them. It was dry enough to plow, and the farmers were still using a mold board plow. In Alabama, the farmer used a disk plow pulled behind the tractor.

Along about that time, Ford Motor Company came out with a new tractor (they had merged with Massey-Ferguson in England). Massey-Ferguson had developed a hydraulic power lift with a three point hitch, which could hook equipment to a tractor in a minute or two and be ready to cultivate or plow. That would become a big item with the farmers who had small farms, but not right away, because Ford still had to establish dealerships. John Deere and International Harvester had saturated the whole United States with dealerships within reach of and sometimes overlapping each other. They did not have to worry about competition from Ford Motor Company for some time.

Machinery was getting scarcer and scarcer. At that time Mr. Butler owned Allen Lumber Company. Permits were required to buy lumber — or to show what the lumber was to be used for, and there were various restrictions on almost everything you could buy. By 1945 he began to worry about it. He called Caine and me in one day and said, "I want to sell you the lumber yard." So we bought the lumber yard from him, paying $13,000 for it. One year later Bruce Harkins, superintendent of education for Fayette County, was anxious to get into business himself, so we sold the lumber yard to him for $25,000 and took a note.

Business continued to be stronger and better, but Mr. Butler began to get more and more worried about the restrictions the government had put on. He had read in the papers about penalties for violations of regulations, and he talked Caine into offering to sell to me. I was surprised one morning, when they came in and said they wanted to sell out to me.

"Well, I believe your half is worth $45,000, I said. I'll be willing to give that if I can borrow the money. Give me a day or two, and I'll go to Birmingham and see if I can get the money." I went up to the Citizens Bank in Fayette where I did business, and Mr. Lindsey, the president of the bank, told me that their limit was $25,000, and he couldn't lend me that much.

In the meantime, John Deere would give a five percent cash discount if you paid for the equipment. Times had gotten so good and the farmers were doing so well, the banks were anxious to get the note if you sold a piece of equipment. So this is what I did: I had some note forms from both the Citizens and First National banks in my briefcase, and I would ask the buyer what bank he did business with. If they said the First National, instead of using the finance plan which would be a few hundred dollars on a John Deere contract, I would put it on a First National Bank note and take it to the bank, and they would give me the money for it. Then I would send the money to John Deere and get my five percent cash discount.

I told Mr. A. M. Grimsley, Sr., the President of the First National Bank, that the Butlers wanted to sell out to me, and I needed to borrow $45,000. He said, "Fuller, I'll write you a letter to the First National Bank in Birmingham. They will loan you that money."

I made a statement on the business, and Mr. Grimsley wrote me a letter. I went to Birmingham and took the letter and statement to Mr. John Hand, the president of the First National Bank, and he said, "Mr. Kimbrell, we have never heard of you before. Farm machinery business is still in its infancy. I just don't know if we can approve that or not. Mr. McMillan is chairman of the board. Let's go talk to him and see what he says about it."

We went into Mr. McMillan's office. He looked at the statement and letter from Mr. Grimsley, and saw I had the note for $25,000 from Harkins Lumber Company. He asked, "Can't you get him to pay that off? Then you won't need but $20,000."

"Mr. McMillan, probably so, but I agreed to let him pay $5,000 a year. I really want to do this, but I don't want to do it bad enough to go back on my word," I said.

Mr. McMillan looked over at John Hand and said, "John, I like this boy. Let him have the money." They gave me a letter stating that they would let me have the money and told me to bring them my information, which would go into mortgages on the farm and Harkins Lumber Company. When I got back home, Mr. Butler and Caine came in.

Mr. Butler said, "We have been talking about this, and Caine has decided that he would like to move to the farm. How could we work out for you to have everything and let us have the farm?"

I thought a minute and said, "We have some equipment. I'll bring the equipment in and give you $25,000 for your half of the farm machinery business."

"Caine, that's a good trade. We need to keep that farm with that fine spring down there, and he has a few cattle down there," Mr. Butler said.

"Fine," Caine said.

"Let me go back to the bank and tell them what I've done. I won't need but $25,000," I said.

Mr. Lindsey, the president of the Citizens Bank, and I had a good relationship. At lunch I walked to the bank and told him I had retraded with the Butlers, and only needed $25,000. He said, "I can let you have that much."

I told him to go ahead and get S. T. Wright, the lawyer I used regularly. He was related to the Kimbrell family, attended school with my daddy, and was a very settled man. It didn't take them but a day or two to draw up the mortgage. Two or three days later, we met at Mr. Wright's office and signed all the papers, and I became sole owner of my first John Deere dealership.

A funny thing happened: we all came back to B & K Tractor and Implement Company, housed in the big old lumber company building that was heated by a big Warm Morning heater. Mr. Butler was waiting — as were other people — and everybody was gathered around the big heater in front. Two fellows walked in and said they wanted to see the manager. "That's me," I said.

That was the beginning of a very profitable business with those two men from Arkansas. One was Jim Wood, who was manager of the John Deere dealerships at West Memphis and Earl Arkansas. He had a store in West Memphis and one in Earl, Arkansas — People's Tractor & Implement Company. The other fellow bought used cars and trucks for the Ford dealer at West Memphis, Tennessee. They took me to one side and said they were from Arkansas and wanted to buy equipment — almost anything I had to sell. I got busy and sold them $19,000 worth of equipment and got a check from them for $16,000 that very day.

"Caine, he's sold enough to nearly pay the mortgage off before we leave the building," Mr. Butler said.

"Dad, he didn't know anything about these folks coming. It's just one of those things that happen once in a while," Caine said.

Since I had such a good connection with Jim Wood with People's Tractor & Implement in Arkansas, I could take anything the branch managers offered me. What I would do was, if they offered me big tractors, I would swap them with Jim Wood for his smaller tractors. In my area they had not yet started using and buying bigger tractors. My relationship with Jim Wood continued to be a wonderful thing.

Along about the second year, he came down to Fayette, and we talked about it. We had traded some equipment, and he had trucks. He said, "I'll tell you what let's do. Mr. Dickey says he will furnish the money, and a fellow named Johnson, at Coleman, Texas, wants to come in. If you will come in we will form an organization—not a corporation—and we will buy equipment and ship it to West Memphis, Arkansas."

At that time we had connections in Iowa, California, and Wisconsin. We were swapping equipment with them and also selling them a lot of equipment. My connection with New Holland had also gotten bigger and bigger. I would take all the balers they would let me have and I would swap them to other dealers for tractors and other equipment.

One time Jim came to Fayette on Sunday morning at ten o'clock, and with him was one of his customers, Tom Kennedy who was a large Arkansas cotton farmer. We got in the car, with Tom in the back. We decided to drive to Dothan, Alabama. While driving down, as customary with farm machinery dealers (They were always bragging about some of the deals they made), we talked about trading for corn, syrup, pigs, calves, cows, and mules. Tom Kennedy was enjoying his Early Times. About 100 miles down the road, after he heard our brag stories, he asked, "Didn't you SOBs ever make a bad deal?" We drove to Dothan and spent the night. The next morning we started up through Georgia and we stopped at every John Deere and International Harvester dealer along the way. We had shipping tags made out to ourselves, and we bought anything they would sell. We would give them a check and a tag to ship it, or we would send a truck to pick it up. We went up through Georgia, South Carolina, and up to Hickory, North Carolina. We went to the Hickory wagon factory and bought three carloads of wooden wheel wagons and had them shipped. Two of them went to West Memphis and one to Tuscaloosa. Incidently, I sold all the wagons, except four, in one week. I don't remember how many, but there must have been forty to a carload. People had the money to buy anything they needed or wanted. It wasn't a matter of selling. It was a matter of having it to sell.

That went on for eight months, and we even went up to Pennsylvania and bought tractors and equipment and shipped it to West Memphis. We accumulated a lot of equipment there, and along in January 1953, we decided the times were not quite as good anymore and it might not continue to work so easy. We needed to have a big auction sale.

We advertised for hundreds of miles around that we were going to have a big auction sale. I rode the train — caught the Frisco in Winfield — and Jim Woods met me at the depot. I spent the night at his home in Earl, Arkansas.

The next day the folks were there, and we sold $108,000 worth of equipment, which was a lot of money in those days. We divided it between the four of us, and I put $26,000 cash in my little suitcase.

Jim Wood was carrying me to the depot to catch the train back to Winfield and pulled into a service station to get gas. I looked up and saw an automobile with an Alabama license plate numbered 60 for Sumter County, Alabama, so I walked over and asked the man if he was driving the car. He said, "Yes, Fuller Kimbrell, I know you!"

"You do?" I asked.

He said, "Yes, my name is Nelson Fuller, I'm with the ABC Board from Alabama, and I'm on my way back home to Emelle in Sumter County. What are you doing?"

"I'm fixing to go catch the train," I said.

"No you're not. Come on and ride with me," he said.

"All right," I said.

About the time I got my suitcase out of Jim Wood's car and put it in the trunk of Mr. Fuller's car, here comes two tall slim boys who had not shaved in a week. They'd been to the men's room around the back, and Nelson told them to get in the back seat. I looked at him, and he said, "It's all right, I'm with the Alabama Beverage Control Board, and I'm well protected. I just picked up the boys and am taking them back to Alabama." The two boys crawled in the back seat and were asleep before we got across the Mississippi River at Memphis.

We got to the edge of Mississippi—about thirty or forty minutes out of Tennessee—and one of the boys woke up and said to the other one, "You're the ugliest old SOB I've ever seen."

Nelson pulled over to the side of the road and said, "Not another word out of you. If you say another word, I'll get you both out of here and rub your noses in the dirt." We never heard another word from either.

"Well, when we get a little further down the road, I'll call my wife and have her meet us in Reform," I said.

"No, I'm going to put you out in your yard," Nelson said. He drove me right up in my front yard and put me out. But before we got home he said, "I didn't want to tell you at first, but I was going to come see you before the week was out. I wanted to buy a New Holland baler." That very night we traded on it, and I sent it to him with a bill. He sent me a check back for a hay rake, a mower, and a baler. I had been really worried with the $26,000 cash in my suitcase, but it turned out all right.

Since Reba and I had to move from the farm, it meant I had to get busy and find a place to live. My friendship with Caine and his wife, Madel, was good, and he was not hurrying me to move. However, I looked and looked for a house. Finally, somebody told me that Mr. E. M. Grimsley — who was a mule dealer and partners with his two brothers, Mr. A. M. Grimsley and Mr. J. C. "Cliff" Grimsley, in the First National Bank — wanted to go back to south Alabama near Headland, where the Grimsleys originally came from when they moved to Fayette, to open up a bank. I went to Mr. E. M. Grimsley's office and told him that I heard he might want to sell his house. I also told him that I had traded my house on the farm to Caine Butler as part of the deal to buy B & K Tractor & Implement Company. Mr. Grimsley said, "Yes I do want to sell my house. Come on and let me show it to you."

We went up and looked at the huge lot and the large house he had lived in for thirty-five years. The house was built of the finest lumber that could be bought then—or now for that matter. He priced it to me for $12,500. Then he suggested that I needed to buy some of his furniture, so I bought a stove, a living room suite, and some carpet, which added another $1000 to the price of the house.

Along about the same time, I had sold a big order out of the Tuscaloosa office, amounting to $7500, to a man at Demopolis that Farm Credit was going to finance. I had received that check and put it in the bank in a separate account. A short time before that there had been a Defense Bond sale, and I had bought a $1000 bond. In fact, I had bought $11,000 worth of bonds, but the bank, at the beginning of the deal, had taken over $10,000 of the bonds. So I had a $1000 bond in the bank and I put the $7500 in the First National Bank, and I had some other bonds that Mr. Lindsey knew about.

After looking at the Grimsley house, I went to the bank and told Mr. Lindsey that the house was for sale, and that I had to find a place to live. He stood and looked at me without saying a word. I said, "Mr. Lindsey, you know you have $2500 worth of bonds for me in your vault, and I've got $7500 deposited in the First National."

"You go buy that house, The land is worth more," he said. He was wondering how I was going to finance it to start with, but once he saw that I had the money he encouraged me to go right away.

Before I told Mr. Grimsley that I would take the house, I took Reba up to look at it. It was a dark, cloudy, rainy day. The interior of the house had high ceilings and huge beams painted a really dark mahogany color. The venetian blinds were a dark color, and it looked so dreary. But I could see outside the big lot and a nice barn behind the house, a garden, and even a place for a milk cow. We talked about it, and she asked me if we could fix it up before we moved. I told her we could. I asked Caine Butler if he was in a hurry for me to move and he said, "No, take your time."

I bought the house and paid Mr. Grimsley $2500 down. He waited and waited. I thought he never was going to settle the deal. So one day I went and told him that I was going to be out of town for a couple of days. He said, "Son, you go ahead. I'm not going to try to back out on you and give you any trouble. My wife is raring to go, but I'm having a little trouble moving and going back all the way to south Alabama."

When I got back from the sales meeting in Memphis, he had the deed ready. I went back and gave him a check for the difference.

It was about four to five weeks before we moved into the Grimsley house, but that house finished up the nicest I've ever seen. The beams were painted white, and we bought new light colored curtains to replace the old blinds. We had the floors sanded and refinished, and they were as smooth and pretty as any mahogany dining table top you have ever seen. We put a concrete driveway back to the barn and redid the back stairs. It turned out wonderful, and we were so happy with the way it looked. However, it was an old house and had old plumbing and fixtures, including a bathtub with legs.

After we had moved in and lived in the house a couple of years, we added a sun porch with a breakfast room on the back. We also re-modeled the bathrooms with modern tubs and sinks. Two of the bedrooms had no closets, so we added closets. It was really a fine place, and we enjoyed living there.

I got a chance to buy two cars at $275 each from the Education Department. I gave Reba one, and Caine Butler wanted one. I let him have the other one for what I paid for it. Those folks from Memphis came back a little while after Reba had been driving her car and offered $1100 for it, so I sold it to them. I think selling her car and leaving her without transportation was one of the worst things I had ever done to my wife, but I was trying so hard make good the $25,000 mortgage I had made at the bank and to get started. It wasn't really a big problem because my business was good, and I had developed a good relationship with the Atlanta branch. I had a good relationship with Nashville already.

I was doing really well, so I went to Columbus, Mississippi. One of the best communities in which to do business was in Caledonia, Mississippi, about forty miles west of Fayette. Quite often I drove over there and came back through Columbus. Or maybe I would take Reba with me, and we would go over to eat.

One day while I was visiting around, I decided I might try to buy the Columbus John Deere dealership. I went by to see the dealer. He was one of those farmers from out in the prairie, and they thought they were better than us folks back in the hill country. He had on a fine hat, and I bragged on his Texas hat and his Texas boots. "Would you want to sell this business?" I asked.

"Yeah, my wife wants to go back to Texas. I think I'll sell my farm, and we will go back to Texas," he answered.

He kept showing his hat in his hand, and I asked, "Does the building go with it?"

"Yeah, I have twelve acres of land right here," he answered.

"What will you take for it?" I asked.

"I'll take $25,000 for the land and the dealership," he answered.

"Can I pay you $5000 down and pay the other at $5000 a year?" I asked.

"Yeah," he answered.

Then, interest was only four to six percent, and I got the loan at five percent. I walked into a lawyer's office, told him what I had done, and he said, "I'll draw up the deed."

"I'll be back tomorrow to pay you," I said. I didn't know where in the world I was going to get that $5000. In the meantime, I had gone deer hunting with Lynn Dodd, who was a cotton buyer and owner of the Coca Cola plant in Fayette. I told him I had bought the Columbus dealership and I needed to borrow $10,000.

"Well, I guess I could let you have $10,000," he said. He wrote me a check on a New York bank for $10,000 and did not even ask for a note. But two or three weeks later he called and said, "Fuller, I've made out a note. When you get time stop by and sign it."

I went by to sign the note, which was a note for demand, and had six percent interest on it. I took the check for $10,000 to the First National Bank in Columbus to deposit it. The bank clerk looked at it and said, "We don't know what to do with it." I told him I had bought the Columbus dealership and twelve acres of land, and I told him I was going to write a $5000 check on it today and he said, "We don't know if this check is good or not."

"I believe the man who wrote it could almost buy this bank if he wanted to," I said. I suggested they call the Citizens Bank in Fayette, and I gave him the telephone number. Mr. Showtard was the president of the bank, and he did call the Citizens Bank and talked to Mr. Lindsey. He deposited the check and said, "You will need some checks."

"Yes, the name of my company is Kimbrell Tractor & Implement Co.," I said.

"All right," he said. He gave me some counter checks so I could write the $5000 check, but I paid everything out of the Fayette account except that one check I made out to Leon Bell, the man from whom I bought the Columbus John Deere dealership.

I had to find someone to operate the dealership in Columbus, so I sent a young man from Fayette over for a few days. Later I moved my nephew, Billy Thomson, over there to manage the company. He had received a B.S. degree in business administration from the University of Alabama, and earlier I had given him a job in the parts department in Fayette. I still went to

Columbus at least two or three times a week. Columbus was really a wonderful place for a farm machinery business. That gave me three dealerships, one out of Nashville, one out of Memphis and one out of Atlanta, which actually gave me three chances to get equipment the farmers might need.

The war was still going on and had moved more into the Pacific Area Theater, but machinery continued to be scarce. I kept my relationships good by going and visiting the dealers. I would get my wife to go with me. Our son, Donald, was in Columbia Military Academy, so Reba was free to go with me when she would. At least once a month we would visit each one of the branches, and we would always take the branch manager to lunch or dinner.

By that time my business was good, and I was feeling secure. I realized that I should devote my full time to my machinery business. I had paid the $3500 mortgage down to $1020 on the farm I had bought from my father. My oldest brother, Arthur, had been crippled for several years and had ten children. He was not getting any better. I went to see him and told him he had a fine family, and if he wanted to pick up the payment on the $1020 balance, I would deed the farm over to him for him and his family. He agreed to it right away.

Today, it is a real pleasure for me to think what a fine family he raised. Instead of three houses on the farm, there are twenty-three houses on the farm today. Some are mobile homes, but the others are all nice homes. Arthur's family are all very devout

Christians. Many of them drove all the way to Bessemer and Birmingham to work, and saved their money and built nice homes. They are well thought of in the community, so I am really proud of what I did. Not only for my family, but it turned out to be wonderful for Arthur's family and for the community.

Today, the farm would be worth about $600,000. After Arthur's sons took over the farm, they started strip mining and got at least $100,000 for the coal. They don't do much farming anymore because most of his family are retired. Some of the houses now belong to Arthur's grandchildren. There are five preachers in the family, but most of the others do public work, driving to Birmingham, Tuscaloosa, and even Fayette daily to do their jobs. One of the grandsons, Bob Kimbrell, who is a preacher, also has the most successful heating and air conditioning service in the area.

SEVEN

FIRST TERM IN THE SENATE

s was customary and by Law, Governor Sparks, the outgoing governor, gave his report to the legislature in the organizational session. It was quite an interesting document and well received. Also, Governor Sparks sent several appointments for the various vacancies to be confirmed, including two members of the Auburn Board of Trustees (none could be confirmed in the organizational session). The organizational session went very smoothly. Lieutenant Governor Handy Ellis announced incoming Lieutenant Governor Clarence Inzer's appointments to the various committees.

As a first term senator, I was not versed in what a legislator was supposed to do or what kind of plans he was supposed to make before the session. So I had not gone to Lieutenant Governor Inzer, who appointed all the members to the various committees, and asked for any special committee appointments for myself, which was customary. For instance, if you had campaigned that you were for roads, schools, or welfare, or if you wanted something special for your county or district, the experienced legislators knew to go to the speaker of the house or the lieutenant governor in the senate, and ask to be put on that particular committee. When I got to Montgomery, the lieutenant governor had assigned me without me having any idea what committees I would be appointed on. I got fairly good committee appointments, but only one chairmanship on a committee which was never active nor important. I was vice-chairman of the Agriculture Committee and vice-chairman of the Local Legislation Committee, and I served on the Educational Committee, which was one of the things I was most interested in. I was also a member of the Rivers and Harbors Committee. The committees I was appointed to were really helpful for my district later.

The organizational session recessed the following Monday after Governor Folsom was sworn into office. Lieutenant Governor Inzer was also sworn in and took over the senate. We went back into session after hearing Governor Folsom's inaugural address. He repeated the previous announcement of all the senate committee appointments, approved the chairmen and vice chairmen and the secretaries, who were set up by law, along with the reading clerk and the various officers of the senate. All business being taken care of, the senate adjourned and went home, but Governor Folsom had notified us that we would be called back to confirm the appointments of the Auburn Board of Trustees.

Pretty soon after the end of the organizational session, the governor called the legislature back, and the first thing he put in was to send the voters a bill giving authority to the legislature to revise the Constitution of Alabama. While campaigning, Governor Folsom very strongly explained to the people that it was time to revise the Constitution of Alabama, which had been written in 1901. It had been amended several hundred times since then and really needed a complete overhauling.

Immediately after we went into session, the bills Governor Folsom's leaders had drawn up were introduced in regards to revising the Constitution. They were read the first time and sent to committee, but were never considered during that special session. Incidentally, the Governor called several special sessions afterwards, and that was always one of the first things in the call — to revise the Constitution — as well as when we went into the regular session in May. This strong belief that the constitution should be changed was proof of his desire to correct the inequities in the present constitution.

By that time the opposition was well-organized. The opposition of Folsom had eighteen or more votes on almost anything that came up, so anything they objected to had no chance of passing. Since appointments to the various boards Governor Sparks had recommended and sent to the senate were laying on the table, they were immediately confirmed — all of them — including two Auburn Trustees. By that time, there were four more vacancies to be filled, and Governor Folsom sent up four names. Immediately they were rejected in committee. Then the senate adjourned. He called us back almost immediately and sent the names up again — maybe with one or two changes. Still they were not confirmed. Then, we went to the regular session of the legislature on the second Tuesday in May. As always, after the governor made his speech to the joint session of the legislature, the first bills introduced were for revising the

Constitution of Alabama and confirming the Board of Trustees for Auburn and other vacancies that had come about at that time. They were sent to the rules committee and never came up again.

The first Tuesday in May we began the regular session. The budget was approved by the house. Governor Folsom's program fared much better in the house than it did in the senate. He got most of the things that he promised the people and recommended to the legislature in the house, but when it got to the senate it was scrutinized so closely and changed so much that you hardly recognized it. His program fared a little better when it went to confrere committee. A bill to become law had to be passed by both the house and senate with exactly the same wording. When the house and senate failed to agree then a confrere committee was appointed, usually three members appointed by the speaker of the house and three members appointed by the lieutenant governor in the senate. Usually in fairness the lieutenant governor and speaker of the house would appoint a majority of the committee in favor of the way that particular body passed the bill. Since the house agreed a majority of the time with Folsom's program, and the speaker was picked by the governor, it was not uncommon for them to have all three members favoring the particular bill in question. In fairness, the lieutenant governor appointed one in favor and two in opposition which most times gave the governor's program a majority in the confrere committee. Most often the house and senate would approve the action of the confrere committee.

In Governor Folsom's campaign — which I explained before — he went to almost every community and to every county courthouse and explained that he was going to pave all mailbox roads in Alabama. That sort of thing was never heard of in the South before. He was also going to build better schools—separate but equal schools—for blacks and whites, raise the teachers' salaries, and raise the appropriation for education and old age pensions.

Of course, to finance his road program he proposed a one cent gasoline tax. He told the people he was going to put a one cent gasoline tax on for the purpose of road construction and bridges. The opposition was very strongly against that. They weren't strongly against roads and bridges, but they didn't want Folsom to have credit for doing it. The Chamber of Commerce was very strong with the legislature, and certainly the Farm Bureau was strong. Since all tax and revenue increase had to originate in the house, the tax bill never got out of the house, so the governor never got his road program through.

One fortunate thing about the situation was that Governor Sparks had been a very conservative governor, popular and well accepted by everybody. He was serving during the war when everything was frozen and could not spend any money for equipment. Employment was low, especially among men, and you had to be an able-bodied man to work on the highways. They were off in the army or working in some defense job. So even if people were for it, it was just not possible to do much in the way of road building. Sparks left $17 million in the state highway fund, which would compare to approximately $300 million or more today. The opposition found out about it and just didn't know what to do.

Finally, in the senate, the opposition introduced a bill to build three bridges that would cost $10 million from that $17 million. Of course, the bill originated in the senate, so the minute it came out of the committee, I — along with the other four senators who were really loyal to Governor Folsom — filibustered it for several days. Finally, I came up with the idea to start amending it. At first they said they would not agree to any amendments; the opposition was going to hold fast. My amendment was to put a bridge across the Warrior River, so the president and officers of Alabama Power Company, whose offices were in Birmingham, wouldn't have to come all the way to Jasper on Highway 78 and back down a run-down county road to Gorgas Power Plant. Senator Albert Boutwell represented Jefferson County, and Eddie Hatch, who later became president of the Southern Company, that controlled several utility companies including Alabama Power Company, was a lobbyist for the Power Company. I called him over and asked him to go get Tom Martin, the president of Alabama Power Company, and tell him that my amendment to the bridge bill would put a bridge right above the Gorgas Power Plant across the Warrior River and would shorten the route from Birmingham to Gorgas by at least fifty miles. It looked like they had enough votes to pass it if they could ever get it up.

Eddie Hatch called and told Tom Martin what I said. It was only a minute before one of the clerks came over and told Senator Boutwell that Tom Martin was on the phone. Boutwell slipped out of the senate chamber, then came back (he had a way of shaking his head when he was going to try to make an impression), and said, "Gentlemen, Senator Kimbrell has an amendment to this bill that is a must. That's over the Warrior River to the Power plant, which is the leading source of energy in Alabama, and it will shorten the route from Birmingham to the Gorgas Power Plant by fifty miles. I'm going to recommend that we accept his amendment." Immediately, the opposition accepted it, but later they felt it was the wrong thing to do. They finally agreed to let every senator add one bridge to the bill, which would be thirty-five bridges instead of three, and it went through.

This thing went on for twenty-two days. Then, folks like myself, who represented three counties, said, "We can't get by with that. We have to do something for the other counties."

"I can't get by with doing a bridge just for Walker County. I have to put a bridge in Fayette and Lamar Counties," I said.

They said they would accept an amendment from any senator that included a bridge proposed across a federally-recognized navigable river. Guerry Pruitt, who later was highway director under Governor Persons, got his records of navigable rivers, and one of the first ones was the Sipsey in Fayette, which was navigable at one time and was on the Federal record as being a navigable river. Pickens had the Tombigbee at Aliceville, which was supposed to be a navigable river. So we kept on until we added 135 bridges to the bridge bill.

Finally, when we got all that done, and we were still filibustering, Senator Harvey, who represented Blount, Cullman, and Winston Counties, got up and said, "Gentlemen, I want to tell you how stupid we are. You have accepted my bridge up in Blount County. It is five miles from a branch that don't go dry;

that won't run all year around. I'm going to move to knock that off." That got things started. I had a bridge over the Luxapallila at Kennedy, so I got up and asked to take that amendment off. Rankin Fite had one in Marion County, and he asked to take that off. Every senator began to take their bridges off, and we got back down to the original bridges.

By that time, the papers were beginning to claim we were wasting the taxpayers' money, so one of the authors of the original bridge bill got up and moved it be postponed indefinitely. That was the end of the bridge myth, but we had used up twenty-two legislative days to work out a solution.

Killing the bridge amendment left the $17 million intact — which as I've said before — built miles and miles of roads. At the end of Folsom's administration that $17 million had done an awful lot, because dirt could be moved for about twenty-nine to thirty cents a cubic yard. Later, it increased to five dollars a cubic yard. Stone could be bought for less than two dollars a ton, delivered to the job. Later on, it took three to four times that amount of money. So it turned out that Folsom's administration during the four years almost fulfilled his promise to pave all mailbox roads. As I remember, the record shows over 100 miles of roads paved out in the rural areas where people never dreamed of having a paved road before. A lot of the mailbox roads had the base, but they didn't have the steady traffic of heavy trucks and all the logging trucks you have today, so you could pave a mile of road for a fraction of what it would cost today.

Later, there was a vacancy on the Agriculture Board. I asked Governor Folsom to appoint me to fill the vacancy, and he did. I was never confirmed, which was true of many of Folsom's appointees, but they left my name in the committee. That way I was eligible to serve. Of course, I went to the Agriculture Board meetings. The Board had control over the state agricultural buildings. The Board also governed regulations pertaining to insecticides and various fertilizers recommended by Auburn Experimental stations. There was a Center Board appointed, by the governor and the agriculture commissioner, Haygood Patterson, who lived in Montgomery and was very friendly to Folsom, and got along with the administration and the opposition as well. The Center Board controlled and supervised the actual building and construction of the Cow coliseum and eight district coliseums.

One of the things brought up and passed during the regular session of the legislature, that was really wonderful for Alabama and had practically no opposition, was what was then called the Cow Coliseum in Montgomery. It is now one of the largest coliseums in the South and is used for many, many purposes that require accommodations for a large crowd. In that bill, we also set aside eight districts for district cattle coliseums, and approved a $2.5 million bond issue to finance the Cow Coliseum. The Cow Coliseum was started during the Folsom administration and finished during the next administration.

As the coliseums progressed and each of the eight districts was getting its coliseum, I decided I would like to have one for Fayette. Since I was on the Agriculture Board and stood in with the administration, I told Haygood Patterson I would like to have a coliseum. I had talked to my County Board of Revenue, which were County Commissioners at that time, and they said they would buy the land, which was one of the requirements for the district coliseums. Patterson said, "Let's call Frank Stewart, the assistant agriculture commissioner, and see if we have any money left." He called him in.

"Yes, each one of those districts got $37,500," Frank said.

"We'll build the coliseum for you if you can do it for $37,500. I think the rest of the Board will go along with it," Patterson said. He called them by telephone while I was sitting there, and they all agreed, as most the of others were getting one already anyhow, or didn't want one.

I came back home to Fayette. They sent the plans up, and Bo Renfroe, a young Auburn graduate with a degree in architectural engineering who lived in Fayette, had just started a construction business and was low bidder. But instead of his bid being just $37,500, he bid $42,000. The county would not put up the extra money.

Bo Renfroe and I went back to Montgomery right at the end of September, and they were fixing to begin a new year and close out the old year. Back then, no department ever turned any money back. They would issue purchase orders or hide the money somewhere or another so they would have that as surplus the next year. Haygood Patterson called Frank Stewart in again and asked, "Do we have any money so we can give Fuller that extra money, about $5000?"

Frank said, "No we don't have any in that fund, but you know we have a $10,000 purchase order made out to Standard Oil which we may not ever use," Frank said.

"Just cancel enough of it to give Fuller that extra money—whatever he needs," Patterson said. They awarded the contract to Bo Renfroe, which was his first contract. That way we got the only coliseum outside of what the legislature specified.

Another drawback was that I was not a favorite of the Fayette County Probate Judge, J. C. McGough. To buy the land, we had to raise a little money. Since Fayette, Lamar, Marion, Tuscaloosa and Walker Counties were going to be part of our district, Judge McGough suggested I get $1000 from each one of the counties. I agreed to do it, but before I called on any of them, he had called and told them not to give me the money. He was trying to kill it, because he didn't want me to have credit for it. But Reverend A. M. Nix, the pastor of the Fayette First Baptist Church, which I attended, was originally from Marion County, and I got him to go with me. Also, he was real close friends to the chairman of the Board of Revenue of Marion County. Rankin Fite was my closest friend, so I got him to go with us, too, and we had no trouble with Marion County. Then I went to Lamar County to see Judge Johnson, who was a very strong Folsom supporter and a good friend of mine. I got him and rode out to the middle of nowhere and stopped, and he said, "Yes, we will give you the $1000." So I got that.

I went on to Walker County and had no problem there, but in Tuscaloosa, Judge Walker, the probate judge, said, "I'll have to get a ruling from the attorney general, and I don't much believe he is going to approve it."

"Have you asked for it?" I asked.

"I'm fixing to," he answered.

"Go ahead and ask for it. I'll see that you get the ruling," I said.

"What are you saying?" he asked.

"The attorney general is a very personal friend of mine. I'm not saying he won't abide by the law, but I have already checked it and I know it is legal. I know you will get the ruling right back," I said.

"Well, I'll think about it," he said. It was quite sometime before I got the $1000 out of Tuscaloosa County, because of the opposition from my home town. Fayette was going to put in the rest, whatever it cost to buy the land. They did their part all right.

In the organizational session the senate passed a resolution setting up several special committees. As I've pointed out before, Governor Folsom was most anxious to move Alabama forward, not only industrially, but also agriculturally. One committee was to study agriculture and make recommendations to further promote agriculture in Alabama. I was vice chairman of the Agriculture Committee, and Worth Thaggard, the representative from Butler County, was the chairman. We visited all the experimental stations in Alabama. It was most interesting for me since I was in the farm machinery business. I had only been to one experimental station before, and that was at Crossville. One of the finest things about the experimental stations, and I noticed it immediately, was for fifty or sixty miles surrounding each one you could see a hundred percent difference in the crops. The corn was bigger and the cotton finer.

When I started selling farm machinery and tractors in 1937, the average yield of corn in Alabama was fifteen bushels an acre, and the average yield of cotton was 135 pounds to the acre. Just recently, I was driving up Highway 171, I had a friend with me; we passed a ten-acre field of corn that I was sure would produce 100 bushels of corn to the acre or more. In 1937 a ten-acre yield of 150 bushels of corn would have brought $75. The 1000 bushels of corn in 1999 produced on the same acreage would bring $3000 or more. But near those experimental stations, corn was fifty, sixty, and seventy-five bushels an acre, and a bale of cotton was 500 pounds to the acre.

We promoted that and set up another experimental station in Clanton to be used to study fruits and vegetables. The one in Fayette County had already been passed by the legislature, but had not been pushed. We got busy and bought the land agreed on with Marion County. It was to be called the Upper Coastal Plain Experimental Station. Fayette County would buy the land if it could be inside the county, but close to the Marion County line, which is inside the Winfield city limits now. It is a wonderful thing for Fayette, Marion, Lamar, Walker, and Winston Counties.

One of the outstanding things we did was pass a bill giving free business licenses to veterans who had twenty-five percent or more disability. Also, we set up a salary for the director of the Department of Industrial Relations. I'm not sure of the amount, but not more than $5,000. Incidentally, none of the cabinet members at that time were ever paid as much as $5000, and the governor's salary was only $6000. Needless to say, the total appropriation was much less.

One of the things that Governor Folsom was so proud of —
and all his leaders were also — was that he almost doubled the
appropriation for education. Governor Sparks was considered
an outstanding governor and had an outstanding administration,
although it was during the war. The total education budget
during his tenure was only $42 million. We passed a $63 million
appropriation, a fifty percent increase for education, and almost
doubled the general fund appropriation.

Another thing we did: since machinery was still scarce, we
decided in our committee that five of us would go to John Deere,
International Harvester, and Allis Chambers plants and see if
we could persuade them to ship more equipment to their dealers.
The war had not been over long, and equipment was not plentiful
since they had not been able to manufacture it. The South had
not advanced in the way of power equipment like Illinois, Iowa,
and even Texas. So we talked within our committee.

I had a new Lincoln Continental, and five of us including
Thaggard, the chairman from Butler County, Senator Bob
Kendall from Evergreen, Paul Colburn from Colbert County, and
the representative from Madison County, went to Chicago to
the International plant, and from there to Moline, Illinois, and
up to Waterloo, Iowa. It was a very successful trip, because they
agreed to get with their branches and allot extra equipment to
the Alabama branches. International had branches in Atlanta,
Birmingham, Memphis, Nashville, and New Orleans. John Deere
and Allis Chambers had branches in most of the same places.
They got the message out that they were going to allot them
extra equipment to further the use of power equipment in the

South, and — more particularly — in Alabama.

EIGHT

WORKING WITH THE FOLSOM ADMINISTRATION

The coliseum in Fayette was only one of the many things that I was able to obtain for Fayette County, by working with the Folsom Administration. The Folsom Administration had shown its appreciation to me, as well as other people who stood by them. We had helped with their programs and put forth every effort possible to get their programs through. In the main, it turned out to be a very outstanding administration. There were many things that I was able to get for my district, the most important being new roads in Fayette County.

Fayette County had decided to put in the unit system for road building. The unit system lets all commissioners or the county Board of Revenue go together and buy equipment to build their own roads instead of letting contracts. One county commissioner could not afford to buy equipment to build roads in an economical manner, but the unit system would let him pool resources with the other commissioners. Fayette had done just that, but they were not happy with the success they were having. The road they first started to build was what is now State Highway 107, the road from Highway 18 west of Fayette to Guin, Alabama. The probate judge, who had turned his back on me during my campaign, asked the commissioners' court clerk to get the approval of the commissioners to ask me if the state would finish building the road. The following Tuesday, I went to Montgomery to the office of Ward McFarland, the highway director, and asked about it. He said, "Yes, we'll do that." He immediately prepared a resolution, and I took it back to Fayette. They took the road construction over without delay.

In Fayette County, part of it was already engineered. Maybe the clearing was done on most of it, and it was about to be finished before it ever started in Marion County. Senator Rankin Fite, whose district included Marion, Franklin, and Colbert Counties, came in one morning and said, "Fuller, you know they haven't done a thing in Marion County on that road, and I understood you to say it was supposed to go to Guin."

"It is," I said.

"Will you go with me to see Ward?" he asked.

"Yes, let's go," I said. We went over to see Ward and turned the heat on him pretty strong. That was the only time I've ever known the engineering department to get out on Saturday. They got that road from the Fayette County line on into Guin in Marion County going pretty quickly and finished it right away.

At that time Fayette County had road equipment that it had paid a little over a $100,000 for. The commissioners court's clerk, Roy Martin, came to me and said, "Fuller, the board thinks maybe you could get the state to buy that equipment from the county. They don't need it, but they need the money." Well it was a good thing that the state had gotten its money released, since the war was over, and they were buying equipment. I went back to the highway director and asked.

"I think so," Ward said. He sent two people to look at it, Charlie Dale Propst and Rex Edwards, who were heads of the Bureau of Equipment for the state. Propst and his family lived in Fayette, and, incidentally, were very close personal friends of mine. They offered the county less than half what they had paid. The county agreed to take it.

Before they moved the equipment, a good old fellow, Marion Jones, who had a drugstore on main street across from the courthouse and the bank in Fayette, came to me and said, "Senator, I wonder if you could get the road paved in front of my house. My neighbor would not sign the easement when they were paving the sidewalk and street, so they stopped two doors from me. I've lived in dust, and I'm just two doors from the other street. I wonder if you could get the state to pave it up to that other street."

"Brother Jones, I don't know, but I'll try," I said.

In the meantime, we had just passed a bill in the senate to give the City of Mobile authority to sell $1.5 million worth of bonds on the old tunnel that went under the Mobile River. The bill specified that the City of Mobile could use that money for feeder roads that came into Highways 90 and 98, which went through the Mobile tunnel. On the way to Montgomery I got to thinking, on Highway 18 in front of my house was a terrible curve which people whipped around at high speed, so starting at the Jones' we could go through West Highland, where there were two black churches and the new West Highland School. I knew Governor Folsom had promised to help the blacks to improve their schools. I thought that could be a relief road, and we could pave that and come into Highway 96. It would take a lot of traffic off Highway 18 coming through town. I went to Ward McFarland again, told him my idea, and showed him on the map what I had in mind. He said, "Yes, we will do that. We'll give him a sidewalk, and widen that road in front of West Highland School. I know the governor won't mind that at all."

While they were building what then was known as Sipsey Street, Joe Caine, the Mayor of Fayette and a very good friend of mine, came to me and said, "Fuller, we sure have a lot of streets in Fayette that need paving." Of course the state had kept the equipment they bought from Fayette County to do the work on Sipsey Street. He asked, "Reckon we couldn't just get them to stay here and pave some streets in Fayette? We need to take the median out of Temple Avenue, and Highway 43 comes right down Temple Avenue through the middle of town in front of the bank and courthouse. It has two big trees in the middle of it, and maybe we could get them to take those trees down and four-lane Temple Avenue, since it is a state highway."

I went back to see Ward McFarland and laid this all out. He said, "I've got two members of the legislature, one from Colbert County and one from Chilton County, that we rely on to look at these things. Let me get them to go and look."

Charlie Cox was the man from Chilton County, a really good joke teller. In the smoke-filled rooms at night, we got together, with three or four good joke tellers, and he was one of them. I had a good relationship with him. He and the other representative of Chilton County had sponsored a bill creating an experiment station to study and promote the growing of fruits and vegetables. He knew I had been instrumental in getting this bill passed in the senate.

When he visited, I took him to my home and Reba cooked a delicious fried chicken dinner. I also invited Mayor Joe Caine. After dinner, Charlie Cox said, I'm going to recommend to Ward McFarland that the state do this for you."

I went back to Montgomery Tuesday morning to see Ward McFarland. He said, "Charlie Cox said that some of those little streets in Fayette you want paved need a little dirt. Does the city have a little truck? We can send a loader in there, but we need a small truck to haul the dirt to fill in and widen the street."

"I'm sure the Mayor will do it," I said. We made a trade and paved about thirteen miles of streets in Fayette, which was unheard of before.

To take the median out of Temple Avenue took some doing because nobody would help me get the easement below the railroad, which we had to have. Also, there was a lot of static about taking down those big, fine oak trees from the median. The merchants were all for it, but some of the elderly people did not feel too good about cutting down the trees. The traffic was getting heavier and heavier, because Highway 43 was getting busier and busier, and the traffic came right through downtown. I came up with the idea that maybe we might get a little bypass or something. I went to see Ward McFarland again, and he agreed to build Aylette Street, later known as Second Avenue, and renamed Fuller Kimbrell Drive all the way through in the spring of 1998.

The city had to get the right-of-way, and since Ward wanted to put a sidewalk on each side of the street, the property owners had to pay fifty cents per foot for the sidewalk. The street, however, did not cost the people anything. Almost everybody who owned property signed the easement or right-of-way immediately. I believe they had to condemn two pieces of property. The owner of these said he wasn't in the habit of signing things like that, but to go ahead and condemn the property, he wouldn't protest. Without delay the City condemned it, and the Highway Department started working on it immediately.

One thing most interesting: I went with Mr. P. W. Caraway and Mr. E. A. Bagwell, two elderly successful businessmen who were outstanding citizens of Fayette, to get a Mr. Jones to sign the easement. Tears rolled down his cheeks and he said, "I've been 30 years growing those fine little oaks. They were pretty out in front, and they are going to be taken from me in an hour. I'm not going to give you any trouble because I know the road is needed, and it we be nice and everything." He signed it.

About a year after the road was finished, and it was nice, Mr. Jones came to the Kimbrell Tractor & Implement Company's office, and said, "Senator, I just want to tell you. I noticed you had tears in your eyes, too, just like I did. But I wouldn't have my trees back and do without the road now because I'm really proud of the road. I thought it would make you feel better if I came and told you." Which it did.

One bad thing was the Highway Department had still agreed to go ahead and finish four-laning Temple Avenue all the way up to Five Points, but the city attorney was so slow about getting the easement where the Civic Center is now on up to Five Points that the Highway Department moved off it. They had been spending a good deal of federal money, and when they moved the highway from Temple Avenue to Aylette Street, the highway director said there was no way he could get by with it. So we didn't get Temple Avenue four-laned all the way to Five Points. Later, we did get Highway 43 four-laned up farther.

It was really rubbing the probate judge the wrong way since all the paving was getting done, but I was getting no credit because my opponent was the editor and owner of the local paper, the Fayette County Times. I was going back and forth to Montgomery getting all these things done, but they never gave me any credit for it, like most politicians now who come home, call a press conference, and make an announcement. I was not doing it to get credit or recognition. I had been elected to do something for my district, and I was feeling just as good knowing that it was being done. It kept going along that way for a good bit. Finally, the editor of the local paper, Jim Ayres, did not put it in his paper, but he called Hugh Sparrow, a political reporter for The Birmingham News. Hugh Sparrow came and took pictures of all the work being done in Fayette County. Fayette County and Fuller Kimbrell made the headlines in the Birmingham News for three Sundays in a row, while they were paving those streets. Ward McFarland called me, and I walked from the Capitol across to the Highway Department. He said, "Fuller, I'm getting so much pressure from all over about this, we are just going to have to pull that equipment out. How much do you lack being through?"

"I promised one more street," I said.

"I just don't know whether I can," Ward said.

"They can do it in about three days," I said.

"We will do that street, but don't promise any more," he said.

When I got back to Fayette, I told Mr. Bagwell, who owned the Fayette Concrete Pipe Company and Ready Mix Concrete business what I had done. When they first announced they were going to pave all the streets in Fayette, he owned three or four blocks where the grammar school is now and the football stadium and playground, and he got busy and put curb and gutter there so it would be paved under the state program.

I never said any more about the road from Fayette to Townley. Part of it went right on into Walker County and came into Highway 78 at Townley. Finally nearly at the end of the administration I went to Folsom, and said, "Governor, I know you promised Representative Dobbs you would build that road from Fayette to Townley and shorten the route to Birmingham. But he didn't vote for your choice for speaker as he had agreed to. That road is needed badly by the people of Fayette and Lamar Counties. It's a shorter and better route to Birmingham, and I would like you to build it, and make it a state highway."

The governor asked, "Would the county get the right-of-way?"

"Yes, I think I can promise you that, but I'll be sure later on," I answered.

"If they do, you tell Ward I said build the road," he said.

I went back to Fayette to see Clyde Cargile, who had become probate judge by that time. I told him what the governor had said. He said, "Yes, we can get the right of way." The Farm-to-Market Program had already built the first nine miles out of Fayette. They picked up there and built it. Part of it went right on into Walker County and came into Highway 78 at Townley. It was the second road we got built by Folsom during that administration.

Reba and I were in the theater one Friday night. Senator Broughton Lamberth, who was the president pro tem in the senate and the leader of our five senators helping Folsom in every way we could, called me out of the theater and asked, "Senator, would you like to have a National Guard Unit?"

"Yes, but I don't know what you are talking about," I said.

"It means a pretty good payroll for your county and employment. We have four, and we are going to give one to the speaker of the house from Fort Payne. Rankin is going to get one, and I'm going to get one," he said.

"Yes, we want it," I said.

The county and city had to furnish the land in order to get the National Guard Armory. The smaller towns like Fayette and Hamilton were not getting an armory, but Alex City and Fort Payne did get an armory. So I went to the county and city officials , and they agreed to buy from Mr. Bagwell some of the land close to the high school that he didn't curb and gutter. I forget the number of acres, but they paid $12,000 it. They built offices and fixed a place to keep equipment, and they put a fence around the area in order to store trucks and various things they had there. Almost immediately the National Guard Unit was the third largest payroll in Fayette County. The unit was equal to a pretty good industry for Fayette.

I got four or five people together and we went to Montgomery to see the governor. We made arrangements for him to come to Fayette and make a speech, and we activated the National Guard Unit. More than 75 men enlisted that day. But the bad thing about it was that the Korean War was going on, and within five weeks from the time the guard unit was organized, the young men were shipped off to Korea.

NINE

LAKES, HIGHWAYS, AND SECRETARIES

I was a member of the Fayette Lions Club, and one night at a meeting, Mr. P. W. Caraway who helped get the easement for Aylette Street—recently named the Fuller Kimbrell Drive—stood up and said, "I just read in the paper that Alabama has enough money to build two fishing lakes. I suggest that we insist that our Senator Kimbrell see if he can get Fayette one of those fishing lakes."

Tuesday morning I went to see Phillip Hamm, the Conservation Director. He lobbied in the senate nearly all the time, and we five Senators—Broughton Lamberth, from Tallapoosa County; Harvey, from Blount County; Tom Blake Howle, from Calhoun County; Rankin Fite, from Marion County, and I—had developed a good relationship with him. I told him what had been in the paper and what happened in the Lions Club meeting. Most of the members were friends of the governor's and mine. He said, "All right, Senator, you are the first one to ask, so you will get the first public fishing lake. Not only is it the first one in Alabama, but it will be the first one in the United States built with public funds. We will have to get the county or someone to furnish the land for it."

I went back and saw O. C. Anders, a friend of the probate judge, who had a place where you could build a twelve acre lake, which he later built. It is a very pretty lake now, but we were hoping to get a bigger lake. My friend, Bruce Harkins, the county superintendent of education, had a place where we could build a fifty-five acre lake, and which could be bought for about the same amount of money. I insisted they buy it and got the conservation director to approve buying it and approve the site. Since that time Fayette County Lake has been a very nice recreation area for Fayette County and surrounding areas. A little later, after there was some more money available, we got a smaller lake for Lamar County. The second lake went down to Luverne in Crenshaw County, south of Montgomery.

Rankin Fite wanted a lake, so he and I came up with the idea to put an extra fifty cents on fishing licenses. We introduced a bill to increase the fishing license from fifty cents to $1.50 and to use the money to build fishing lakes around. Over the weekend the president of Farm Bureau, Walter Randolph, who was not our friend and was with the group fighting the Folsom administration, put an article in the paper. I didn't see it, but Rankin saw it over the weekend. It had a picture with caption, "Nigger, what you doing trying to catch that catfish? Don't you know it's going to cost you $1.50?" Rankin had the article and he said, "Fuller, if you will call Walter Randolph, (Walter was from Fayette County originally), I'll get him told."

I called him into the Rotunda, and we went over to the corner. Rankin sure did pour the heat on him about it. We got our bill passed, and Rankin got his fishing lake. Since he wasn't the only one who wanted a fishing lake out of it, we did enough trading with other folks to get it passed in one day when there weren't so many senators in the chamber. He got his fishing lake, but it was smaller than Fayette County's. Fayette County's lake is one of the nicest in the whole state because it is located in a very appropriate place and has good roads that are easily accessed by surrounding areas.

Things I was able to get for Walker County: Walker County had a National Guard Unit, so I went to see the adjutant general and told him Walker County ought to have a better armory for their unit. He checked and said, "Yes, there is some money." We met with the county officers and agreed to update the National Guard Armory, which was right inside the city limits of Jasper. Their unit worked out, and Lamar County got a National Guard unit later, but not during that four years.

Another good thing was that Pee Wee Burgess, a very good friend of mine in the construction business, was building a bypass around Jasper, just a two-lane road. He came to me and said, "Fuller, see if you can get it made a four-lane, and while I'm working on it amend the contract."

I went to see Herman Nelson, the highway director, about amending the contract and making it four-lane, and he said, "It will be above the amount that we can amend the contract for, but let me look at it a little bit." He called me from the senate, and I went back over the next day. He said, "Fuller, I tell you what. We have nearly all the engineering work. We will start advertising and have a special letting for that second lane on the road. I'm satisfied that since your friend is the contractor he will be low bidder. He already has his equipment on the ground, and it will save the cost of moving in and moving out." That developed into four-laning the bypass around Jasper, which right now is probably the busiest highway in west Alabama going right through the city limits of Jasper today. It runs by two shopping areas and several restaurants and other businesses located right along on that bypass, which has been a wonderful thing for Highway 78 going from east to west.

Along about the end of his administration, Bibb Graves made a statement: "The setting sun gives off no heat." What he meant by that was: along at the end of the administration people quit coming to the governor's office hoping to get favors and things done for their districts and counties. Governor Folsom had his secretary, Bill Lyerly, who had also served in other cabinet positions during the four years, called me one afternoon. Bill said, "Senator, the Governor wants to see you at eight o'clock in the morning."

I got to thinking, and I called Bruce Doughty, the representative of Pickens County. I knew he had voted with the administration, and I said, "Bruce, the governor has called me to come to Montgomery. If you will meet me in Tuscaloosa in the morning I'll bet we can get the road (now Highway 159) from Fayette to Gordo made a state highway."

"What time?" he asked.

"Be there at six o'clock, because he wants me in Montgomery at eight," I said.

"I'll be there," he said. I met him in Tuscaloosa, and we rode down in his new Lincoln Continental.

When we got there Governor Folsom was sitting behind his desk with his size fourteen-and-a-half brogan shoes, which he wore all the time, on top of the desk. He welcomed us, and we visited a little while. Finally he asked, "Senator, what brings you all to town so early?"

"Bill Lyerly called and said you wanted to see me. I asked Bruce Doughty to come with me," I answered.

He said, "Aw foot, I didn't mean that early. I just wanted to talk about the branch heads and see how things are getting along back up in the country." I told him just fine.

"Can I do something for you boys?" he asked.

"Yes, Bruce and I would like to have the road from Fayette to Gordo made a state highway. We sure would appreciate it," I said.

The Governor punched his button for Bill Lyerly to get Ward McFarland, the highway director, on the phone. He said, "Ward, we got two old country boys here, Representative Doughty from Pickens County and Senator Kimbrell of Fayette County. They are pretty good boys. They are wanting something all the time, but I think this is needed. They want the road from Fayette to Gordo made a state highway. Get the resolution ready. They will be over there to pick it up in a little bit. Bye." And he hung up the phone. We went by and picked up the resolution, and that was how the road from Fayette to Gordo became State Highway 159.

At that time the newspapers, the "lying dailies" as he called them, had been accusing Governor Folsom of drinking. When we started to leave, Governor Folsom followed us to the back steps of the State Capitol. Mr. Doughty and I were about the same height about 5′8″, Governor Folsom was 6′8″ tall. We were down about three steps looking up at him — like looking up at a tall tree — and he said, "Senator, you know they started lying on me again."

"Lord have mercy Governor!" I said. "What are they telling this time?" I asked.

"They are telling that I've stopped drinking," he said.

For quite sometime, when I first moved to Fayette in 1939 and even before then, they had promised to pave the road called the Newtonville road from Fayette to Newtonville. Two or three governors had promised it. Sparks had promised it, and Bibb Graves had promised it, but it never got done. I had pushed for that road to be paved during the administration, and at the very last letting in the Folsom administration that was one of the contracts that was let. Governor Persons was elected, and Rankin Fite had a contract that was let in that letting. Senator Broughton Lamberth, a friend of the Folsoms and one of the floor leaders, had one, which was a bypass around Alex City. They got A. A. Timmons, the AAA Automobile Insurance agent in Birmingham, to file a suit and hold up those three contracts. They had not awarded them, and it looked like they were not going to. While Governor Persons was making his inauguration address, I went to see Guerry Pruitt. Before that time Guerry was a lobbyist and advisor for Ward McFarland, the highway director, and during the bridge bill we would ask him how long a bridge would be at a certain place. He had his maps and his figures, and he would look at them and come back and tell us. He counted every bridge

$15,000 a foot for an estimate in order to keep up with how much of that $10 million we were getting.

Pruitt was really friendly, and I noticed that he was really friendly to one of the clerks in the senate. So I went to her and told her the Newtonville road—now Highway 171—had been promised for twenty years, and it went into one of the finest communities in Fayette County. I asked would she go and whisper in Guerry Pruitt's ear and ask him to let that contract, but not to tell him I had talked to her. While Governor Persons was making his inaugural address, I slipped over to the Highway Department—Guerry Pruitt had been appointed highway director—and he was sitting at his desk already. I said, "Guerry that road is really needed. It's goes into a fine community, and it's been promised time and time again."

"Fuller, we are not going to let that contract, but I promise you we will make it a state road and I'll pave it," he said. About a year later, he not only paved it to the Fayette County line, but on down to Moore's Bridge, and widened it, which was better than I hoped to get. That was one of the things that came to pass that had been talked about for many years. Today we are trying to get the road improved and brought up to date from Moore's Bridge to Highway 82 in Northport.

When Governor Folsom was campaigning, usually he would have a flatbed one-ton pickup. He would get upon the back to speak. Before he pulled into town, someone would go ahead of him and announce "Big Jim" Folsom was coming to town and tell when and where he was going to speak. When he came to

Berry, he got upon the back end of the pickup and he saw a beautiful little brunette.

"Bring that beautiful little brunette standing out there and put her on this truck with me," he said. She came walking over and they helped her up. He spoke to her and told her who he was, and she told him she was Jamelle Moore. When he finished his speech that night, he was going to have a rally at Carbon Hill. He called her mother and daddy, and asked, "If I send somebody to pick up you and your daughter Jamelle, will you come to the rally at Carbon Hill?"

"Yes," they said. In a small town like Berry, gossippers would pass around stories from one to another, and it was a favorite pastime because they only had a few radios and no televisions at all. He sent for her several times during his campaign to come to his rallies.

Earl Speight, the clerk of the senate, came to Fayette one day and brought Agnes Quinn. She was Mr. Lynn Dodd's daughter. Mr. Dodd called and said, "Senator, the clerk, Earl Speight, and my daughter Agnes are coming for lunch, and they want to know if you and your wife will come have lunch with us."

"Yes, we'll be happy to," I said.

Earl Speight said, "Senator, I don't know if you know it or not, but all the senators are entitled to a clerk if they want one. Some of them don't have one, but almost everybody does, and all the members of the committees or the more outstanding committees have their own clerk. Agnes has experience and has worked two or three sessions in the legislature. I've used her as kind of a foreman and supervisor. If you don't have anyone in mind that you want to be your clerk, I would appreciate it if you will take her as your clerk."

"I'll be happy to. I've never met her before but if she is anything like her daddy she will be the finest," I said.

"She is just that fine and that dependable," he said.

I had my clerk, but I didn't know that I needed one. I don't remember writing but a few letters in the full four years while I was in the senate.

We had only been in the regular session a few days when O. H. Finney, the Governor's executive secretary, came one day and said, "Senator, the Governor wanted to know if you would mind bringing Jamelle Moore down as your secretary."

"I'll be happy too. I'm so new at this, let me see about it," I said. I slipped up to Earl Speight's office, and told him the Governor wanted me to bring down one of my home town constituents, Jamelle Moore to be my secretary.

"You can get what you want from me, Fuller. She can be your secretary," he said. I went back and told O. H. Finney. They sent to Berry and brought her down, and she lived with her cousin in Montgomery. Of course, she was not a qualified secretary by any means, but she was very ladylike and a beautiful lady.

She was my secretary, and later she and Governor "Big Jim" got married. During "Little Jim" Folsom's campaign, I made the statement several times, "I was the only man I ever heard of whose secretary became the Governor's wife and was a Governor's mother."

TEN

MORE WHEELING AND DEALING

L ate in 1947, a group of Fayette leaders got together and decided it would be good if Fayette had a Chamber of Commerce. Several leading citizens and businessmen in town met in the office of Lynn Dodd, a local cotton buyer, and organized. It was agreed that Dr. Banks Robertson, a Fayette surgeon, would be president, Alex Smith, a local attorney, would be vice president, and Bill Sanders, the owner of Sanders Insurance Company, agreed to be the secretary and treasurer. Soon after, Dr. Robertson became sick, and it was apparent he would not overcome his illness and be active in any public or civic function. Alex Smith was asked, but said he could not serve as president due to unexpected legal work. The group got back together and asked if I would serve as president, and I agreed to.

The first thing I thought would be good for the county and give a start to chamber activities was to get Fayette's county agent an assistant. While serving with the legislature in 1947, which was the regular session and several special sessions, I learned Chilton County had an extra assistant county agent. Instead of having one county agent, as did the rest of the counties, they had two. I came up with the idea that Fayette County could have an assistant county agent to work with the farmers. There was a good deal of talk at that time of producing cucumbers and selling them to Whitfield Pickle Company in Montgomery, plus the chicken broiler business had just begun to come to life all over the South. Arkansas was doing well with it, and the northern part of Alabama had begun to produce broilers. I talked to the board. Bill Sanders and I decided we would go to Auburn to talk to P. O. Davis and Jimmy Lawson, who were heads of the extension service at that time, and see if they would be willing to give Fayette County an assistant county agent. It worked out that the county would need to put in $175 a month, as it was customary for the counties to participate in the salaries of the county agent, assistant agent, and Home Extension agent. We came back home and went before the County Board of Commissioners. Judge McGough was still probate judge at that time. And after we told them what we had done, the county passed the resolution immediately to furnish the $175 a month.

Judge McGough, as I've said before, had fallen out with me and had been fighting me every way he could. He would never let the commissioners court's clerk put the resolution in the minutes, and we kept going to them. I didn't know they had not recorded it. I called Jimmy Lawson and he said, "We don't have the resolution here."

One of the funny things about it was: back then, if you made a long distance telephone call from Fayette you had to call the Jasper operator, and she would place your telephone call. Nell Chaffin, a telephone operator whose mother lived in Fayette, came to Fayette about that time. I talked to Nell a lot over the telephone, since I was making a lot of calls trying to find machinery to stay in business as you could sell almost anything you could find. She told me that she and her mother were going to Louisville, Kentucky, to visit her sister or some relative. Since she had been so good about getting my calls through, I gave her a $25 check for her and her mother to spend on the trip. I never thought much about it, but when she got back home, she would call me every morning and say, "Mr. Kimbrell, if you will give me your calls, I'll get them through for you. Otherwise you might be all day getting just one call through." A lot of people were doing the same thing I was doing, calling trying to find merchandise, and making other business calls. One morning she called and said, "Mr. Kimbrell, you can't say a word. You must not say a word."

"All right," I said.

She connected me to a conference call between P. O. Davis, Judge McGough, Jimmy Lawson, and the local County Agent, P. R. Pettus. My ears were really burning because they were trying to figure every way possible not to give us an assistant county agent, and they were successful. We never got the assistant county agent at that time because Judge McGough held on to the resolution, and even when the county commissioners got on to him about it, still he never put the resolution on the books. Of course, it went on until my time ran out in the senate. I quit trying, and I was elected to serve one year as president of the Chamber of Commerce.

We did some other things for the county during that time. I

came up with the idea to build a high school stadium. I didn't get it through right then, but when it came time for J. C. McGough to run for re-election, I had become quite popular because I was calling on the farmers. The rural people went to the polls and voted by a larger percentage than they do now, plus the fact I was calling on them trying to sell equipment. They would come into my place of business and visit and talk. Judge McGough had not only fought me, but I thought he could have done a better job as probate judge.

Clyde Cargile, the county superintendent of education, was real popular, and well liked. The people were happy with the job he was doing as superintendent of education. His office was upstairs in the courthouse. One day I called him and said, "Clyde, how about coming down. I want to ride you around the block." He got in the car and we rode up Temple Avenue and back down Aylette Street, and I took him back to the courthouse. I had put $400 in my pocket, and I took it out and said, "Clyde, here's $400. I want you to run for probate judge."

He looked at me funny and said, "I'll admit, I've thought of it a little bit. You giving me this as a campaign contribution?"

"Yes," I said.

"I'll just tell you, I'll run." he said. He ran and was elected.

After he got into office, I went before the commissioners court and I said, "I've come up with an idea. Behind Fayette High School you could go in and dig that bank out, push the dirt up, put concrete seats on that dirt you dig out and level it down inside. For a minimum cost we can make a stadium over there that will be the envy of all West Alabama."

One of the commissioners spoke up and asked, "What's your proposition, Fuller?"

I said, "I'll organize a committee and get out and raise the money if the county will put their equipment over there. They won't be out any gas or cost." The commissioners agreed to do that. I got several local citizens together, and we decided to push for it.

As it turned out, I was the only one that decided to do any work on it. Farm machinery was still very scarce then, and I had a brand new Model A John Deere. I told the committee, "I'll sell the committee that tractor at regular retail price and we will get out and sell chances on it." As I remember, we sold chances for twenty dollars each, and we sold enough tickets that we got about $6700 for about a $1200 tractor. I went to see a lot of folks — Yellow Front store, Hill Grocery Company, the A&P Store — and they all put in twenty-five dollars each. Sumter Farm put in $200. At that time I had developed a real good relationship with Mr. O. J. Henley, the president of Sumter Farm Stores, and he contributed more than any other business. Local businesses put in a good bit, and we raised enough money to make a 4500 seat stadium in Fayette, which is still being used and is one of the main attractions for ball games in Fayette and West Alabama.

Along about 1943-44 the farm machinery dealers in Alabama, including Allis Chambers, John Deere, and International, met in Montgomery at the Whitney Hotel for the purpose of organizing the Alabama Equipment Association. Caine Butler and I attended. The first president was Mr. Scott, the International dealer in Mobile, and we got it going good and it was working out well. At the regular annual convention in the fall of 1946, I was elected president, to serve in 1947, and J. B. Wilson, a professor in the Auburn Agriculture School, was elected secretary. In Auburn, J. B. Wilson was working with farmers and promoting power farm equipment, which was just beginning to be talked about and was getting more and more popular for cultivating and harvesting crops. Of course, that was during the time I started serving in the Alabama Senate. While serving in the senate, I came up with the idea that Auburn needed to do more in the way of training their agriculture students about power farm equipment. I went to see the branch manager, C. S. Masterson, of John Deere, who was on the board of directors of the parent company in Atlanta. I also went to Birmingham and talked to the branch manager of International Harvester Company. I got one of the Allis Chambers dealers up at Athens, Alabama to call his branch manager, and they agreed that if Auburn would set aside some land for demonstration, they would put their newest and most modern equipment there so the students could learn how to operate it and learn the advantages.

When I got to Montgomery, I decided to introduce a bill in the legislature to set aside 100 acres of land owned by Auburn University for the study and use of power equipment for farming. After a little research work with Dr. Fred Coumer and J. B. Wilson, we worked out that what was really needed was more of a storage barn, warehouse-like with garage. Then they needed to do some work on the land that was to be set aside. So I got the legislative referencing service to draw up a bill, and I introduced it as Senate Bill 189. I almost didn't get it out of the committee. It first went to the Agriculture Committee, which came out very easy because I was vice chairman of that committee. But since it carried an appropriation, the chairman of the Finance and Taxation Committee insisted it come through his committee — which was customary really. I did not know exactly what was coming, but I found out right quick. The leaders from Farm Bureau were punishing me for voting with Folsom for the Auburn Trustees. And of course it was apparent that the Auburn leaders did not want me to have credit for this new idea. They were sure if the trustees were confirmed by the senate, the governor would fire P. O. Davis and Jimmy Lawson, because they had been so politically active in the farm area, particularly against him. I finally got my bill out, but only by agreeing to a conditional appropriation. That meant that if the governor said the money was there and the budget officer told the finance director the money was available it would happen. So we got it out, and it passed the senate, and it went over to the house.

I was working with a fellow named Walter Givhan, the representative of Dallas County, who lived near the small experimental station at Marion Junction, and he was going to handle it in the House. Just before time for it to come up in the House, Givhan came through the senate and said, "Fuller, I'm going to have to leave. I won't be able to handle your bill, but I've worked it out with Dr. Taylor from Greensboro, (who was another one of Farm Bureau's henchmen so to speak. On many Tuesday mornings, Dr. Taylor would introduce a resolution calling for the impeachment of Governor Folsom!) and Dr. Taylor will handle it." Right away I knew they were trying to throw me a curve.

When it came up on the calendar, E. L. Roberts, one of the House Floor Leaders for Governor Folsom, came running over and asked, "Senator, who is suppose to be handling your bill?"

"Givhan left, but I understand Doc Taylor," I answered.

He said, "Doc Taylor isn't here either. Why don't you just come over here?" So by permission of the Speaker of the House, which is most unusual for a senator to come in an explain a bill before the full house, they let me explain the bill. In so doing, I killed the senate committee amendment in the House, which left it with an absolute appropriation, and otherwise it was just as it was.

When it got back to the senate, the budget officer had a separate substitute for it drawn up, because he wanted to specify that so much would be spent for the warehouse and so much for the fences and the equipment in the shop, as well as the equipment the various companies would put there. I accepted the substitute, but by that time they discovered that the amendment making it a conditional appropriation had been deleted, so they sent it back to the committee. I didn't know they were going to bring it up, and as president of Alabama Farm and Equipment Association, I had gone to Cincinnati to attend the annual National Retail Equipment Association meeting.

Earl Speight, the senate clerk, a very close friend of mine, called me in Cincinnati that Monday and said, "Fuller, they are going to bring your bill up while you are out, and they are going to kill it. I've just gotten word because one of the clerks who is your friend came and told me." I jumped on the plane, flew almost all night, got into Montgomery by six A.M., and showed — up to their surprise. The first thing they did was to try to postpone it indefinitely, but they didn't have enough votes to do that. Then they put the conditional appropriation back on, and I moved to lay that on the table. I didn't have enough votes to do that, but after ten separate votes in the senate alone, I finally got the bill passed. But I had to accept the conditional appropriation.

The bill went to Governor Folsom's office that afternoon and so did I. The governor signed it and immediately called the budget officer and put the money back in. So it came through just like I wanted it. Coming down the hall I met Senator Jim Allen Sr., who later became U.S. senator, and I said, "Thanks to you — but no thanks to you — I got the money put back in."

"I knew you would get it put back anyway," Senator Allen said.

Allen was a funny fellow, he was very able and a very smart senator, but he never introduced any bills. He never really tried to do anything for the state of Alabama, but he tried to stop legislation a lot of times. He voted against a lot of bills, but never tried to help Folsom in any way. You could might-near say the same thing about him when he went to Washington later.

The bill passed, and until this day, Auburn has never invited me to come see what I worked so hard to get for them. But some of my friends, who are Auburn graduates and later became county agents and worked over there, told me it covers about 500 acres now instead of 100 acres and is heavy in dairy, poultry, and other experiments.

Another bill that passed during Folsom's administration was a bill regulating the study of forests and horticulture. This bill helped the farmers realize the value of looking after their forests and woodlands, keeping the fires out, watching the pines, and cutting out the trees infected with pine beetles. Back then you hardly ever saw a hardware store, and certainly not department stores, selling potted flowers or plants and shrubbery. Just a few of the merchants sold seeds, cabbage plants, onion plants, and onion sets. Now a lot of the stores in small towns sell flowers and such. You never heard much talk of people planting flowers, shrubbery, or shade trees. People would go to the woods and cut a dogwood bush to sweep the yard and kept it real clean, instead of planting grass. Of course that was before we had lawnmowers. I credit the Folsom administration in its promotion of forestry and commend his friends, also, in the promotion of horticulture. Various plants certainly contributes a lot to the beauty of Alabama and the South. Of course the other states have come along too. Horticulture's gotten to be one of the biggest industries in the state. I believe when I was on the Board of Agriculture, during Little Jim's Administration, it was the fourth largest industry in Alabama.

Another thing: Temo Callahan, who at this time lives in Tuscaloosa and is 95 years old, introduced a bill to put a one-cent sales tax in Tuscaloosa County to build and promote the Druid City Hospital in Tuscaloosa. They immediately started construction where it is now located, and fortunately they had the foresight to plan it for future expansion. From that day on they have hardly stopped building it. It is one of the leading hospitals in the South, certainly among the smaller and medium-sized cities. The one-cent sales tax to build the hospital was the only tax I ever voted for. I would have voted for a one-cent gasoline tax, but it never got to the senate.

We also passed a bill regulating the use of state automobiles, so that only the elected officials could legally use state automobiles. The governor, lieutenant governor, and a few cabinet members could use them, but not legislators. Back then it was not uncommon for a senator or representative to call the State Highway Patrol to pick him up and drive him wherever he wanted to go. Of course, the lieutenant governor and cabinet members were driven various places, but only for the purpose of conducting state business.

Big Jim's main subject, and the main theme of his platform, was to pave all the mailbox roads. That was the reason that he introduced the one-cent gasoline tax, which never got out of the House and never got to the Senate. I've said before, it was a very serious and costly mistake by the opposition.

In my district, which represented Fayette, Lamar, and Walker Counties, we had Walker College in Jasper, which was an outstanding institution and was well-thought-of in Walker County. A couple of members of the Board of Trustees of Walker College came to see me one day with Chester Black, the representative of Walker County and a very outstanding one. We went to lunch, and they asked us about getting around $10,000 in state money for some specific project at Walker College. I agreed to him the money and went to the Legislative

Reference Service and had the bill drawn up. I had a lot of hollering and carrying on about it, but I knew that Senator Pinson from Sumter County was on the Board of Trustees at Tuskegee and was the first white person to ever serve on the Tuskegee's Board of Trustees. The population of Sumter County was predominately black. We talked about it and heard about it, so he immediately put a bill in to give $5000 to Tuskegee. That made it a lot easier because he — being from the Black Belt — had voted with the crowd that was fighting Folsom most of the time. In order to give him his money, they didn't dare not let Walker County have the $10,000. Those were the first two state appropriations ever for private schools in Alabama. Now, it is quite common that the schools get state monies and additional appropriations for specific purposes.

A funny thing that happened: Kenneth Griffith from Cullman was Governor Folsom's legal adviser and enjoyed going out with the boys at night and having a drink and playing poker. They talked him into getting the governor to sponsor a bill creating the Department of Examiners of Public Accounts. Kenneth got the bill drawn up and brought it up and it came to my desk first. Rankin was standing there, and he said, "The governor wants this bill."

I talked it over with him, and I noticed Senator Coleman from Green and Hale Counties was standing there. He took a look at it and said, "Yes this is good for you boys."

Rankin looked at it, and he was a lawyer, and said, "What this is doing is setting up a separate department and taking the auditing of state departments of cities and counties out from under the governor's office, really." He added, "Kenneth, you sure the governor wants this?"

Kenneth answered, "Yes, I've just talked it over with him."

So I signed it, Rankin signed it, Senator Coleman signed it, and Senator Bob Kendall, from Conecuh County, signed it. They introduced it and it passed without any slow-down. Everybody voted for it. And it went over to the house and got ninety-seven votes. A few members were absent, but it didn't have a single vote against it. By the time it got to the governor's office, he found out that the bill was going to take the Department of Examiners of Public Accounts out of the governor's control, so he vetoed it.

Kenneth Griffith brought it up and said, "Senators, the Governor vetoed this bill, and you all signed it."

We looked at each other and Rankin said, "What!"

Griffith said, "Yes, the Governor has vetoed it and wants you to go along and help sustain the veto."

"Kenneth, there isn't any way we can get enough votes to sustain that veto," I said.

"I tried to tell him that but he vetoed it anyway," he said. He took it on up and laid it on the clerk's desk.

Rankin and I talked about it. We said since ours were the first names on that bill, how were we going to be able to vote to sustain the veto? Rankin said, "I'm not going to do it, I'm going out in the hall and wait until it comes up." This practice was known as "cabbage patching."

I said, "I'm going to stay here and vote to sustain the veto."

Rankin went to the hall and they brought it up and had enough votes to override the veto in the senate. They sent it to the house. They did not sustain the veto, and we were put in a position to try to kill our own bill. That bill really survived, and it is one of the most active departments in the state of Alabama connected with the state government. It has also been the most criticized by the cities and counties, because so often cities and counties have clerks, commissioners, boards of revenue, city councils, mayors, and probate judges, that are not all that well-versed about the law. It is not uncommon for them to put in their minutes things that are not supposed to be there. This bill really did haunt Governor Folsom.

ELEVEN

MORE ON THE FOLSOM ADMINISTRATION

One of my favorite senators was Early Barrett, who represented Pickens County, just south of Fayette and Lamar Counties. He owned some farms, too, and we visited a lot during the legislative sessions. One day we were talking about farming, and I said, "I've been thinking about opening up a John Deere place in Aliceville. I have one in Fayette, Tuscaloosa, and Columbus, Mississippi."

"I'll build you a building," he said.

"All right," I said.

Something happened and we didn't discuss it anymore. That was Thursday when we recessed, and we usually came back Tuesday morning.

Tuesday morning when we came back, Barrett said, "Well, I started your building."

"Oh!" I didn't know what to say.

The next morning, since we didn't usually meet on Wednesday, I got up really early and drove to Atlanta to see the John Deere assistant district manager. I told him what happened, and said, "I think I will let him go ahead and build the building and open up in Aliceville if I can get the dealership for Pickens and that area."

He looked at the records and said, "Yes."

I signed the contract for the dealership in Aliceville, and Senator Barrett went right ahead with the building. I opened up and kept it for — I don't remember how many years — five or six, and it turned out to be a real profitable venture. I made good money while I operated it and later sold it for a nice profit.

Back to other personalities: I have mentioned Rankin Fite, who represented the district right north of me — which was Marion, Franklin, and Colbert Counties, one of the other larger districts. I had never met him until we were both elected to the senate. As I said before, the very first day we made a good alliance with the Highway Director, Ward McFarland, and it held good all the following four years and was very beneficial for our districts.

I've mentioned several times about Folsom working so hard trying to get the Auburn Trustees of his choice confirmed. But that was not the only problem that Governor Folsom had with the legislature, particularly the senate, because Folsom in his campaign speeches said he was going to change the Constitution, which was originally drawn up and passed in 1901 by the Legislature which represented the counties that had large plantations. Many of the owners' parents had previously owned slaves, who were counted for the proration of Legislature, but not allowed to vote, and they were determined to stay in control of the Alabama State Government. After Governor Folsom was sworn in, the very first few days in the regular session he had a bill introduced calling a constitutional convention for the purpose of rewriting the Constitution, which would then go to the voters. It was one of the reasons why the Senate was organized so strongly against him. They didn't want it to happen.

Many years ago, you had to own forty acres of land and a mule, be able to read and write, and pay poll tax before you could vote. When I was old enough to register to vote, I had to pay a $1.50 poll tax. Later, the federal government ruled that paying poll tax was unconstitutional. Of course, the Black Belt leaders, in cooperation with the big businesses and the leaders of Farm Bureau, were trying to work out some way to get the $1.50 poll tax reinstated, because, to tell the truth, they wanted to keep the poor folk and blacks from voting. They could see their power diminishing very much if that became true.

The 1901 Constitution disfranchised more whites than it did blacks percentage wise. It affected mostly small farmers in the hill country of north Alabama. Although that constitution has been amended 600 plus times, those small farmers are still penalized today.

One of the funny things that happened: Bud Boswell, a close friend of Governor Folsom's who was leading this group, thought he had it worked out to get the poll tax reinstated. It was called the Boswell Amendment, but the courts had already ruled it unconstitutional. One day Senator Fite, Senator Lamberth, Bud Boswell, Kenneth Griffith, the legal adviser to the governor, Governor Folsom, and I were at the old Exchange Hotel trying to work out something with Bud Boswell to satisfy their crowd. We hoped to get some advantages for the people in the hills of Alabama out of the deal. Bud Boswell had picked up a navy boy to drive him there; Bud was kind of an elderly-like fellow. We were having a few drinks, and the whiskey ran out.

"Kenneth, send and get us some more whiskey," the governor said.

Kenneth reached to his back pocket and said, "My pocketbook is gone."

Bud Boswell had his grandson with him, and the boy said, "Grandpa that navy boy that was here got Mr. Griffith's pocketbook."

Mr. Boswell asked, "Why didn't you tell him?"

He said, "I did, but he said just let him steal it. I can make it faster than he can steal it."

As I said, Kenneth Griffith, Governor Folsom's legal adviser and I worked on it, but were never able to get anything pertaining to poll tax that we thought would come out of the committee. Of course, poll tax was dead anyway, and there was no way to ever salvage it.

At each session, Governor Folsom introduced a call for a constitutional convention in some form or other, but it never got out of the committee and never happened.

I didn't realize then that it was not that the opposition was so strong against reapportionment, but they did not want to give up their voting control. For instance, I represented Fayette, Lamar, and Walker Counties, which was the Twelfth Senatorial District. It had 38,000 registered voters. Senator Henderson, who represented Wilcox County, had 2000 voters, yet his senatorial district had two representatives. I had a senatorial district with three counties, but I had four representatives, one for each county except Walker County, which had two representatives. Senator Fite had three representatives with about 20,000 voters in his district. That was true in several other senatorial districts in north Alabama and down in the Wiregrass section of Alabama where there were small farmers. One of the things we tried so hard to do, and we almost begged them, was to pass a bill to have one senator for each county and leave the House of Representatives like it was. That would mean sixty-seven senators instead of thirty-five, but we could never get it going. We finally got it passed in the House, but when it got to the Senate, we lacked one vote getting enough votes. We thought surely Senator James Allen, who I mentioned before, would come with us, but we never could move him because at that time he was running for governor. He didn't get too far in his race for governor, but later he was elected to the U. S. Senate.

One of the things I was telling about Senator Fite and I riding together: the senior senators, by time served, would whip us with the rule book one way and another. Of course, right at the point of order, Lieutenant Governor Inzer, who was an Alabama Power Company lawyer, was on their side, and ruled in their favor every time, and we didn't know whether they were right or not. I'm not saying Lieutenant Governor Inzer wasn't honest about it, but they were whipping us to death. We just really didn't know the rules. So what we would do while riding to and from Montgomery was this: I would drive, and since Rankin was a lawyer and could read legalese, he would read the rule book. Senator Fite's father had served twelve years in the Legislature, but not in the Senate. Rankin would go home and talk to his Daddy about it, and Tuesday morning on our way back to the Legislature we would read our rule book. He would say Pa said this and Pa said that. It didn't take us long to get familiar with the rules, and they didn't work us over quite so bad after that.

One morning we were riding along and talking about it, there were only five of us who would stand up there getting our ears beaten back one way or another and getting whipped. We didn't know whether we were coming or going, and I asked, "Rankin, you know what?"

"What?" he asked.

"I've decided the State Treasury divided by five is lot more than if it is divided by thirty-five," I said.

He was silent for a long way, and then he said, "By God, you are right."

We operated on that basis pretty good, but later I'll tell you just how effective it was. I've told a good bit about the things I've done for Fayette County, and that was part of the reason — because we cooperated with the governor.

The Highway Department was not controlled by the general fund as it is now. It was almost left with a free hand to spend the money that was coming in. Most of the money was going into the State Treasury anyway — like sales taxes and gasoline taxes and so on.

Another outstanding thing: as I said before, the probate judge and his followers, after they insisted I run for the senate, had turned against me because I wouldn't promise them I would be against exempting the gasoline tax for farmers. So it was introduced in the House, of course, and when it came to the Senate, I was the floor leader. They kidded me a lot because I was one of the larger farm machinery dealers in the state, plus the fact that I was president of the Alabama Farm Equipment Association. They would say: "You vote for yourself there, you know." I did farm some at that time, but power farming was just coming into its own and there was no doubt that it was going to be an outstanding thing for Alabama.

We revised the code so that the industrial schools for boys and girls would have more attention, stronger leadership, and better management—I guess I should say—particularly the one at Mt. Meigs. It was set up for the blacks who lived in Macon County. Then you had the Boys and Girls Ranch, which straddled the Blount and Jefferson County line. It was strengthened. We gave a larger appropriation to Bryce Hospital, and the hospital for blacks at Mt. Vernon got a larger percentage of the state appropriation than it had ever gotten before.

More attention was given to the prisons. Governor Folsom was strongly against the fee system, because he said so many rich boys stood to gain more favor in court than the poor who were unable to hire a lawyer. So the governor appointed a prison commissioner who was willing to turn a lot of folks out, particularly the people who were unable to hire lawyers. The opposition was successful in getting the law changed to a three-man prison commission, but they didn't realize they were still leaving it under the governor's jurisdiction. The law stated that he could appoint three prison commissioners, and Governor Folsom appointed all three of them. Along towards the end of

Folsom's first administration, in 1950 and early 1951, those three commissioners turned people out almost wholesale to the extent that Governor Persons, who followed Big Jim as governor, thought he had caught Governor Folsom doing something illegal. He called a special session to investigate, but it turned out in the end that they spent $300,000 for a special session and indicted nobody. It really benefited Governor Folsom in his second campaign, because the newspapers had a field day with the story, and it made the people who had never taken time to go the polls realize how important it was to go the polls and vote for their man. Four years later, when Governor Folsom ran for re-election, poor folks, farmers, and average factory workers realized who their friend was and turned out on election day and gave him a clear majority.

For four years during Governor Sparks' Administration, the war had caused a shortage of lawyers and personnel in the Judiciary. The case loads in almost every circuit in the state had built up to the point it was impossible for judges in many circuits to handle their case loads. It became apparent that most of the circuits needed to be divided, or a new circuit judge needed to be added. During Folsom's first administration, I was one of eight senators who introduced bills to add an additional circuit judge in our senatorial districts. My bill was to add an additional circuit judge in Walker County. Senator Fite had one for Marion County, as well as Senator Albert Boutwell from Jefferson, Senator Joe Langan from Mobile, Senator Cater from Montgomery, and Senator Broughton Lamberth from Tallapoosa County, Senator Patterson from Russell County, and Senator

Mize from Tuscaloosa. Guy Hardwick from Houston County, and Senator Glover from Washington County were really strong against it, the reason being they didn't want Governor Folsom to appoint the judges. They were filibustering the bills to keep them from coming up and had them all bottled up, even though they were on the calendar. Senator Hardwick from Dothan was one of the strongest opponents to it. He later became lieutenant governor. I found out through a friend that one of the circuit judges in Walker County was Lieutenant Governor Inzer's roommate when they were in law school. I sent for the judge to come down and got him to talk to the lieutenant governor about it. Inzer ruled that it was a general bill with local application and permissible.

According to the rules you could not get a bill up, except by unanimous consent. But during most filibusters you could bring up local bills and general bills with local application. I got the judge to talk to Governor Inzer and rule that these bills were general bills with local application. So the next Tuesday morning I got up and asked for my bill to come up. I said, "Governor, this is a general bill with local application, and I would like to bring it up."

"The Senator is right. It is a general bill with local application," Lieutenant Governor Inzer said.

With that, we passed all eight of the judiciary bills. Senator Guy Hardwick came over and whispered in my ear, "You little bastard."

I'm reminded of one thing: during the interim between the 1947 and 1949 session Governor Folsom called three, four, or maybe five special sessions. Senator Bruce Henderson, who was one of the largest and most profitable farmers in the Black Belt, and Representative Wallace Malone from Dothan, a very wealthy banker, who was the father of the present president and CEO of South Trust Bank, got together and rated all the senators. When we came back to the regular session in 1949, Guy Hardwick, the senator from Dothan and later lieutenant governor, had a list of the ratings, and he told Senator Fite and me about it. He stayed in the Jeff Davis Hotel, as we did, and when we recessed he whispered in our ear, "If you all come by my room, I'll let you read your ratings."

We had just gotten to his room when the telephone rang. As Hardwick walked over to answer it he said, "Probably some SOB wanting to know his grade." Rankin had been a little more vicious in the senate than I had and did not get too good a rating. Of course, I had made the paper so strongly about paving the streets, etc., that my rating was BB. I remember it really well. I had hoped to get a copy of the rating sheet, but Guy would never let anybody have it. Mine said: "Senator Kimbrell is a quiet, easy-going fellow and able to get what he wants without much fanfare."

Governor Folsom, as I've said, was the poor man's and working man's friend. He had a running battle with Grover Hall, the editor of the Montgomery Advertiser, who really had a lot of fun criticizing the administration and Governor Folsom personally. One of the things that made the headlines and tickled the readers was in an editorial he wrote: "The hicks have come to town and there will be no gracious ladies in the Governor's mansion with their beautiful bonnets and frilly dresses and no up-town ladies." Two or three days after this came out in the paper, Governor Folsom got up, took his shoes off, rolled up his britches, and walked up and down Perry Street. He made sure it was going to be known by the press so the photographer would be there to take his picture. The editor really had a good time writing about it.

Not all the legislators were elite people. I remember one time Folsom was really taking advantage of the situation because he knew the restrictions were pretty loose. He knew the papers were going to take him and his administration apart—whether he was right or wrong—so he gave a party at the mansion and served champagne. The law had not been passed to restrict whiskey agents. They had almost a free hand. The ABC Board was in effect but not restricted as it is today, and the liquor agents had whiskey they could give to anybody at any place and supply any party the administration wanted. If you were an outstanding senator, you did not have to worry about getting the whiskey of you own choice.

One of the agents closest to the administration was Senator Harvey's brother from Blount County, who was a sales representative for Early Times. So all the Folsom leaders drank Early Times; it was free. During my tenure in Montgomery, I had kept my home in Fayette. Bobby Cobb, the owner of Cobb Theaters, lived next door to us in Fayette and was one of our closest friends. Our daughters were best friends and are still friends. Once, when we were home from Montgomery, Reba and I invited Bobby and his wife Alice over, and I grilled steaks. We all had a drink while we were waiting for the steaks to cook. Bobby, Alice, and Reba had Seven-Up with their bourbon. I drank water with mine. When I was fixing the drinks, I told them, "Go light on the Seven-Up. I have to buy it." After that, every time I saw Bobby he would ask if I still had to buy the Seven-Up.

As a member of the legislature back then, you could do favors for your constituents who asked you, things needed for the community and schools, etc. I remember one time Ed Faulkner, an uncle of Jimmy Faulkner, who ran for governor twice and is still an outstanding businessman and politician in Alabama, got in trouble with his sales tax. He was charged with $6800. His lawyer, Newman Strawbridge—a brother of Cecil Strawbridge, who later was Circuit Judge for this district for many years— who lived in Vernon and his auditor, Roy Martin, who lived in Fayette and did tax work for people, knocked on my door one night at ten o'clock and said Mr. Ed wanted to know if I would go to Montgomery and see if I could save him some money on his sales tax. He only had another day or two before the penalty started. I told them I would. They called Ed Faulkner in Vernon and told him I would go. Faulkner called back and asked me to tell Governor Folsom when they passed the "suds bucket" in Vernon he put in a twenty dollar bill.

To explain about the "suds bucket:" Governor Folsom ran a very cheap and conservative campaign, and had what he called a "suds bucket", an old-fashioned wooden mop bucket with a mop made of corn shucks. He told the people he was going to mop out the Capitol when he got down to Montgomery.

I drove to Montgomery next morning, went to the governor's office, told him what I came for, and that I wanted to talk to the Revenue Commissioner about it. I said, "Incidentally, Ed Faulkner put a twenty dollar bill in the suds bucket when you had your rally in Vernon."

"That's too much. He ought not to have put but five in it," the governor said.

I went on up to see Phillip Hamm, the Revenue Commissioner, and he said, "Senator, I'll tell you what. I'll send for the records, and any part we know is absolute he is going to have to pay it. But the part we kind of estimated and the other, I'll exempt."

He sent for the two auditors who had done the auditing. The head of the department brought the records and said, "Mr. Hamm, if you split the amount almost half into, it would conform to the above statement. But let me tell you this, tomorrow is the last day he can pay without penalty, and if we don't get the check tomorrow, then we can't take the money without adding penalty and interest, and we will have to go to court or negotiate a settlement."

Mr. Hamm asked, "Senator, you think you can get the check here tomorrow?"

"I'll bet I can. Let's just call Mr. Faulkner right now," I said.

I called Ed Faulkner and he said, "I'll have it in Mr. Hamm's office in the morning at eight o'clock." They almost divided the amount in half. His lawyer got $500; his auditor got $500; and I got the pleasure of doing him a favor. This is a good place to say that I never charged anybody anything, not even the gas in my car to go to and from Montgomery, or the long-distance calls I made on my private phone on their behalf.

Along toward the end of the Folsom Administration, the Highway Department ordered some industrial tractors, which were probably the first John Deere tractors that were ever sold in the state. I sold them six John Deere "D" industrial tractors. I have a picture in my memoirs and photo album of all those John Deere tractors parked in front of my Kimbrell Tractor & Implement Company. I don't remember the dollar amount. Back then you could buy a tractor for about what it cost to buy a tire now. But anyway, for me it was my largest sale.

Also during that time Kenneth Griffith, the governor's legal adviser resigned. Governor Folsom appointed Annie Lola Price, a lawyer from Cullman to that position. Pretty soon after her appointment, there came a vacancy on the Supreme Court. I walked into the governor's office, and there were quite a few people close to the governor in his office, trying to get appointed to the vacancy. All of a sudden I realized the best way for the governor to settle this was to appoint Anna Lola Price to this judgeship. Not only was she the first lady legal adviser to a governor, but also the first lady to serve on the Supreme Court.

TWELVE

FUNNIES, ETC.

During the 1949 regular session of the legislature, Grace Scott, the daughter of Mr. Scott, a former Alabama Highway Director, was lobbying to get money to renovate Fort Morgan at Mobile Bay. Since she was kind of a unique lady and a daughter of a former highway director, she was granted privilege of the floor at all times. She wore a broad brimmed hat and prissed around kind of old fashion-like on the senate floor. When she found a senator out of his seat, she would go and sit in his seat. One time we were trying to get the Sixty-seven Senators' Bill passed that I talked about previously, and it was certainly a very fine thing. Senator Cooper from Centerville, who represented Bibb and Perry Counties, was a big farmer. Since he knew I was a farmer and in the farm machinery business, if I was sitting by him, usually I could influence his vote. He was rather a feeble kind of fellow, but a very fine old gentleman. I was sitting by him to be sure the opposition didn't get to him, and Grace Scott came prissing over and asked, "May I sit by my old friend and sweetheart, Senator Cooper?"

"No, you sure can't, and I'll clear this floor if you try to influence him," I said. About that time somebody made a motion to adjourn for lunch, and it carried. Everyone went out. I thought no more about it. We got on the elevator to go downstairs, and she got on, too. There were eight or ten senators and two lobbyists in the elevator, and she stepped in, looked at me, and said, "This man insulted me." She didn't tell how it happened nor offer any further explanation.

Everyone went their separate ways to lunch. When we got back, Senator Rankin Fite had heard about it. Rankin and I were in our seats, and I was leaning back in mine. She came over and asked, "Senator Fite, did you know Senator Kimbrell insulted me?"

"He did? Why don't you hit him with that walking stick?" Rankin asked.

I was really worried because she was the type that just might. But she didn't, and I was much relieved. It took me a little while to explain what had really happened. Of course everybody understood, but they had a lot of fun at my expense.

Another thing that was most unusual: in the first administration after the first session, Governor Folsom was accused of getting a young lady, a clerk at the Tutwiler Hotel, pregnant. I reckon it turned out to be true; she went on and had the baby. The governor replaced Kenneth Griffith with an attorney from one of the biggest law firms in Birmingham to settle it. The attorney wrote the lady a check for $10,000, and she accepted it. The newspapers and some periodicals had a field day about the situation. Although, they did not know about the check at first, later they got the check, made a photostatic copy of it, and ran it in the papers. It was similar to what they are trying to do to President Clinton today. Anything they could use to diminish Governor Folsom's power, they used it.

During the recess, Governor Folsom's wife, Jamelle, called and said, "Fuller, Jim wants you to pick up Rankin Fite and come to the house in Cullman for breakfast at seven thirty in the morning."

"All right," I told her.

I called Rankin and told him I would pick him up in Hamilton the next morning at six o'clock, and we drove Highway 278, which was a very narrow crooked road, and got to Cullman by seven thirty. Jack, the prisoner who drove Governor Folsom a lot and went to Cullman with him as kind of a handy man, let us in, and we sat there waiting. About nine o'clock here came Governor Folsom and Jamelle downstairs and he asked, "Why didn't somebody tell me we had all this distinguished company?"

"Jim, you remember telling me to call Fuller and tell him to pick up Rankin and be here for breakfast," Jamelle said.

The Governor said, "Oh yeah. Why didn't you remind me of it again this morning?"

We had country ham and eggs with grits, biscuits, and red eye gravy. Governor Folsom ate about as much as a baby and ended up with a beer. We sat and visited a while and he said, "Boys, here is what I wanted you to come for. I want you to drive me on to Birmingham. I have a business proposition I want to talk over with you all."

He told Jack to fix him up a "go package." So Jack fixed him a plastic bag with ice in it and a bottle of Early Times, which was a favorite brand of his whole administration, and a beer each for Rankin and me. We got in my Studebaker. The seats were not divided, and I had the seat pushed back as far as it would go. Governor Folsom was six feet eight inches tall. I had to make as much room for him as I could in the front seat.

We had just gotten into the highway — that was before the days of the interstate — and started down the road. He said, "What I wanted to talk to you boys about is I'm going to resign as Governor. Since you all have been my leaders and best friends, I wanted you all to know first."

Rankin was sitting in the back seat. He quickly raised up and asked, "What are you saying?"

"Yes, I just found a business I can go into that's much better than being governor. There won't be all those problems and the job will be a lot more pleasureable for me. I'm going to do it," the Governor said.

"Governor, you know you can't do that. Rankin's and my relationship with Lieutenant Governor Inzer has not been good, and we won't even be able to go to Montgomery much less go back to the senate chamber," I said.

"I've thought about all that fellows, but I've decided it's best I go on and get out of it," Big Jim said.

Rankin asked, "What in the hell kind of business you going into that would be better than being the Governor of Alabama? You know this is the best job you've ever had in your life."

"Well, the way they have built me up, I think I can resign and hire myself out for stud fee," the Governor said.

As I've said before, the strongest opposition to my bill setting up acreage at Auburn University for the study of power equipment were the people that voted with Farm Bureau altogether. They weren't exactly against it, they just didn't want anybody to pass a bill who had voted for those trustees earlier. It was generally known that the Farm Bureau represented only the biggest farmers in Alabama, and didn't have much regard for the small farmers in the state. In fact, it was well known that the small farmers knew very little about what was going on with the Farm Bureau and its activities.

One thing I've talked about a good bit is that Walter Givhan, the representative of Dallas County and leader in the house, was supposed to be Farm Bureau's most outstanding legislator. He served in the house many, many years and later he moved to the senate, but he was serving in the house at this time. For the legislators he would always give a barbecue at Marion Junction, which was the smallest experimental station in Auburn's Experimental Department. He would give it in the name of the Farm Bureau, and everybody knew that the Chamber of Commerce paid for it altogether. But everybody ate the barbecue and drank the beer and enjoyed it without talking about it. The press was also invited. The press people represented big industry in Alabama much more than they did the people, and their views were seldom challenged. Of course there was no television then, and radios had not become that effective.

Along at the end of the administration, Governor Folsom

was anxious for somebody from north Alabama to be elected to succeed him. But then, neither a Governor nor a lieutenant governor could succeed himself, and the attorney general could not succeed himself. The Governor tried every way he could to get somebody to run. Along about that time, the legislature had passed a bill whereby if a petition was signed by a majority of the legislature, they could call themselves back into session. Governor Folsom was not for it, and he went all over the state in an effort to defeat it—which he did. He called it a "report to the people." He came to Vernon, in Lamar County, which was my district. I met him there and introduced him. I had gone in my car and took one of the good citizens from Fayette County over with me. Senator Rankin Fite and two or three of Folsom's other leaders were there in a Packard limousine.

After his speech Folsom said, "Fuller, you and Rankin meet me at the back door, and we will take a little ride. I want to talk to you all." We did. My car was locked up, and I didn't even tell my good friend and constituent who had ridden over with me, but he happened to see me get in the car.

We started up the road toward Sulligent. He was going to make a speech later at Hamilton, so he said we would just ride on to Hamilton. On the way he just talked and never brought up anything in particular. After the governor had made a little speech at Hamilton, we got back into his Packard. Winston Craig was his chauffeur at that time, and the governor said, "Winston, drive out Highway 278." Highway 278 was on the way toward Decatur. Governor Folsom had come from Montgomery that day, but we kept riding and talking. Of course we had a fairly good supply of Early Times in the car. The Governor said, "Winston, get Judge John Snodgrass, on the radio and tell him to meet us at Knox McRay's house in Decatur, and call Knox McRay and tell him to get some of that good fish that we get on the river bank ready for us. We are on the way to his house." Judge Snodgrass was the representative of Jackson County, and a loyal supporter. Winston talked to them on the short-wave radio, since there were no car telephones back then, and Judge Snodgrass said he would be there.

When we got to Decatur, Judge Snodgrass was there. We had a few drinks and ate that fish. By then, it was midnight, and we hadn't called our wives to tell them where we were. But it so happened that somebody knew and called our wives and told them we were in the car with the governor. What Folsom wanted us to do was to all get together and just make Judge Snodgrass run for governor. Judge Snodgrass didn't yield, and he didn't run. We told the governor we needed to go home, since our wives didn't know where we were. He said, "Winston go out to the car and radio the highway patrol. Tell them to come take Senator Fite and Senator Kimbrell home." A highway patrolman came, and we both got in the same car. It was daylight by the time we got to Winfield, and the highway patrolman there picked up Rankin and took him home, and the one we were with took me home.

Judge Snodgrass had no idea of running for governor, and he didn't. After we got back home, Phillip Hamm, the Revenue Commissioner who had first started out as Conservation Director and later moved up to Revenue Commissioner, decided to run, and he made a good showing. But he didn't do well enough to beat Gordon Persons. Gordon Persons had served two terms as Chairman of the Public Service Commission, and he led the ticket easily. Rankin and I were called to Montgomery to try to keep him from making the runoff, and Governor Folsom never quite forgave us for not helping Phillip Hamm enough to make the runoff. We were just going to call on the Folsom friends to finance the campaign, as it didn't cost a lot of money to finance a campaign back then, but there was no chance of him winning.

One of the very first things I was able to get done for my district was to persuade the Highway Department to build Highway 69, which became an outstanding highway for Walker County.

March 7, 1947, Cynthia, our daughter, was born, and Governor Folsom was calling the legislature in for one special session after another. It was keeping me in Montgomery an awful lot. In fact, I drove from Fayette to Montgomery and back every day for several days. Finally, someone told us that Bess Davis, a retired registered nurse who lived north of Oakman, would come stay in the house and take care of the baby. After we heard about Bess, the next Sunday afternoon we drove over to her house. It was a nice, modest little white house. She was a very clean, neat, nice looking lady and very pleasant. I told her what we had come for. She said she would come for twenty-five dollars a week, so we took her back with us.

While she, her mother, and Reba were in the house packing her bag, her father, Mr. Davis, who was a quite elderly man, and

I were sitting on the porch and he said, "Senator, I've lived here on a dirt road all my life. I'm an old man now, and I sure would like to have a paved road before I die."

I said, "All right, brother Davis. The only promise I made during my campaign was that I would do as near right as I know how, but I'm going to make you a promise that I'll try to get you a paved road."

Tuesday morning when I got to Montgomery, I went to Ward McFarland's office, and said, "Ward, I made a promise Sunday that I sure hope you can take care of." I told him the story, and suggested the road be paved from Oakman and come into Highway 78 at McCollum, which was a few miles west of Jasper."

Ward said, "All right Senator. That's good. The Governor wants a highway and paved road from Jasper to Cullman. We will have to build a bridge over the Warrior River, and I want to build a road to the upper end of Tuscaloosa County by my good friend and constituent Jess Dunn's. We will just build a paved highway from Tuscaloosa to Cullman."

The road was started immediately, and when it was finished it became state Highway 69 all the way from Guntersville to Jackson through Greensboro and on down that way. It is a very popular road. In fact, out of Tuscaloosa there is about seven or eight miles four-laned, and the other ten miles to Moundville are in the process of being four-laned now.

During that time, I also tried to get a road from Jasper through by Gorgas Power Plant to Fairfield. The mayor of Fairfield came down several times to talk to me. I went with him to see the highway director a time or two, as he was pulling for a highway from Fairfield through Fayette to Columbus, Mississippi. In addition, I was trying to get the highway department to build the Fairfield-Columbus road via the Gorgas Power Plant. This would accommodate the president of Alabama Power Company and other officials, as well as some of the people, in that it would give them a direct road from Birmingham to the Gorgas Power Plant, rather than going out Highway 78 to Jasper then down on a county road to the power plant. A saving of about forty miles each trip. When power company officials came to visit the power plant down at Gorgas, they had to go all the way to Jasper and then down a very common county road to Gorgas. This new road was only going to be about ten or twenty miles all the way from Bessemer to the power plant.

I could never get the Walker County people to help. They didn't want the traffic coming from Berry and that area to be changed and used as a short cut to Birmingham instead of going through Jasper. Later, during Governor Albert Brewer's administration, it was done for me. Governor Brewer made it a state highway, and fortunately, I and my children owned the asphalt plant in Jasper and were in the construction business at that time. We did $1.3 million worth of work on that project the first year after Albert Brewer made it State Highway 269.

I pushed awful hard trying to get Herman Nelson, who was the highway director later on, to build a road from Jasper to Decatur, because travelers were having to go all around through Cullman. You could already go the direct way, but it was a very common road. It was paved but not very desirable to travel. I never could get him to do it, but later I did get him to widen the road to the Winston County line. He built a bridge and made it a twenty-four foot wide highway up to the Winston County line. They changed it then to Highway 57 out of Jasper. It ran close to Musgrove Country Club and up through what used to be the Bankhead homestead.

From the very beginning, I realized how important it was to be nice to the state employees, cabinet members and other personnel. If you recognized them, called them by their names, and were nice, they would do all they could to help you. One of the fellows who was most beneficial in helping me accomplish so many things I was able to do for Fayette County was Dick Sherer. Dick was the maintenance engineer for the Tuscaloosa highway division, which represented Fayette, Tuscaloosa, Pickens, Lamar, and several other counties. His assistant was Grady Zeanah. If I was trying to get the highway department to pave a road or something, I would go to him and tell him what I was going to do. He would advise me right away how important the highway department thought it was, the amount of traffic that would be on it, and give me a rough estimate of what it would cost to do what I had hoped to do. Dick Sherer was one of the finest fellows I've ever known. He was always a gentleman and helped me in every way possible.

Senator Barrett wanted to sell some land he owned over in Barbour County. He got Senator Rankin Fite and me to go in to see the governor. The governor sent somebody to go look it over, and Barrett sold the land. It was quite a sale back then, $55,000 which would probably be a $5 million sale today. It was just nice to be nice to everybody, and the state employees would really work with you if they knew you were not trying to finagle something out of them.

Another funny thing that happened involved the people in Randolph County trying to get a bridge across the Tallapoosa River. There was only a ferry to get across the river. After the bridge was built, a crowd gathered to dedicate it. Herman Nelson was the highway director at that time, so he got over there and waited for the Governor to come make the dedication speech. They waited and waited and the governor didn't show up. So Herman Nelson decided to speak. He got up and said that the Governor really didn't want to build the bridge, but he himself wanted to go ahead with it because it would be so fine for that county. He said the Governor just didn't have any interest in it, one way or another, etc." About the time he finished talking, the Governor finally showed up. He had been enjoying Early Times a little bit on the way, so he got up and told the folks, "I'm just so proud we finally got this done. Herman was so slow getting started on it, and I said, 'Herman, build the bridge,' and he would find every excuse in the world not to do it. And I said, "Herman, build the bridge."

I was recently invited to Representative Pete Matthews' 80th birthday party in Montgomery. He could make the best story out of the Tallapoosa River bridge dedication you've ever heard, and they made him repeat it before the crowd at his birthday party that night. Its just too good not to put in the book.

As I've said before, Ward McFarland, the highway director, still did a windfall business as an attorney in Tuscaloosa. When he had clients who were going to have to go to jail or something or other and the governor had the power to pardon them or take care of the situation, Ward would usually come to the senate chamber and get Senator Rankin Fite and me to go with him to the governor's office for moral support, as we were getting along well with the Governor. McFarland had a client, Dee Cunningham, in Tuscaloosa County—kind of a character. He was a fellow who, around home, wore a dress, had long hair, and kept his hat on all the time. But when he went to town he would put on his big overalls with a cotton plaid shirt and overall jumper, and wore a hat all the time regardless of where he was. He was a big, heavy-set fellow, and very personable. It was no secret. Everybody in Tuscaloosa knew of the situation. He came to Montgomery to Ward's office, and Ward sent up to the Senate Chamber and asked Rankin and me to go to the governor's office with him. We got downstairs and there stood Dee Cunningham. Ward McFarland said, "Dee wants to get somebody out of prison and wants you all to go in with him."

We went into the governor's office. Governor Folsom had heard of Dee Cunningham and knew a lot about him. Dee was the most unusual country fellow you've ever seen, but very personable and likable. He sat down—all 250 pounds of him— right in front of the governor's desk, and sat forward with his hands on his knees. Rankin was standing on one side and I on the other, and Ward McFarland was kind of backing up the line. Of course, the governor, as usual, passed the time of the day and asked Dee about the branch heads and everything back in Tuscaloosa, then finally got around to asking, "Dee, what can I do for you?"

Dee said, "Mr. Governor, you know you've got Mr. Fields locked up out yonder in your Kilby Prison. He don't need to be locked up because he makes the best whiskey of anybody in Tuscaloosa County, and I want to take him back with me." Needless to say, Governor Folsom let Dee take Mr. Fields back home.

Another incident that happened with Ward McFarland was when I first opened my business in Tuscaloosa. I didn't realize that you had to buy city licenses in the month of January, because in Fayette you had until March lst to buy your city license. I had just found out, and I wasn't in Tuscaloosa on the last day of January. But I went down the very next morning with a check to see the city clerk, and I said, "I'm sure you haven't closed your books." In Fayette where I have a John Deere Tractor Agency, you don't have to buy your license until March, and I assumed the same was true in Tuscaloosa. I figured since you haven't closed your books I wouldn't have to pay the penalty."

"Mr. Kimbrell, don't you insinuate that I might do something wrong," the clerk said.

"I didn't insinuate anything. I just thought you would make an exception for a country boy from Fayette County who didn't know any better," I said.

"I certainly will not," the clerk said. I paid the penalty.
After I got to the senate, Ward McFarland sent for Rankin and

me to go with him to see the governor and there was a man with him who had been convicted for getting his hand in the cookie jar. He and another fellow were in cahoots about money from the parking meters. Of course, I recognized him and he did me, but I never said anything. And he didn't either. Ward presented his case to the governor and the man came back home without spending the night at Kilby. That was the same city clerk that said I better not insinuate that he would do anything wrong when I went to buy my license for my John Deere Agency in Tuscaloosa.

Another incident of the same nature: Senator Fite had a client who committed a serious crime in Fayette County and had received a sentence of five years. When it came time for him to report to prison, Rankin asked me to go with him to see the governor, and I did. That fellow came home that day without spending a single night in prison. Later, I was hoping the Fayette County Democratic Executive Committee would nominate me to fill the vacancy in the House created by the untimely death of Representative Truman "Red" Simpson, who was killed in an automobile accident while coming home from the legislative session. I was hoping I would be able to serve the balance of his time, because the only reason I didn't run for that office was Red and I were good friends. He had told me all the time he was going to run when the time came. When it came time for the committee to nominate me, the same man Rankin had asked me to go with him to see the governor about pardoning was on the committee and voted against me.

I was still a member of the State Democratic Executive Committee. At their next meeting, I got a resolution passed whereby the State Democratic Executive Committee would nominate candidates to fill vacancies in the House of Representatives—which was true of state senators already.

THIRTEEN

FAYETTE CITY COUNCIL AND CHAMBER OF COMMERCE

In 1952, after being approached by numerous community and civic leaders, business and professional men, and elected officials to seek a position in local leadership, I was persuaded to run for the Fayette City Council. In a field of about nine candidates, five were elected: E. A. Bagwell, Grover Propst, Curt Haughton, Guthrie Smith, and me. I lead the ticket, receiving more votes than any other candidate. It was a most interesting time for me because I felt like incorporating with members of the council and the Mayor, Joe Caine, a long-time, much respected citizen of Fayette, and a very progressive person. We did have a very successful administration. E. A. Bagwell and Grover Propst were also very liberal and progressive. Together, we were able to accomplish a great deal. Many times, Mayor Joe Caine, Grover Propst, E. A. Bagwell, and I voted the same way, but most of the time the vote was unanimous among the Council.

One large achievement was to get a natural gas system put in the City of Fayette. Southern Natural Gas had built a line across Alabama at Brownville, if I remember correctly. The distance was about seventeen miles from Fayette to the line. The

Council worked out with the Ray Loper Lumber Company to go down the right-of-way of their old abandoned railroad track and put in the line that would bring the natural gas to Fayette. At that time Loper Lumber Company's headquarters was located at Brown Lumber Company, in Brownville. It was easily worked out at no cost to Fayette as, Mr. Loper was very civic minded and was glad to help improve Fayette. The natural gas system was installed in Fayette. We set up the Gas Board, and it is still operating under the same system as it was originally. In the minutes of the meeting that I reviewed today, I was reminded that the three people I nominated — R. C. Cobb, V. E. (Dick) Poe, and Frank Jefferies — were unanimously elected as the first board members.

Among other things, we did a lot of street paving. I was still in good standing with Governor Person's Administration, so we got them to help move a lot of debris off the streets and clean up the town. The Highway Department staff had not changed from the time I was in the senate, and I had worked up a wonderful relationship with the district manager and the construction and maintenance engineer in Tuscaloosa. I was able to get them to do favors for people along the rights-of-way in the City of Fayette and Fayette County. Two things we were able to achieve with their help were to widen Aylette Street from the railroad south down to the "Y," where Highway 159 leads off to Highway 171, and widen Temple Avenue from the railroad down to the same "Y," which helped divide the traffic entering and leaving town. We also got Temple Avenue four-laned most of the way — a short distance is only three-laned as we could not get the right-of-way because it was too close to residents' houses.

While I was on the Board — I'm not sure if it was while I was also president of the Chamber of Commerce — the Chamber of Commerce, along with the Industrial Board, sponsored building a cheese plant next to City Springs, but it was not in operation very long. Afterwards, we sponsored a dairy business in Fayette. After a lot of searching, we finally got Joe Huffman to manage and operate it. The Chamber of Commerce helped him build a dairy on part of the old National Youth Administration (NYA) property, which was built during the Depression, while Bruce Harkins was superintendent of education. The City voted to sell Huffman one of those buildings — a 100' X 400' structure — to put in a milk processing plant. When Huffman opened the milk processing plant, many small dairies sprung up all over Fayette County. A lot of people would milk one, two, and three cows, but it still was not enough milk to process. In order to get enough, Huffman bought a large quantity of milk from dairies in Mississippi.

Later Huffman came up with the idea of processing and selling all Jersey milk. While I was in the legislature and on the Agriculture Committee, we set up a Milk Board, and I was able to get him appointed to the Milk Board. Somebody protested him calling his milk "All Jersey Milk" and filed suit. This caused everybody to sell their Holsteins and get Jerseys because the milk was one percent higher in butter fat than the mixed cows such as Holsteins and Guernseys. But he had to quit selling "All Jersey Milk," so he came up with the name of Flav-o-Rich, and Flav-o-Rich turned out to be one of the most outstanding milk processing plants in Alabama.

While I was serving on the Fayette City Council, some of the ladies in town organized a garden club, and the Council worked with them to help build flower planters, and to plant flowers and trees to beautify the city streets, particularly Temple Avenue downtown. A group of Garden Club members came before the Council and asked permission to plant shrubbery and flowers along on the sides of the streets. These plants really added to the beauty of the town and made it more pleasurable to drive through Fayette.

Also, Fayette added several thousand feet of much-needed sewer pipe to the sewer system, paving the way for the City to get into a major sewer project later.

Billy Partlow, a good friend of mine, called and asked, "Fuller, do you want a nice sewing industry for Fayette?"

"Yes," I answered.

"Meet me at the Dill Motel in Tuscaloosa in the morning at seven o'clock for breakfast, and I'll have some folks there who are looking for a place to locate. I've shown them York, Alabama, but they don't like York. I told them that I believe they would like Fayette. They are paying me, so I won't need any pay for it," he said.

I got Bobby Cobb to go with me. We were both on the Chamber of Commerce and Industrial Boards. Sam Norwich, the president of Simon & Mogilmer, Inc., came to Fayette the next day, and met with the Chamber of Commerce and Industrial Boards. Mr. Norwich built what started out as the Simon & Mogilmer plant south of town, a 185,000 square feet building where Oneida is today. Later the plant name was changed to Fayette Manufacturing Co., and worked 200 or 300 people — I don't remember just how many — but it was one of Fayette's largest industrial plants at that time and operated successfully for several years before it was sold out.

As was happening in many towns and cities in Alabama, Fayette Exchange Club started an annual event naming the "Man of the Year." The first year, 1950, E. A. Bagwell was named Fayette's Man of the Year. He was the oldest man on the City Council, and was very civic minded. He owned and operated a sand and gravel operation, a ready mix concrete plant, and a concrete pipe plant. This combination employed several people, and was one of the larger employers of Fayette County. Bagwell had a record of being one of the most civic minded people in the county. The next year, 1951, they selected me as "Man of the Year" and presented me with a nice trophy, which I still have and am very proud to show.

While I was a member of the Fayette City Council, almost every individual in town — including the Mayor and every member of the City Council — agreed something needed to be done about the City Hall building. I pushed to build a new building. However, by the time it was finished, I was no longer a member of the Council. I had to resign when Governor Folsom appointed me Alabama Director of Finance. I asked the Council to appoint Gus Woodard, a good friend of mine who had worked for me about seventeen years, to replace me — which they did. They built the City Hall building where it is today.

Since my first job was in Walker County, particularly around

Parrish, Oakman, and Gorgas where Alabama Power Company had one plant, but now has two, I was interested in getting better roads there. I had pulled and pushed for sometime for Highway 18, which comes through Vernon, Fayette, Berry, Corona, Oakman, and on to Parrish to go straight through Cordova on up and come into Highway 78 at Sumiton, instead of turning at Parrish, going to Jasper, and ending at Jasper. I started working on this project in 1957 and worked, worked, worked, and finally the last section from Oakman to Parrish was completed and opened to traffic in 1997. For people in Fayette and Berry going to Birmingham, traveling Highway 18 is a much shorter route. While I was in the paving business, I was successful in getting Highway 18 widened from eighteen feet to twenty-four feet from the Mississippi line all the way to Oakman.

One of the finest industrial plants in west Alabama is Arvin Industries. The president of Arvin, a personal friend of Reverend Bob Atkins, the pastor of the First Baptist Church in Fayette, was on his way to Florida and stopped in Fayette to spend the night with Brother Bob. Brother Atkins showed him around town and told him what a nice place it was and got in touch with me. I was vice-president of the Industrial Development Board at the time. When they came to my office, we talked further. I remember telling him that he would find the people who would be employed at his plant to be very dependable, because Fayette County was made up of small farms which averaged about 135 acres per farm, and these farms had been in the same families since the early 1800's. I showed him a piece of land we could buy that belonged to T. L. Lindsey, the cashier at the Citizens

Bank.

He brought his committee down to Fayette and we agreed to buy Mr. Lindsey's land. Arvin moved their plant to Fayette, and it's been one of the finest industrial additions Fayette has ever had. The Arvin plant in Fayette manufactured after-market tail pipes and mufflers for years. More recently, they have gotten the contract to manufacture mufflers for General Motors' Saturn plant in Franklin, Tennessee, one of the finest branches of General Motors. Saturn is a very moderately priced automobile, and General Motors has brought it up to modern standards, which is something to be desired by people who want a second or third car. A great number of high school and college students buy the Saturn because the price is affordable, and for the ease and maneuverability of driving and parking. Arvin continues to be one of the steadiest, employers of any plant in Alabama, I guess you could say, from the very time it came in. They have employed from 300 to 550 people at all times, most of the time running two or three shifts a day.

Another funny thing: when Big Jim Folsom's son, Governor Jim Folsom, Jr., was running for re-election recently, he was invited to be the guest speaker at the thirty-fifth year Anniversary Celebration of the Fayette County hospital, now a branch of Druid City Hospital. "Little Jim" and I were talking before he got to Fayette, and I said, "One thing you might need to know is when your father was governor, the state could put up as much as $80,000 and the federal government would match it with another $80,000. The state did put up $80,000 during your father's first administration, and the federal government matched it, and the county passed a four mils tax to finishing funding the hospital and buy the land."

Little Jim asked, "Reckon Pa ever knew about it?" I didn't answer. Because he really didn't know about it.

I learned early, if all the cabinet members knew a senator, such as I, was really close to the administration and worked with the governor almost 100 percent, the senator could go to any department and get a lot of things done for his senatorial district, without seeing the Governor.

While in the Senate, I got an Industrial Act passed, which was patterned after the Mississippi Industrial Act, called Balancing Industry and Agriculture. I patterned a similar local bill for Fayette County, although I had to change it three times before the House of Representatives would let it pass.

Soon after that, while I was president of the Fayette Chamber of Commerce, we had gotten rather far along negotiating with a company planning to relocate in Fayette. But, the president of the Alabama Cotton Mill sent us word that if we permitted this company to locate in Fayette, he would close his plant in Fayette. A group of us local citizens—three carloads—went to see him. Alex Smith, the attorney for the city at that time, did the talking, and the president of Alabama Cotton Mill said in no uncertain terms, "If you do bring it in, I'll close the Fayette plant."

As I remember, Alabama Mills had ten cotton mills in Alabama; maybe one or two were in Georgia. They had one at Fayette, Winfield, Aliceville, and Wetumpka, but some of these other cities had gotten an industrial plant without Alabama Mills leaving. The big thing the president was fussing about was that other plants were paying much higher wages; he was paying, you might say, starvation wages at that time. Better to say minimum wages, because the Wage and Hour Law was in effect then, but the minimum was still below fifty cents an hour. Some of the other cities had gotten plants, and he didn't close theirs. So the next year we did get another plant here. I'm not sure if it was Simon & Mogilmer, but it was another plant. That was one of the things we were confronted with and able to work out satisfactorily when I was president of the Fayette Chamber of Commerce. We got the new industry, and Alabama Mills, after a lot of threats and posturing, stayed put.

FOURTEEN

DEMOCRATIC EXECUTIVE COMMITTEE MANAGING CAMPAIGNS FOR KEFAUVER AND FOLSOM

My experience working in the legislature and serving as a member on the Fayette City Council pointed out to me just how important it was to be civic minded and spend a certain amount of my time serving my community, county, and state. The more I got into it, the greater success I enjoyed for the people, and the bigger thrill it was for me. Therefore in 1950, I decided to run for the State Democratic Executive Committee.

At that time, the State Democratic Executive Committee consisted of seventy-two members, eight from each congressional district. There were nine congressional districts, and eight were to be elected from each congressional district. You ran for the whole district. I lived and ran in the Seventh Congressional District, which consisted of Etowah, Fayette, Lamar, Marion, Pickens, Walker, and probably Franklin and Winston Counties — I'm not sure. There were fifteen or more candidates who ran, but only four were elected without a runoff: Judge Roy Mayhall from Jasper; Leonard Wilson, Sr., an outstanding attorney who lived in Jasper; John Miller, who was the Mayor of Cordova and operated a theater there, and I was the fourth one. I was continuously elected to the Democratic Executive Committee nine times and only had a runoff twice during the whole time. Three times I ran without an opponent. Later, they broke it down so you ran in a certain district within the congressional district, and that was when I ran without an opponent three different times. Once I had one opponent after the district was divided, but I won very easily.

I was very active from the start, because I had established some degree of notoriety, I would say, by serving in the senate from 1947-51. Newspaper editors and reporters made sure everyone in Folsom's administration got a lot of publicity — not always favorably — but we made the papers. That was one reason I was elected so easily, I guess, because there wasn't that much advertising. There was no television and very little radio advertising. What advertising we did was by newspapers. People voted for somebody they had heard of a lot. Fortunately they didn't remember that I had come up with a lot of criticism in the daily papers, especially the Birmingham News, Post Herald, and Montgomery Advertiser. As I've said before, when I ran for the senate my opponent was editor of the local paper in Fayette, and I didn't get much publicity either way during the time I served in the senate.

The Jefferson-Jackson dinner is a fund raiser put on each year by the State Democratic Executive Committee. There was usually an outstanding Democrat speaker for the event. All senators and congressmen were invited, as well as state and county elected officials. I attended all the Jefferson-Jackson dinners and continue to do so. If I remember correctly, I've only missed two since

1950 until this day.

Estes Kefauver decided to run for president in 1952, and it was time to elect delegates to the National Democratic Convention. I don't know how he got my name, but Kefauver wrote and asked if I would manage his campaign in Alabama. I took the letter and showed it to former Governor "Big Jim" Folsom. As I've said before, Governor Gordon Persons had been elected following Folsom and had called a special session to investigate the prison system. Kefauver had investigated crime in Phoenix, Arizona, Las Vegas, New Orleans, and places in California and had quite a reputation. So when I showed the letter to "Big Jim" he said, "Senator, I don't like no SOB who investigates." But later, after he learned more about Kefauver, he was very supportive of him.

I agreed to be Kefauver's Alabama campaign manager. I invited Billy Partlow, an outstanding lawyer in Tuscaloosa, who later became the state adjutant general, and Jimmy Mayfield, also an outstanding lawyer in Tuscaloosa, who later became an Alabama Supreme Court Judge, to travel with me. We traveled an awful lot. I still had my Studebaker President. It seemed Jimmy Mayfield knew where there would be a pay telephone around every bend in the road. We would be going down the road, and he would say, "Senator, slow down now. Just around that curve is a pay phone. I want to call in a press release." Of course, he had a credit card he used, and Billy Partlow had a credit card. When we spent the night in Dothan, Florence, Gadsden, or Mobile, or wherever, Billy Partlow would put his and Jimmy Mayfield's nights lodging and meals on that credit card. But I paid for my own expenses all the time. In fact, I paid for the gas out of my own company, although several salesman made contributions, and it was never questioned later by tax folks. They didn't think of it, I reckon, or if they did they didn't let me know about it. We traveled all over the state, when we did spend the night away from home we would get two rooms, and I always paid for mine.

Politically we were well-accepted. The Partlow name was well known statewide, since it was associated with Bryce Hospital. Dr. Partlow, Billy's father, was the superintendent of Bryce Hospital for many years. And one of Jimmy Mayfield's uncles served on the 1901 Constitution Committee. As for me, most people we called on had read many of the newspapers articles — some good, some bad — printed about me while I was serving as one of the Floor Leaders in the Alabama State Senate in the first Folsom Administration. Needless to say, this made for a favorable acceptance in our endeavor.

We had a good time calling on all the delegates. I forget how many delegates there were, but we had thirty-three votes, although some of the delegates' votes only counted as half a vote. We felt Alabama was going for Kefauver easy enough, but Kefauver made the mistake of running against President Harry S. Truman in New Hampshire, where they had the first primary.

In the presidential election year of 1952, both parties started electing delegates to the national convention who were pledged to certain candidates. That was the beginning of the custom where the presidential candidates ran in states, and it was determined who the delegates to the Convention should vote for. In New Hampshire, Kefauver won over President Harry Truman, getting thirteen electoral votes over Truman's nine. That rubbed President Truman the wrong way, so he got in touch with Alabama U. S. Senators Lister Hill and John Sparkman and told them, according to the story that went around, not to support Kefauver and to take part in the Convention. They had previously told they were not going to take part. Suddenly they switched to Adlai Stevenson, who had been governor of Illinois twice, and whose father had also been governor of Illinois twice. They sent word to us that they could no longer support Kefauver. Then Governor Persons threw his support to Adlai Stevenson. However, we finally mustered eight and one-half votes, and that was all we ever could muster.

Before the convention the entire Alabama Delegation met in the old Tutwiler Hotel in Birmingham to organize a committee and to discuss the situation and decide how we would manage it. The chairman of the Democratic Executive Committee, Jim Smith, an outstanding lawyer who lived at Florence, stayed neutral. In the discussion, it was very obvious Senators Hill and Sparkman were going to support Adlai Stevenson. Since I was supposed to be the campaign leader for Kefauver, I got up and said, "I will continue to support Kefauver." Somebody on the Stevenson's side nominated Cooper Green, the Mayor of Birmingham, for vice chairman. It was already determined, without a vote, that senior Senator Lister Hill would be chairman, and it was whispered around that Senator John Sparkman was going to be the nominee for vice-president. I might as well say now, I had the honor of nominating him for vice president. Lister

Hill was up on the platform to make the nominating speech.

The statewide elected delegates' votes counted as half a vote only, however the congressional district elected delegates' votes counted as a whole vote. After Cooper Green was nominated for vice-chairman, someone nominated me for vice chairman. They called the roll, alphabetically of course, and Cooper Green's name was called before mine, and he voted for me. So when they called my name, I voted for Cooper, and everybody laughed out loud because they knew I was losing half a vote. Fortunately, when the votes were counted, I won by six votes. So I went to Chicago as vice chairman. I think that incident was really responsible for Governor Folsom asking me to be his north Alabama campaign manager when he ran in 1954.

Before we went to the convention, Kefauver had started campaigning and was covering a lot of territory. He called one day and asked if I would meet him in Birmingham as he was going to Jackson, Mississippi, Little Rock, Arkansas, etc., and I did. We flew to Jackson to see Governor Hugh White, who was a very strong Dixiecrat. It was apparent there was no way he was going to support Kefauver. He was not very cordial, but did invite us to the mansion for lunch. I could tell he was in a hurry for us to leave, so we didn't stay too long.

Needless to say, Governor White was a very strong segregationist. I'll always remember that the next time I ate at the governor's mansion was twenty years later. Reba and I were invited to dinner, and we sat at the same table with Probate Judge Branch of Green County, Alabama and his wife, and another black couple.

From Jackson we flew to Little Rock, Arkansas and saw Governor Sid McMath, who later ran for U. S. Senate but was defeated by William Fulbright. He warmly welcomed us. Senator Kefauver and I spent the night in the mansion. The next morning we flew back to Memphis and went to the Union Planters Bank where they had planned a luncheon in the Executive Suite with political leaders and officers of the bank, and we were well accepted.

We flew from Memphis to New Orleans and were guests of the New Orleans State Docks. Eddie Reed, who was the director of public relations for the City Docks, met us at the airport and took us to the hotel where he had rooms reserved for us, and everybody registered. That night, a man who invented some kind of guiding device used on ships during the war—I don't know what it was and didn't try to know, but evidently it must have been very important—and had built a mansion in New Orleans, invited us for cocktails and dinner. Several very impressive people were at the dinner, including the Lieutenant governor of Mississippi, the Mayor of New Orleans, and several other dignitaries, But I am not sure about the senator. It was quite a party.

Afterwards, Eddie Reed took us to Bourbon Street. Back then, if you went to Bourbon Street you had been somewhere in the south. We started at one end of Bourbon Street and had a drink at every bar for about four blocks. Of course, we learned to take a couple of sips of each drink because we were going just next door and have another one. I finally stopped about two o'clock, left the crowd, returned to the hotel, and went to bed. The next morning, I heard some of the others in the group stayed with Eddie including Kefauver, who stood up well and went all the night.

The 1952 National Democratic Convention in Chicago was really something. It was most interesting. We went from early morning until ten or eleven o'clock at night and sometimes later. Kefauver got 585 votes, but he had to have 720 to win. I don't know how many times roll was called, but we never gained or lost a single vote. California, Minnesota, and some of the other states were going 100 percent for him.

During recess, visitors, spectators, and supporters were allowed into the convention hall. They would come marching in waving banners and flags with the names of the candidates they were supporting, such as Kefauver, Stevenson, and others. They marched all over the place and hollered and whistled every time their candidate was named. At the end of the day, the floor was littered with banners, flags, and other trash. That afternoon about three thirty or four o'clock, I saw a man set a banner on fire, which started a lot of confusion. The chairman, Sam Rayburn from Texas, who was the Speaker of the House — and he was tough — dismissed us and said, "This is Friday, and we are coming back in at eight o'clock this evening and we are going to nominate a president."

During that time, a fellow senator, Albert Patterson, who voted with "Big Jim" Folsom's administration in his 1947-1951 term was a candidate for state attorney general. Albert was the father of John Patterson, who later became Alabama's attorney general and governor. John later served on the Supreme Court until he reached the age of 70 and is still working in the court. But by an Alabama law, he had to resign at the age of 70. I kept Albert voting with us by telling him I would be sure to get him up on the platform and let him make a speech. I did. The very last day of the convention, I was able, by prevailing on Senator Lister Hill, who had a lot of influence on the platform, to let Senator Patterson have five minutes to speak and be heard in Alabama. His speech was broadcast in Alabama via radio as only a few people owned television sets.

I bought my first television set in 1948, and I was the second person in Fayette to have a television, but by 1952 there were several televisions all around. While I'm talking about televisions: I sold Studebaker automobiles then, and a fellow came in after I got back from the convention and bought a new pickup truck from me. Brand new pickups sold for a high price of $625, which was about the same price as Ford, Chevrolet, and Dodge pickups. It was interesting, I knew where he lived, and he was as fine as he could be. He had a little house that probably didn't have but two rooms, and I bet it wasn't over 20' X 30' in dimension, and he had a television set. I'd been to his house before. When I visited him this time his daughter was sitting in my office and she said, "Daddy, I saw that man on television."

Of course, Senator Hill stayed on the platform most of the time. Even though I was the vice-chairman, I acted as chairman and announced Alabama's votes most of the time, which never varied. We still had eight and one-half for Kefauver and others for Adlai Stevenson all the way through. Eventually, Adlai Stevenson was nominated as presidential candidate and John

Sparkman was the vice-presidential candidate at the 1952 convention.

In November 1953, Governor Folsom called and said he would like to talk to me. I told him I had planned to go to Chattanooga the next day and was meeting someone, and would probably have lunch with him, but I could get back to Cullman about four o'clock. I asked if that would be all right. Governor Folsom said, "Yes, that will be fine. Come by my home."

I was going to Chattanooga to see the president of Blue Bell Overalls. His first name was Fuller, also. His mother had bought a tractor from me at my Aliceville store and owed $3000 to Kimbrell Tractor & Implement Co. I was going to see if I could collect it from her son, which I did. When I met with him, he asked, "Why don't you take that 1200 acres she owns in Pickens County for that $3000?"

I said, "Well, I'm sure it is worth that much, but I operate on a very close budget, and I don't need to let that much money out of my business at this time." If I had taken the land it would probably be worth a $1.5 million now, including the timber, but I didn't. That was one of the biggest mistakes I ever made. A couple of days later, I went to Birmingham where she lived to see her. She gave me a check for $3000 plus interest.

That afternoon on my way back from Chattanooga, I did stop by Governor Folsom's home in Cullman. It was a very pleasant, warm day. We sat on his porch and talked. He said, "Senator, what I wanted to talk to you about is, I'm planning to run for Governor again in the 1954, and I wanted to ask you to be my north Alabama campaign manager. I've talked to Judge George Wallace, and he has agreed to be the south Alabama manager. Charlie Pinkston, who is a prominent attorney in Montgomery, has agreed to be the Montgomery and central Alabama manager."

I didn't have to think long about it because I was sold on his philosophy and what he had tried to do in his first administration for Alabama. I thought it would be a wonderful opportunity for me to help further the cause of the economy and general education in northwest Alabama, so I agreed to be his north Alabama campaign manager. He asked, "When do you want to go to work?"

"I'll be willing to go to work almost anytime," I replied.

He said, "I don't plan to announce officially until the latter part of January, and the Democratic Executive Committee usually meets the last Saturday in January to set up the rules and regulations. But I'm going to let it be known anytime now. In fact, I'll announce that you, Judge Wallace, and Attorney Charlie Pinkston are going to be my campaign managers, and I'll officially announce that later on." He did in late January.

On the way home that night, I got to thinking about his 1946 campaign and remembered he was strictly elected by the people. He had no organized campaign statewide and no organized campaign leaders. But he had done something I had never heard of before, and which was almost unheard of, really, at that time. He had rallies in every county and spoke at the courthouse, or on the courthouse square, and in some parks. He told the people what he hoped to do when he became governor and that was to pave mailbox roads, increase old age pensions, and advance education in Alabama statewide. He spoke with such enthusiasm and sincerity that people knew he was speaking from his heart, and he had a genuine desire to make Alabama a better state.

In 1946, when Folsom was campaigning for governor, I went to several of the Folsom rallies. During that time I was running for the senate, and that gave me an opportunity to shake hands while campaigning. It was gratifying to see the common people, the hard working people, in our section of the state where I was running. The majority of the voters were still mostly one-mule farmers or two-mule farmers, whose children walked to school because school buses were very uncommon then. There were a few school buses in every county, but not every child was able to ride to school. When Folsom promised all that and to increase the old age pension, to build more and better school buildings, and separate but equal schools for the blacks, it was plain to see that he was really selling the people.

I thought about it and realized that to have a successful campaign, he needed the support of the probate judges, county commissioners, mayors, city council members, and small bankers, which he didn't have in his first administration. I knew there was no reason for me to go to the bigger bankers and businesses in Birmingham, Mobile, or Montgomery, as they were not going to support the philosophy and the program that Governor Jim Folsom had tried so hard to make come to pass in his first administration. I decided the best thing for me to do was to go to every county and city and call on the elected officials and small bankers.

While I was in the Alabama Senate I had done so much for Fayette, Lamar, and Walker Counties, and particularly the City of Fayette, but the newspapers had just taken me apart. Most of the publicity related to my achievements was not very favorable. But it had a very favorable effect on the people, because they felt if I could do that in Fayette County under Folsom and if he was governor again, my position would be such that I could help him continue his program that he began in his first administration. The whole state would prosper. He had paved over 100 miles of mailbox roads during his first administration. The economy had begun to improve and there was more money, and the gasoline tax was bringing in more money than ever before. The war was over, and all the equipment was readily available. Automobiles had become plentiful for people who were able to buy, and many, many more people — a much larger percentage of the population — were able to buy automobiles.

By that time, it was beginning to be common for most of the farmers to buy and cultivate with tractors instead of mules. As I've said before, I like to say, "I took the man from behind the plow." When I started selling farm machinery in 1937, no one was cultivating with tractors or using power equipment in west Alabama, but when I quit in 1957, just twenty-one years later, almost everybody in Alabama was cultivating with tractors.

As I was saying, publicity about me, particularly in the Birmingham News, had spread all over Alabama, but mostly north Alabama. The Montgomery Advertiser carried a lot of it, too, and the fact that I had been president and was still on the board of Alabama Farm Equipment Association, put me on first base when I went to call on the bankers and elected officials. They knew immediately who I was, for they had read about things I had done for Fayette County and my senatorial district. So when I sat down to talk to them, they were willing to listen.

One thing I did as I traveled around the state was go to farm machinery dealers in each county and get them to go to the probate judges' offices or go see the chairmen of the Board of Revenue or Board of Commissioners or mayors and some of the council members and even go into the banks and visit with them. In no time at all the word got around that I was out building the fences and paving the way for Governor Folsom's campaign, that would start in the early spring of 1954. It was amazing to me the reception I got almost everywhere I went. I traveled all over north Alabama at first. I did go down into what was called the Wiregrass country, which is southeast of Montgomery, but I didn't travel too much in the Black Belt, because I figured Folsom would not have much support there. And at that time the blacks had not registered or had not been permitted to register to vote, so I didn't spend the time and effort in those counties like I did in northeast, northwest, and central Alabama. I spent virtually no time in Birmingham.

My brother, Basil, was a good booster for Governor Folsom. He operated a barber shop in Monroeville, in Monroe County. He was a very personable fellow and quite a good conversationalist, and as was customary, people loafed in the barber shop in those days more than any other place, since Alabama had no pool halls or bars of any kind. Basil's wife, Louise, was the Monroe County health nurse, and also a really good booster for Governor Folsom, because he was the first governor in her lifetime that talked about welfare, or elderly people's needs, or even talked about helping the blacks in any area. Louise was the county health nurse during Folsom's first administration, and she told me several times when I went to Monroeville to talk to her that it was very common talk at their monthly and quarterly meetings that they hoped Folsom would run for governor again, and that he would be elected. For the first time in their lifetime they felt like they would have a friend in the state capitol.

It was interesting and funny about my brother and his wife. They loved each other and had been married several years. Both lived to be in their eighties, but a good bit of the time they would get to where they couldn't live together, so he would sell his barbershop and go buy one in another town. He had barbershops at different times in Mobile, and one in the Moulton Hotel in Birmingham for quite a long while. He operated one in Berry, Alabama for a little while, one in Fayette County, and even had one in West Virginia and stayed there about a year. But they were married at least fifty years, and he told me that every night when he was away from home he would write her a few lines, put a dollar bill in the envelope and mail it to her. Needless to say, when they passed away they had no children and left quite a nice estate to some of their nieces and nephews.

They were a funny kind of people but loved everyone. One of the highlights of their visits to my father's and mother's was when we would all get together, and Louise would draw from her repertoire of hundreds of jokes she had collected while treating her patients. She would just tell one good funny story after another, and we would sit up late at night listening to her stories.

Another amusing thing happened when Basil had a barbershop in Mobile. I traveled some then and would go see him occasionally. One time when I visited him he told me, "Fuller, I want you to come see me. I have a house rented in Mobile and an extra bed, and you come anytime you want to. But don't come on Thursday night, because that's the night I cook for the nurses." I didn't go on Thursday nights, but he and Louise came to see us once and brought the nurses. They were friends of Louise's. Early in her lifetime she had worked at Guntersville as a nurse and met these two ladies, and they later moved to Mobile and lived at Mobile at that time.

So I did work in the area of Monroe County, and made a real good friend of the probate judge, Shorty Millsap, who was always called "Shorty." He was a strong supporter of Folsom already. We didn't know at the time who our strongest opponent was going to be in the upcoming campaign. It turned out to be Jimmy Faulkner, a partner of Judge Millsap's in a radio station in Monroe County, who lived in Bay Minette.

Another man who was a strong supporter was Judge Beeland from Greenville in Butler County. Judge Beeland was a friend of Governor Folsom's in the first administration. When I called on him he said, "You can forget about Butler County, 'cause we are going to carry that for Folsom."

There was a convention delegate from Monroe County named Scott. I went to see him, and he said, "Fuller, you know

I voted for Adlai Stevenson."

"Yes, I know that, but this is a different election," I said.

"Well, ordinarily I wouldn't say I would vote for Folsom. But since you are going to be heading it up, you can count me in," he said.

Since Jimmy Faulkner, our strongest opponent, had a radio station in Monroe County, it turned out that we did not carry Monroe County.

I had a very successful business, the John Deere dealership in Pickens County, and had developed a really close relationship with Senator Early Barrett, who had served in the senate in Folsom's first administration. I stopped by to see him. When I was at my store in Pickens County the farmers would come in to talk. I was not only the John Deere dealer there, but also in Fayette and Columbus. By that time I had sold the Tuscaloosa store, but still had the other three stores, and it was well known that I was a very successful farmer, born and raised on a farm, and at one time I was the largest farmer in Fayette County. I raised more hogs, and cows, and grew more corn and oats than anybody in Fayette County. The word about me got around in Columbus, Aliceville, and Fayette, so when I went to see the leaders and elected officials who talked to the average voter in Fayette County, they were willing to listen from the very beginning.

Earlier I mentioned that I didn't want to work in Birmingham much because of big business, and the newspapers had not supported Governor Folsom, and we didn't expect they would support him in this upcoming election. Fortunately, in Governor

Folsom's first administration he had appointed Dee Kendricks as chairman of the Board of Revenue. Kendricks ran four times without opposition; after that and he did a lot of work for the campaign in Jefferson County. But Jefferson County had a record at that time of canceling itself out. The two top candidates would not be very far apart in the number of votes. It turned out in the upcoming election that the three top candidates were not very far apart. (which I will talk about later).

Another outstanding appointment Governor Folsom made, and we reaped a lot of benefits from it when the campaign got underway, was Judge DeBardeleben in Calhoun County. He was a vocal kind of fellow, but spoke in a language that people appreciated and understood and had confidence in. That meant hundreds of votes in Calhoun County for Governor Folsom.

It doesn't come to mind at this time, but it was true of a lot of counties, somehow Folsom had been able to appoint people in most incidents who were born leaders and popular in their counties. The fact that Folsom had done so much for every small county, particularly paving roads, buying more school buses than had ever been bought before in any one administration, and building more school buildings than had ever been built before, meant that the people he had appointed judges, commissioners, and sheriffs had no trouble being re-elected. The people obviously thought that if Governor Folsom was elected again, their county, district, and community could expect to receive the same treatment and benefits from the upcoming administration as they did in the first.

In my travels over Alabama during those sixty days, by the

look of anxiety on the people's faces, and listening to their conversations about Folsom's first administration, it was very apparent that hope for a better time for Alabama still existed. I made no bones about it while talking to the people I contacted, such as the mayors, probate judges, commissioners, and bankers. It was important that they elect representatives and senators who would help put in place a progressive program that would really advance Alabama. It was interesting that a lot of times the elected officials and business people would take time to have lunch with me and talk more about the upcoming campaign. They would introduce me to people in the cafes and people would linger and visit for quite a long while, which made me feel that Jim Folsom was — a good country way to say it — on first base already. His campaign was going to be one of the most interesting ever. The next four years in the governor's office was his if he handled himself right and presented the program they expected from him during his campaign.

One of the good things for the campaign effort was my having been vice-chairman of the Alabama delegation to the 1952 National Democratic Convention. I was the acting chairman most of the time, because Senator Lister Hill's involvement was backstage with the leaders of the Democratic Party. We had some delegates supporting Kefauver who were kind of rowdy and pushy, but I kept them quiet and gained the respect of the very conservative delegates who were supporting Adlai Stevenson. One of the delegates, Mayor Cooper Green from Birmingham, who was my opponent and nominated to be vice-chairman, was also the public relations man for Alabama Power Company.

When I went to see him, he said without hesitation that he thought Governor Folsom would make a good governor and would be good for Alabama again, and since I was going to manage his campaign he felt good about it. He gave me a list of several people I could talk to in Jefferson County. One in particular was Judge Gardner Goodwin, the judge who lived out on the Bessemer cutoff, and I picked him to be Jefferson County's campaign manager. Also in the delegation was Bob Gwin who later became a circuit judge in Jefferson County. The Gwin name in Jefferson County was a very outstanding name in leadership. Bob's uncle had been a contractor in Jefferson County for many years, plus the fact that Bob was connected with one of the biggest and most outstanding law firms in Jefferson County.

Another thing Cooper Green did was to introduce me to Claude Vardeman, who was chairman of the Alabama Republican Party, and was one of President Dwight Eisenhower's advisers at that time. Not right then, but later, I got with Claude Vardeman after the campaign got underway and worked out that he would whisper the word around. They didn't have a candidate for governor at that time. In fact they didn't have any candidates for statewide office. I also whispered to him that we planned to support Guy Hardwick for lieutenant governor, in a quiet way, depending on how strong the Folsom campaign might be later. He said, "We will just make a pair of it." He worked all the way through the campaign, and we sure felt a difference, because a lot of the Republicans came to the polls and voted.

One outstanding Republican, Hershel Deavours, from Fayette County who was a very strong leader in the Republican

Party, came to me and said, "Fuller, I'll get you all the Republican votes in the fourth district of Fayette County. There are a lot of people that vote Republican all the time, and there are a lot of people in adjoining Winston County right on the north side that vote Republican. I'll get all those votes if you will get me a paved road." The promise of a paved road was good for the election, although as it turned out it was bad for the City of Fayette later, because I didn't remember Governor Folsom was such a scholar in Alabama history. He remembered the old Byler Road, the old stage coach route from Tuscaloosa to Moulton went right in front of Hershel Deavours' house, so he built a road that took almost fifty percent of the traffic out away from the City of Fayette going north and south. But Alabama Highway 13 was good for the community and is still heavily traveled. It was wonderful for north Alabama.

I kept my standing with the conservative crowd in the 1952 delegation to Chicago. There was a fellow there named Bill Garner, a representative who was a delegate who voted for Kefauver, and one named Dan Davis, a Kefauver delegate from Florence, Alabama. As was customary, people would have banners, and when they called their candidate's name, they would grab their banners and go stomping and cheering around the auditorium. It got embarrassing for Senator Lister Hill, so he tried to take the banners away from them. Bob Gwin — later Judge Gwin — had a banner, too, and he, Dan Davis, and Bill Garner had a few negative words with Senator Hill. I didn't know it, but Bob Gwin's father was the doorkeeper in the U. S. Senate and one of Lister Hill's appointees. A week later, Bob

Gwin called and said, "Fuller, you know, I played hell."

"How's that?" I asked.

"All that carrying on I did in Chicago caused Lister Hill to dismiss my father as doorkeeper in the senate," he said. "Reckon you can do anything about it?" he asked.

"I don't know, but I'll sure try," I said. I called Lister Hill and went to his office in Montgomery. He happened to be there. I told him that I didn't know about the incident at the time, but I felt a little responsible. "I wish you wouldn't fire the old man, as I understand he is a very quiet, nice gentleman." I said.

"Yes, he really is just as fine as he can be. I feel guilty about doing it, but Bob was so ugly up there I thought he needed a lesson," said Lister Hill.

"I believe he got the lesson," I said.

"All right Fuller. I'll bring him back," Lister Hill said. I got Mr. Gwin's job back, and Bob was very happy since he had really worried about it.

Another outstanding delegate was Homer Cobb from Phenix City. We had no trouble getting Russell County because we had a couple of fellows in the legislature who were strong for Folsom to start with, and I called on them during my sixty-day campaign. In Talladega County, Curtis Stalling was a farm machinery dealer while I was president of Alabama Farm Equipment Association. I stopped to see him, and he took me by to meet his doctor, Dr. J. L. Hardwick. As it turned out he was a first cousin to Guy Hardwick, who was a candidate for lieutenant-governor. When I told him we were going to whisper around that we wanted Guy for lieutenant- governor, he agreed to manage the campaign.

He said, "My next door neighbor is Tom Cooley, who is the Chevrolet and Oldsmobile dealer here. We will rope him in." So we carried Talladega County very strongly.

Another fellow I had known a long time as president of Alabama Farm Equipment Association was Clyde Anderson of Huntsville, who was the Ford Automobile dealer and Ford Tractor dealer. I contacted him and signed him up as campaign manager. A couple of other people I called on who were anxious to see Governor Folsom serve as governor again were the Circuit Judge in St. Clair County, Frank Emory, Sr., a very outstanding community leader whose office was in Pell City, and David Morrow, a John Deere dealer at Red Bay, who was a delegate to the Convention. We had a good relationship in the Alabama Farm Equipment Association, however, he was not a Kefauver delegate. But he supported the Folsom ticket.

Bill Garner from south Alabama, a delegate and one of the boys at the Convention in 1952 who had a run-in with Senator Hill, turned out to be a very strong supporter of Folsom. Later, he was also a strong supporter of Jimmy Mayfield and was his administrative assistant in Montgomery after he became a Supreme Court judge.

I was active in the 1956 campaign as Kefauver's Alabama campaign manager, and served on the national advisory committee for the campaign. Kefauver and I attended rallies in Alabama, Arkansas, Tennessee, and West Virginia. We attended a barbecue picnic in the upper corner of Arkansas, almost in Missouri, which was an outstanding event. I had invited a friend, Bob Stapp, from Montgomery to ride with me. Kefauver asked me to leave Bob and go with him to Nashville where a rally had been scheduled. I couldn't very well send Bob back to Montgomery alone, and I didn't.

One reason Bob Stapp went with me was that he was also in the farm machinery business. Jim Wood, my close friend I've talked about in the farm machinery business, had taken on the J I CASE Industrial line of equipment and wanted to tell us about it, so we met him in Memphis, spent the night at the famous Peabody Hotel, and had quite a party. J I CASE Industrial's representative was there, and that night my friend Bob Stapp signed up as a J I CASE Industrial dealer for middle Alabama. After I moved back to Fayette and started my asphalt business, I bought two CASE tractors from Bob Stapp.

I met Senator Kefauver later in Nashville and we went to the Governor's Mansion and met with Governor Frank Clement and the Mayor of Nashville. They took us on a tour of Nashville. I spent one night with Senator and Mrs. Kefauver and the next day drove back to Fayette.

Later, I met Senator Kefauver in Chattanooga to attend a barbecue. We rode a bus to Knoxville and on to Lake Martin — I think was the name of the lake — north of Nashville on the Tennessee River, and attended two different barbecues.

The 1956 National Democratic Convention was in Chicago, also. I was still a member of the State Democratic Executive Committee, and since I was Alabama's Director of Finance, the committee automatically made me a delegate to the Convention. I was still managing Kefauver's campaign in Alabama. Billy Partlow was a delegate again and very supportive of Kefauver, and Jimmy Mayfield, whom I spoke of earlier, had become an Alabama Supreme Court Judge and didn't go to the convention as a delegate, but he did go. We traveled a good bit and called on the delegates to the convention again, as we had during the first campaign.

Billy Partlow's family was politically-oriented. His father was head of the Partlow State School at one time, and Jimmy Mayfield's family was an outstanding political family. In fact, one of his uncles was in the House when the Alabama Constitution was written in 1901, and it has never been replaced. I've said before, one of Governor Folsom's big ambitions was to try to revise the Constitution, but as many times as it was introduced in both administrations, it never got out of committee, because the lieutenant-governor and the Speaker of the House would always see that it went into a committee that would never give it consideration. We never got to re-write it, and to this day it has never been re-written. No governor since has really made it a priority.

It was really an interesting time and new experiences for me—a country boy just from behind the plow traveling with those folks that had finished the University of Alabama Law School. Of course, they knew somebody in every town that had been to law school, and by that time we knew who the delegates were going to be, and we called on them. I think we had sixteen votes in 1956. I was not chairman then, but I was a member of the delegation. Kefauver still didn't have the votes, although he got a lot of votes, but finally in the end Adlai Stevenson was nominated for president, and Kefauver was nominated for vice-president. Senator John F. Kennedy was running for vice-president at that time, but Kefauver won over him.

If Kefauver had been elected President of the United States, I would have had an appointive position with the Department of Agriculture in Washington.

One thing that kept Kefauver from getting votes was something that had been brewing in Alabama from the 1954 ruling by the U. S. Supreme Court regarding integration, and was getting more and more pertinent, particularly in our committee. In Alabama, as well as in other southern states, they organized "White Citizens' Council." It was amazing how many people joined, because almost everybody they ran into wanted to join to help fight the Brown vs. The Board of Education ruling. Membership was only $1.50. They had put signs all over Alabama urging to "Impeach Earl Warren," who was Chief Justice of the Supreme Court, but they never found a way. They did try to in several places in Alabama. It began to affect the Democratic Executive Committee, as well as loyal Democrats in north Alabama, where the black population was a smaller percentage of the counties' total and not that much of a concern. But a lot of people were still sympathetic and would give that $1.50 rather than turn it down.

About 1955-56, every time the committee met, that group would get a little stronger in the committee. But it was actually in 1958 or 1960 before they were ever able to elect any officers in the committee. The White Citizens' Council was getting more influential, but integration finally became a reality. Of course, now the blacks are as strong in the committee as whites and it's causing a lot of people that voted democrat from 1954-1958 and maybe even on up to 1960, to switch parties.

Six years ago in 1994 to this day, the Republicans were able to elect several members to the legislature—the senate and the house. The blacks with "One Man One Vote" began to register until they were strong enough to have a fair representation in the Alabama legislature. The move by the Dixiecrats fighting integration so hard had a strong effect on the Alabama Democrat Party. The South lost its hold in the congress and senate by people switching like this, and the working people and the people who really need help are the losers because the Republican Party had never been very strong. If it had been left up to the Republican Party, as it has been known up to now, we would never have had Social Security, the Wage and Hour Law, or Medicare for that matter. Because, up to this point, there has not been enough votes in the Republican Party to defeat these worthwhile programs, and very few votes to support them.

The philosophy of the southern Democrat is still prevailing in the house and senate in Washington. During Kefauver's campaign he was looked upon as being a representative of the common people, as was evidenced during the really strong campaign he was running in Minnesota. Lyndon Johnson, a Democrat, who was President Pro-Tem in the senate, was scheduling the programs in the senate. There was a farm bill, which was very important to Minnesota and the middle west, and farmers all over for that matter. Johnson scheduled a vote for that Monday. He thought Kefauver would miss it, because this was the day before election in Minnesota. Kefauver went on and campaigned in Minnesota, but slipped in time to vote for the bill.

Kefauver carried Minnesota really strong in both presidential campaigns. But his opposition immediately begin to work on everybody they thought had any influence in California, and several of the folks changed that were supposed to be Kefauver's leaders in California. He still carried California and was convinced he had the full support of their delegates. But they finally kept him from ever being nominated for president, although he did get nominated for vice-president in 1956.

A lot of the fighting against Kefauver stemmed from integration. Many people were so afraid that more common people would be able to vote and have a bigger voice in who might be serving, and elect men such as Kefauver and Governor Folsom. This philosophy, the money behind it, and the political influence it carried would muster enormous power and influence against Kefauver. Even the governor of Tennessee, Frank Clemons, had ambition to run for president or vice-president. He was chairman of the delegation to the convention and withheld the Tennessee votes until the very last, then finally threw their votes to Kefauver. But by that time, the majority had made an agreement with Kefauver, that if he withdrew from the presidential, race he would be the nominee for vice-president.

I wish I had documented a lot of the discussions and people I met at Kefauver's various meetings. As I've said before, I was invited to Washington and Chattanooga and several other places I mentioned earlier. One of the places I was invited to was a buffet breakfast at the Mayflower Hotel in Washington, which I attended. That night, I went to Kefauver's strategy meeting and dinner at the Willard Hotel in Washington. I had to fly there and back, because some of the meetings I went to occurred when I still lived in Fayette.

One of the committee meetings I spoke of at the Mayflower Hotel involved the finance chairman of the National Democratic Committee, Sidney Solomon, Jr., as well as the National Democrat Party chairman, Mike McCluskey. McCluskey was from Philadelphia, Pennsylvania. Later, when I was in the insurance business in Montgomery, we were trying to represent one of the major insurance companies. Mr. Leon Morgan, a partner who managed our insurance company, could not get his foot in the door of the major company. I called Mike McCluskey in Philadelphia and asked him to make him an appointment. Leon Morgan flew up there, and we got the contract. That insurance company developed into a really successful bonding company for our construction contractors.

Another outstanding leader who later became more and more pertinent and ran for president one time was Senator "Scoop" Jackson from Washington. He was chairman of one committee and stayed in office until he just quit running, but he served about 12 years. Another very active man, Sid McMath, who was Governor of Arkansas, ran at the end of his term for U. S. Senator from Arkansas. He was defeated by Senator Fulbright.

FIFTEEN

WEST VIRGINIA TRIP
YOUNG DEMOCRATS NATIONAL
CONVENTION

One of the most interesting trips I made with Kefauver was to West Virginia. He wrote me a letter saying they were going to have the big state fair, and he was going to be the principal speaker. I showed the letter to Governor Folsom, and he said, "Why don't you have Billy Partlow, who was the adjutant general, to get out the National Guard plane, and we will fly to West Virginia." He called it the "Gully Jumper;" it was a DC3 left over from World War II. The National Guard had two of them, and the Governor and other state officials used them for state business quite often. In fact, we flew to New York in one once when I went to sign bonds. Since the governor was going to West Virginia, and Billy Partlow was going as adjutant general, he notified the adjutant general in West Virginia we were coming. Our party consisted of the governor, a couple of senators, me, and Billy Partlow, who appeared, decked out in his dress uniform with all of his honors, medals, badges, and braids. We were a little late getting to West Virginia, but the National Guard troops were there to greet us. When we landed they helped the governor and party off the plane, then gave Governor Folsom the 21 gun salute. I guess that was what it was, anyway they stood out and shot their guns.

We went straight to the rally where Senator Kefauver was already speaking. Someone noticed that Governor Folsom was slightly inebriated and feeling no pain, and gave him his seat behind Senator Kefauver. Folsom immediately began to nod. So I motioned to the person sitting next to him to change seats with me, and I would see what I could do. I moved into the seat next to the governor, but was unable to help much. When he nodded, I would shake him, and he would straighten up and loudly say, "Tell 'em Kef."

I always figured it was a Life Magazine photographer standing in front taking pictures. When Kefauver finished his speech, the program was over, and everybody was shaking hands and talking, I walked over to the photographer as he was taking the film out of his camera. I asked, "Is that the film of the pictures you were taking during the speech?"

"Yes," he answered.

I pulled out a $100 bill where he could see it, and I asked, "Are you a horse trader?"

He studied a minute and asked, "You mean you would give me that for this film?"

"I think I would swap with you," I said. He handed me the film and I handed him the $100 bill. I really don't know what magazine he represented, but I didn't want those pictures to appear in any magazine later, and they never did.

It was a big rally for Kefauver as he was the only presidential candidate speaking, although there were some local candidates speaking. The Governor of West Virginia was there, but I don't remember his name. The state fair was in a valley-like place, and the valley was almost like a stadium. Kefauver and other speakers were up at one end, and you could see them from both sides all the way down, and hear them, as well, since there were no loud speakers set up. It was a wonderful rally. We stayed for it all, but came on back to Alabama that night as soon as it ended.

Another thing that happened before that was when Kefauver was campaigning in California. He called to see if I could get Reverend Martin Luther King to come travel with us around the state, since he was going to be there all the week. I went to Martin Luther King's residence while he was still pastor of the Dexter Avenue Baptist Church in Montgomery, and knocked on the door.

"Come in," he said.

I walked into a small vestibule where he was sitting at a desk reading a Bible. His wife, Coretta, was close by playing the piano. I introduced myself. He motioned for Coretta to stop playing, and I said, "No, please let her finish. She is playing Amazing Grace, my father's favorite hymn." When she finished playing we sat down, and I said to Reverend King, "I am managing Senator Kefauver's campaign in Alabama, and he wanted me to ask if you would come to California and travel with him two or three days. I will go with you, and take care of your expenses."

"No, I haven't decided what I am going to do politically yet, but I do appreciate your inviting me, and I feel honored," Dr. King said.

I went back and told Governor Folsom about it. "Can you

get up $10,000?" he asked.

"I think I can," I answered. In fact, I did have $10,000, but that was all I had.

"Why don't you go out there and take it to him and travel with him a day or two?" the governor asked. I caught the plane out of Montgomery, flew to the San Francisco, and stayed three days and two nights. We flew up into northern California, and Kefauver made three or four speeches, two big ones to large crowds at night. We visited Chinatown in San Francisco, and I don't know how many little restaurants we stopped in, and had coffee or tea and talked to people. It was a wonderful trip, and I flew back home the next day.

Governor Folsom was always anxious to support candidates running for state office. About the middle of his second administration, it was time to elect the national president of the Young Democrats. Senator Neil Metcalf from Geneva County asked Folsom to support him for this national office. Folsom agreed to it right away, and that meant we all had to get busy getting as many Alabama delegates as we could to attend the convention in Oklahoma City, Oklahoma. Everybody got busy, and several secretaries prepared mail outs, and made phone calls. We made several trips to other states. Senator Metcalf and I got busy and made sure that each of our delegates could be financed or had money to get to Oklahoma City for the convention, and that their room would be taken care of. I got in touch with my nephew, Billy Thomson, who was managing my John Deere Dealership in Mississippi, and told him to get three or four people from Mississippi to go, and I saw that they had travel tickets to the convention and their rooms and expenses were taken care of.

Oklahoma City was dry, and they had to have "spirits." Ed Pepper, the assistant finance director was there, and also a young man named Taylor from Ashland, Ed Pepper's home town. Pete Matthews, the floor leader in the house, knew him, so I gave Taylor a purchase order for a panel truck and a dealer's tag to put on the truck, and told him to go to the Chevrolet dealer in Cullman, and pick up the truck. I told him to go to the warehouse in Manchester, Tennessee where the world famous Jack Daniel whiskey was distilled and bottled, and made arrangements to buy 40 cases of Jack Daniel Black Label.

I put him on the train to Cullman, gave him cash for expenses and enough to pay for the whiskey, and told him, "While you have the whiskey in Tennessee you are all right, but when you get to Arkansas you won't have any Arkansas stamps, and when you get to Oklahoma, it's dry. There isn't any such thing as whiskey stamps in Oklahoma, so don't you stop for anything except to get gas from the time you leave the Tennessee line across the bridge at Memphis until you get here, because you are traveling with illegal cargo."

In the meantime, General Partlow took one of the National Guard twin engine planes, which we had loaded with four cases of Jack Daniel to get the party started, and he flew on to Oklahoma City.

Averell Harriman, the former governor of New York, was running for president, and was down at Congressman Boykin's lodge. Boykin, the congressman from the first congressional district, was putting on a big hunt in Harriman's honor. Not only had he invited Averell Harriman as his honored guest, but also the ambassador from Germany, and Governor Folsom, along with Bill Drinkard, the conservation director, Guy Hardwick, the lieutenant governor, me, and several other men who were friendly to the administration. We hunted a day or two. Boykin really put on a feast while we were there. Most of it was game — deer and turkey — killed on his big tree farm. I understand his farm consisted of about 200,000 acres located in Mobile and Washington Counties, and was the finest pine forest you've ever seen.

One of the funny things Winston, the govenor's chauffeur, told was that they had a place picked out for Folsom to hunt. I have an idea that Boykin had caught a deer and had it tied down in a certain place so Winston could drive to it, and Governor Folsom would be able to kill a deer. But Governor Folsom was not about to shoot any kind of wild animal. He would shoot ducks or doves, but he would not shoot deer or any other wild animal. The governor had his gun, and Winston said he pulled up close to where the deer was and said, "Governor, there it is. There it is, get your gun!" Folsom reach down and picked up a bottle of Early Times laying in the floor board instead of his gun and never did shoot the deer.

The press had been talking an awful lot about Folsom using the National Guard plane. We had not bought a state plane for the other departments, but later we did buy one for the highway department. Before Partlow left to fly to Oklahoma City, I had asked him to see if the National Guard people of Tennessee would lend us their plane, and they agreed to. I made arrangements for them to pick us up at Brookley Field in Mobile, and fly us to Oklahoma City.

After the hunt we went on into Mobile and spent the night. We had planned before for Jamelle and Reba met us at the Admiral Semmes Hotel that night. Governor Folsom would never leave for anywhere except at an ungodly hour, so about three o'clock in the morning he woke us up; Jamelle, Reba, me, Bill Drinkard, and two or three other people who were going to the convention. Everybody got up, got ready, and went to Brookley Field where the Tennessee National Guard plane was waiting for us. We boarded in the pouring rain, and took off. We flew to Dallas and on into Oklahoma City. When we landed, there was the press with all their cameras and equipment, so I got off first. Since they didn't know me they said, "That's the Tennessee National Guard plane." They got in their cars and drove off without taking any pictures.

When we got to the hotel, they had set up a two bedroom suite for Governor Folsom and Jamelle, and Reba and I were in a very large adjoining suite. The panel truck had arrived, and several students, boys and girls from Oklahoma University, and a lot of other people who had found out about the Jack Daniels, were in the suite enjoying it. The funny thing about it was when Taylor got to Oklahoma City, he called Pete Matthews and Frank Long, the governor's legal advisor, and told them, "I'm right here in Oklahoma City. My orders were to come to Oklahoma City, and I'm looking right at a sign that reads Oklahoma City.

That's as far as I'm coming, so you all can come get this truck."

Pete Matthews said, "Just drive it on to the hotel down the alley and we'll get it unloaded."

No, I'm not coming any further. I'm going to catch the bus to Alabama," Taylor said.

Pete Matthews and Frank Long got a taxi to drive them to the edge of town where Taylor was, and they drove the truck with the dealer's tag back and parked it behind the hotel. They called two bellboys to help unload the cargo. Frank Long said when they opened the back of the panel truck the bellboys saw those forty cases of Jack Daniels. One of the bellboys' eyes got as big as saucers. "We'll give you fifteen dollars cash for every bottle because we can get twenty dollars a bottle," he said.

They locked the door back, and here comes Pete Matthews and Frank Long to see me. They called me off to one side, and Frank Long said, "Mr. Kimbrell, those bellboys want to buy that whiskey and they'll give us fifteen dollars a bottle for it. We'll have enough money to pay for all our expenses."

"No. It's bad enough to have illegal whiskey, much less bootlegging. We bought that whiskey for folks to drink so bring it up," I said. They brought it up, and as the old saying goes, "A good time was had by all."

The convention went fine. It was a typical political convention. Governor Mennen Williams of Michigan was there. Governor Williams' family owned the Mennen Cosmetics Company. Also, the governor from Minnesota was there with his delegation. Senator John Sparkman, Senator Kefauver, Guy Hardwick, the lieutenant governor of Alabama, the lieutenant governor of Louisiana, and the mayor of New Orleans were there. We had a real collection of outstanding leaders of the United States.

One morning a table was set up for a press conference. Seated at the table was Congressman Carl Elliott, one of Alabama's finest congressmen, and a teetotaler. After the conference started, Pete Matthews and McDowell Lee, the clerk of the senate, brought Big Jim in. They brought him over to where I was sitting. I had saved a seat for him, and Congressman Carl Elliott was on the other side. They sat him down by Carl Elliott, and Folsom had in his hand a jelly glass with a drink in it. Right away the press came over to Governor Folsom and asked, "Now, Governor who are you supporting for president?"

"I'm supporting Harry S. Truman," Folsom said. Harry S. Truman had not been president for the last eight years.

"No, sure enough. We are wondering who you are supporting," the reporters asked,

"Harry S. Truman," Big Jim said beating on the table.

At that point, that was about all Carl Elliott could take because he was running for re-election. Representative Pete Matthews still has a grand time telling about Congressman Carl Elliott getting up and leaving the room at 'table level' to avoid the television cameras.

We worked and worked, but could never get the nine delegates' votes that Michigan had, and Senator Metcalf lost by those nine votes. Governor Folsom and I got Governor Mennen Williams in our suite, and tried to persuade him to give the votes to Metcalf, but he didn't. After it was over, Folsom said, "Fuller,

I believe you are going to make a hard-shell preacher the way you were laying it on Governor Williams."

On the way back to Alabama, Reba didn't think she could fly in the "Gully Jumper" since we had to go down to Dallas and through Mobile and back to Montgomery. So we caught the Frisco train out of Oklahoma City into Memphis. It was a fun trip. When everyone boarded the train there were, Judge Roy Mayhall, the chairman of the State Democratic Committee whom I failed to mention before; Lecil Gray, the probate judge of Walker County; Jim Smith, the former chairman of the Democratic Executive Committee from Tuscumbia; and our wives. We all got in the same car.

Judge Lecil Gray was one of the finest story tellers you've ever heard. It was daylight all the way to Memphis, and he entertained us for two or three hours before he ran out of stories. By that time I had developed into a pretty good story teller, and I would tell about my kinfolks — Uncle Mancy and others — so I took the floor and had it for about forty minutes. One of Congressman Albert Raines' cousins, Joe Starnes from Guntersville, was also a pretty good story teller, and he kept us laughing. So it was a fun trip from there to Memphis. When we got to Memphis, Reba and I flew into Birmingham, got a car, and drove to Montgomery. The people from Jasper stayed on the train and rode back to Jasper. That trip was a good story in itself.

SIXTEEN

FOLSOM CAMPAIGN KICKOFF

After taking off a couple or three weeks for the Christmas and New Year's holidays, I started traveling from Fayette to Governor Folsom's Cullman campaign office, which had been set up in the Ponders' building. Ponders was an outstanding department store on the corner of Main Street and Highway 31 in Cullman. The Ponders donated the use of the whole upstairs of a rather large building for campaign purposes.

I began meeting with Bill Drinkard, Murray Battles, and a little later Myra Hamner, who was set up to be campaign treasurer. Two young girls who lived in Cullman, and worked in the office were the only paid people at that time in the campaign. Governor Folsom told us he planned to have a kick-off rally later and wanted to have it in Hamilton, Alabama, the county seat of Marion County. By then it was known that I would be the north Alabama campaign manager. Judge George Wallace of Barbour County, who later became Governor, was to be the south Alabama campaign manager. Charley Pinkston was to be the Montgomery County and central Alabama campaign manager. Governor Folsom was rather hesitant to call us campaign managers. Most of the time he called us the "committee to take the politics out of politics."

During the first two and three weeks of January we set out to get some printing machines — mimeograph machines since there were no copy machines at that time — to get out letters, flyers, etc. People had donated the use of electric typewriters. An IBM dealer donated the use of one for the campaign, and a business person in Birmingham donated the use of one. That was the first time I had ever heard of an electric typewriter.

A businessman had volunteered to pay for what we called then a WATT line, which was a toll-free telephone line incoming and outgoing. So I begin to call the people I had met while I traveled during November and December in the various counties, recruiting county coordinators from among them. Nobody, as I remember, ever turned me down, and they became a very important part of the campaign.

It became apparent at a certain point that we had to have some campaign money, although all of us were working gratis. Governor Folsom had appointed me as finance chairman and told me, "I don't want you to take over $1000 from any one person." Of course, that sounds ridiculous, because nowadays that kind of money won't do anything for a campaign. We needed some serious money immediately — even before he announced. I had a good relationship with the four industrial machinery dealers in Alabama. I went to see them, and each one gave us $1000 — the limit — and that was enough money to buy paper for printing, bumper stickers, and posters to put along the roads, in store windows, and other places.

By that time we had begun to try to find volunteers with panel trucks. I believe one fellow who owned a station wagon volunteered. We had two fellows who furnished their own station wagons and gas, and after the announcement around January 20th at Hamilton, they went all over the state, stopped at all the crossroads, nailed posters to stakes, and placed them on the side of the roads. They also gave out bumper stickers. It was no problem to get people to put bumper stickers on their vehicles. People everywhere were really anxious to get the Folsom bumper stickers, particularly the farmers, those who had pickup trucks, and those who had voted for him before.

I was convinced while traveling around visiting people in the various counties that he was really going to carry the state and do really well come election time, unless something changed.

It was amazing how the county commissioners and city council members took hold, especially in the smaller counties. Of course we didn't work too much at first in Jefferson County. But later, after Folsom qualified and announced he was running for governor, Cliff Stiles, the owner of the Redmont Hotel, gave me a key to a suite in the hotel. I would go there a lot of times at night to make calls. By that time I had worked out that Judge Gardner Goodwin would be the campaign manager for Jefferson County in Birmingham, which was really a good choice. He was the kind of fellow you would like to have for a brother. He was such a nice, quiet gentleman. He was re-elected three or four times. Incidentally, Governor Folsom had appointed him, and he never had an opponent when he ran for re-election. So he came in, and we set up a room in the Tutwiler Hotel as campaign headquarters for Jefferson County. He would volunteer to man the headquarters when court was not in session.

Charlie Pinkston. George Wallace, and I started in mid January working on the platform. We met in Cullman almost every Sunday afternoon. Rankin Fite would meet with us a lot of times because he was hoping to be the Speaker of the House, and I was hoping he could be. So we worked on the platform program, and finally put together one that Governor Folsom approved. It was obvious that his real ambition was to try to do something to help everybody in Alabama, especially the low-income and no-income people.

We had a pamphlet printed of the platform, featuring a picture of Folsom, ready to hand out at all the rallies. Our county campaign workers would pick up these pamphlets when they visited the headquarters in Cullman.

Meanwhile, back at the office in Cullman, Bill Drinkard, Murray Battles, and I took maps and marked out different places we felt Governor Folsom should have political rallies. We tried to line them up so he would have a rally in one town in the morning, and in another one in the afternoon, ending up in the county seats at night, where there would be bigger crowds. In most county seats there would be a National Guard Armory or unit that Folsom had built, or awarded to that county, as well as a courthouse square to accommodate the larger crowds. We printed folders listing the places we planned to be and we would stamp the date Folsom would be at a certain place. These folders read "I want to see you (or speak to you) at (such and such) time and in (a certain) town." Then we would put them in the mailboxes, and in smaller post offices the postal workers would put them in the post office boxes. Later I found out they didn't do it for other candidates. We tried to circulate within a seven mile radius of where we were planning to have a rally. We were not disappointed, and Governor Folsom was pleased with the turnout everywhere we had a rally. The courthouse squares were full, the courtrooms were full, or the National Guard Armories were full.

As to the kickoff in Hamilton, it was a 100 percent success. People came from all over the state. It was estimated at least 4000 people had come to the little town of Hamilton just for the kickoff of Governor Folsom's campaign.

I remember one time we thought we would try a rally in the Black Belt at Forkland, Alabama in Green County. There must have been 3000 people out there from nowhere. It was just amazing, because in that area a large portion of the population was black, and hundreds of blacks were there. They were trying to register to vote, and it was not all that easy then for blacks to register. In Governor Folsom's campaign speeches when he talked about education, he would say, "separate but equal school buildings." That was the first time improving the school system for blacks had been mentioned that I ever heard. They were all anxious to register which, as I said before, was not all that easy. But a lot of them did, and they all went to the polls. And the rural people, who were enjoying their mailbox roads paved during the governor's first administration, came out and showed their appreciation by voting for him the second time.

To begin with, we had set out to have most of the rallies in north and northwest Alabama, as well as in Etowah, DeKalb, and Jackson Counties, where Folsom had strong support. Then we moved into south Alabama, into the Wiregrass area, since Folsom was very popular there and had some good, strong leaders in Dothan. The Flowers family's support was outstanding, and a family that later built a shopping center and owned the hospital and bank was also among his very strong supporters. Louis Opprey, the sales manager for the Chevrolet-Oldsmobile dealer there, was a campaign manager and a really fine gentleman. We couldn't have picked a better fellow. So we moved into that section, and the rallies continued to be just as strong with large crowds.

When we got over around Barbour County and in that section and moving back through the Black Belt in Lowndes, Dallas, Marengo, and Perry Counties, George Wallace was taking the lead and introducing Governor Folsom. In a lot of places, Wallace would tell Governor Folsom not to shake hands with the blacks during that time, but to shake hands only with the whites. But Governor Folsom never heard a word of it. He would move right out, and if a black was close enough for him to shake hands with first, he did just that. And it didn't affect his popularity. It was that way everywhere we went. I remember one time we went into Selma for a night meeting. Reba and I went down to the rally. We spent the night in Montgomery, and went over that night. All the blacks were over on the right side, and all the whites were on the other side. One of Governor Folsom's opponents was there to hear it, and the crowd was taking the roof down as Governor Folsom told them what he was going to do if he was elected again. When he got through speaking, three of the Black Belt campaign managers formed a line between him and the blacks so he would have to shake hands with the whites first. But it didn't work. He jumped off the stage and started shaking hands with the blacks and worked around to the whites and his opponent to shake hands.

I called a meeting at the campaign office in Cullman with Wallace, Pinkston, Battles, and Drinkard to discuss having a statewide rally in Birmingham, since it had been six or seven weeks after we started the campaign. I thought this would boost the enthusiasm that we had enjoyed at every statewide rally we'd had so far, give the county coordinators an opportunity to swap ideas, and, also bring in campaign funds. Judge Wallace and Charlie Pinkston were to notify the south Alabama county coordinators, and I was to notify the ones in north Alabama. We set the date for a rally and fund-raiser to be held at the Redmont Hotel in Birmingham, Alabama. North Alabama produced the largest crowd and $6700, and a good crowd from south Alabama brought in $1300. A funny thing that happened was Senator Rankin Fite and Aline, his wife came in. Rankin gave a nice booster talk and ended with saying that he and Aline had conducted a poll from Hamilton to Birmingham. The results were that Folsom had 157 bumper stickers, and Birmingham Slag had nine.

In his first administration Folsom had talked about rewriting the State Constitution, and had such a bill introduced as one of the first when the legislature met each regular session. At that time the legislature only met every two years, instead of every year like it does now, but Governor Folsom had called several special sessions. One of the main thrusts in each call was to rewrite the Constitution. But it never passed. It hasn't happened to this day and no state needs it any more than Alabama.

In Folsom's platform, the number two plank was the old age pension. Governor Folsom still talked about the mailbox roads. Then he would talk about a transportation system for all Alabama. Next, he would talk about health and welfare, and then he would bring up his plan for an old age pension. And right about there he would say, "I want to have an old age pension and give everybody age sixty-five and older fifty dollars a month." He went on to talk about improving the hospital system and began to try to promote a system of nursing homes.

Folsom did a wonderful job during the first administration regarding education, and he began to talk about building more and better schools and acquiring more school buses. Labor knew he was very favorable to whatever they wanted. It was hard to get much Labor legislation through then, but is much easier now. Of course, one of the things I insisted he put in was the same thing Mississippi had already passed, promoting an increase of industries in small towns and even crossroads. This was the Department of Industrial Development, which Mississippi called Balancing Agriculture with Industry. So we got that in his platform. He talked about that a lot. He said, "I'm going to get a little plant here if it works. In fact, we may move a lot of sewing industries in here to give the women work. It might even get like it was with the Indians, when the women did all the work and the men did the hunting and fishing." He always talked about women's rights and local government, and he never tried to block any local bills.

One of the beauties of starting the campaign in north Alabama was that the newspapers were still unfavorable toward Folsom. But they had decided that writing too much against him might go against their wishes, because in his campaign speeches he would call them the "lying dailies." He said, "They used to print lies by the thousands and now they have these automatic presses and they print lies by the millions."

Another thing that went over big in the smaller counties was there had been two or three cases in a short period of time where rich men's sons had gotten by with committing serious crimes. Even one with murder, and several with crimes that were too bad to talk about. Some of them didn't even go to jail because they had the money to pay a powerful lawyer. So he spoke out very strongly against the fee system for criminal lawyers, which continues to be a way of life even now. He felt that the poor people and the working people didn't have a chance in court because they were not able to hire prominent lawyers.

Back to the way the press printed about the crowds and Folsom's acceptance up in north Alabama: when he moved into the Black Belt in central Alabama, where he had not expected to be strong, the press got the message that he was setting the woods on fire where we had campaigned and had rallies. Before it was over Folsom had rallies in every county, and even moved into Birmingham and Bessemer for rallies. He attended Labor Day barbecues before the general election and after the primary. Bessemer and Tuscumbia changed the date of their Labor Day celebrations so he could be there. They had a big fish fry in Mobile, which Folsom attended as the main speaker. The campaign was everything we had hoped it would be.

I continued to raise money. We ran a poor folks campaign if there ever was one. Someone furnished us a car, somebody else a gas credit card, and somebody paid for a telephone Watt line for us to use. Enough money to pay the motel bill where his party stayed was all we needed, and this was taken care of by the "toll bucket." That $4000 I talked about early bought most of the supplies, such as printing and mail outs, nearly until the May primary. We didn't have to have a runoff later on. I continued to travel around and go the rallies. I would pick up $100 here and $200 there and take the money to Myra Hamner who would write each one a "thank you" note and sign Governor Folsom's name. It turned out that we didn't have too many people on the list.

Back then, $50,000 was the legal maximum you were allowed to spend on a governor's campaign, but the amount was a lot less for attorney general, supreme court judge, court of appeals, lieutenant governor, or others running for statewide officers. Our expenses for the campaign were less than $50,000. We did it for $48,000. We went back to the industrial equipment people, and two of them each gave $4000 and two others gave $2000 each. We got $12,000 total, but we didn't have the bid law, and I knew I could make a satisfactory business proposition for them at that time.

Radio spots, television campaign commercials, and newspaper ads did not have to be included in the $50,000. We used only $1200 for television time, which Dr. Louis Friedman paid so he could be seen with Governor Folsom often. I decided to stop at several local radio stations and get spots on the air. With cash from campaign funds in my pocket, I could get several radio spots run on Monday morning when people were going to work, and Monday evening at the time people would be getting off from work, and have some run Saturday afternoon. In addition, we decided to put a quarter page ad in all the daily papers in Alabama including Birmingham, Dothan, Florence, Huntsville, Mobile, Montgomery, and Tuscaloosa, which cost a total of $27,000 and was more than half of the amount that we spent under the legal total. However, the cost of the radio spots I requested of the county campaign managers had not been included in the $48,000. I have no way of guessing how much they spent in the various counties, but it was minimal. I called the campaign managers in each county probably three different times and asked them to put campaign announcements on the radio, and this cost ten or twelve dollars each time. So you are talking about maybe averaging twenty-five dollars per county for the whole campaign, because the cost at that time I think was about a dollar per spot. In the larger counties, such as Colbert, Jefferson, Lauderdale, Jefferson, Madison, Mobile, or Montgomery, I don't think I called the managers at all.

In Folsom's 1946 campaign he had a hillbilly band called the Strawberry Pickers, but in this campaign he changed the name of the band to the Corn Grinders. Also, in his 1946 campaign he had the Suds Bucket. But in his 1954 campaign they passed around copper cups (I still have one at home.) for people to pay the toll. He would tell them, "When you go to the mill to get your corn ground, you have to pay the toll. We are going down to Montgomery, and we are going to grind the corn for you. But we got to have a little toll."

Folsom's people passed the copper cups around through the crowd, and they raised just about enough to keep them on the road all the time, due to the fact they already had the gas credit card someone had donated and the automobiles. I furnished my own car and my own gas. Of course, when I spent the night in Birmingham I stayed at the Redmont where Cliff Stiles had furnished a suite, and that was free. But I had to pay for my meals. If the other boys went to a rally or anywhere, they wanted a little gas money for their cars, but I never took a penny of it and never took a penny of campaign money a single time.

During the campaign, most of the statewide candidates, including two or three supreme court and court of appeals judges, had run-offs. The superintendent of education, who ran statewide instead of being appointed by the board of education, had a run-off. The attorney general's race was open, and Senator Albert Patterson won. He was one of Kefauver's delegates at the 1952 Convention, and as I said before, at the convention I kept promising him I would get him on the stand to make at least a five-minute talk, which made him happy. He came to campaign headquarters, and Governor Folsom and I shook hands with him, and agreed to support him. Of course, there was Austin Meadows, who was running for superintendent of education. He came, and we told him we would support him. Agnes Baggett was running for state auditor and we supported her. Sybil Poole was running for state treasurer. She didn't need any special help, because she could pop those high heels and wear that tight dress through all the businesses in town and get the votes. I say that about Sybil Poole with the highest respect. She was a vote getter statewide, a beautiful and very clever lady. When I was in the senate she was well liked by everybody. No one would dare run against her and hope to get elected. There was someone on the Public Service Commission we supported, but I don't remember who he was. These folks I just mentioned all had run-offs.

In the run-off I called my campaign managers and said, "These are the folks that we know will work with us. Please get these spots on the radio again for me." Practically no one used television ads because very few people had televisions then. Although we did finally spend $1200 for television time in Birmingham the very last week. Another thing we did the very last night before election, which I think was very special, was we got 60 minutes on Channel 6 in Birmingham. We got outstanding people—Judge DeBardeleben, of Anniston, George Hawkins, who was running for the House and was an outstanding labor attorney, Dee Kendricks, Chairman of the Board of Revenue in Jefferson County, and others I can't remember, but I think we had seven who each got up and talked just minutes. We left Jim Folsom ten minutes to speak, and we put him on at nine o'clock in the evening. We had it well advertised that the program would be televised, as we had told all our people to put a little ad in the newspapers.

One of the innovative things we did that pushed it over that

I haven't told (it was tried two or three times later, but people fussed about it): Bill Drinkard came up with the idea to have a motorcade zigzagging the whole state of Alabama, starting at Cullman. So we decided to do it. Governor Folsom was afraid of the idea, and I was, too, at first. But Drinkard said it would work. We got to thinking and discussing it, and decided that with the crowds that he had in every county seat it would work. We worked out a route that we could do in a week. What I did was to get on the phone again and call all my campaign managers. I told them to have a crowd to from each town to join us just before we arrived at the city limits and ride with us through town. We gave them a schedule of the time we would be in every little town.

We started at Cullman, drove down through Oakman, down Highway 69 to Tuscaloosa, back up Highway 43, switched over to Berry because that was Jamelle's hometown, then back through Fayette, up to Winfield, Guin, Hamilton and got way up nearly to Hackleburg, where we saw some folks plowing on the hillside. They were waving Folsom banners and had Folsom stickers all over the harnesses. One fellow had a riding cultivator, and he had sticks with Folsom's banners up on his cultivator. We went all the way across and into Huntsville, down through Talledega, over to Anniston, and switched back through Selma. We went back over to Dothan and on into Mobile where we spent the night. That night the owner of the Silver Spoon Restaurant, a big supporter of Big Jim's, told us to come to the restaurant, and he would fix dinner for us. There must have been at least thirty people. He placed us in the back room of the restaurant at a big, long wooden table. He started boiling shrimp, and soft shelled crabs. He would bring them and pour them out on table. Also he brought pitchers of draft beer to go with the meal. He served us plenty of fried fish, broiled fish, hushpuppies, and slaw. Everyone thoroughly enjoyed it and a good time was had by all. It was the highlight of the week of the motorcade, but I wound up with the bill. About the second day of the last week after we started the motorcade, Governor Folsom and I discussed the status of the campaign that morning at breakfast. We were so happy with the way things were going, we felt that with a little extra push we could get by without a run off. The next night we wound it up by having a big rally in the Coliseum in Montgomery.

Judge Wallace was against the rally in Montgomery. He said, "It isn't going to work. Fuller, don't let him say that about going to have six more young'uns." In Folsom's education part of his speech he would say, "I've got six young'uns now. The Lord willing, I'm going to have six more," and it would bring the house down. Wallace said, "These folks are educated here in Montgomery. Don't let him say that." But I knew there was no need to try to get him to stop.

We got to the Coliseum, and they were hanging from the rafters. There wasn't a seat left; it was full. Before the rally, George Wallace kept saying, "You won't have 5000 people there." It seated 15,000, and they filled the downstairs area. I bet there were 20,000 people there that night. George Wallace got up and introduced him with his "sophisticated" speech, you know. And Governor Folsom got up to speak. He was still just Governor

Jim Folsom and brought the house down. That ended the campaign on Monday night before the election, and we went back to Cullman for election day.

We had six strong candidates. Some were about as strong as Alabama ever had. The night of the election, people all around were betting there would not be a run-off. Of course, none of us working in the campaign bet, but we knew some of our friends were betting. One man bet $20,000 dollars there would not be a run-off. He won it.

I was telling everybody there wouldn't be a run-off because I was getting calls from my campaign managers. I would sit in the office all day long and call them. What I did was sit in the office the last week before the election the following Tuesday, and I called every campaign manager I had in every county all over the state. I don't know how many calls I made on that Watt line and don't even remember what I said. But I read them an ad that cost one dollar a spot, and told them to run it ten times. I said, "I want these run over the radio stations on Monday about the time folks go to work and Monday afternoon at the time people get off from work."

Back then, you weren't supposed to campaign on election day, and you were looked on as bad if you tried to campaign on Sunday. None of the ten spots in any place cost over a total of twelve dollars, most of them eight and nine dollars, or about ninety cents a spot. I tried to get those on the local radio stations. Most of the counties only had one radio station then. In the spots—I don't remember the exact wording—but I said, "Just get everybody out to vote. We hope to get this over May 2nd without a run-off so we can go on and prepare to do you a good job next year."

Election night, along about midnight, votes began to come in. From the very start it looked like we had enough votes without a run-off, but it went on down to the very last, and looked like we might lack just a 1000 or 1500 votes. Jimmy Faulkner, our strongest opponent, was in a hotel in Birmingham saying he was going to run it off if Folsom just lacked one vote. It went right on up until after midnight, and the next morning it was still doubtful.

I remember when it looked like for sure we wouldn't have a runoff, Cliff Stiles, a strong supporter, called and made reservations for the Kentucky Derby, and got tickets and hotel rooms in Louisville for Big Jim, Jamelle, Bully Moon, who had been the driver for Big Jim and his wife, and himself and his wife. All the crowd from campaign headquarters went out to see them off. When the train stopped in Cullman to pick them up, Big Jim got on the steps of the train, he turned around and said, "Fuller, don't you sleep until you get me a clear majority." The election had been over for eighteen hours, and everybody laughed because we were pretty safe by then.

Several of our friends did not make it in the run-off. Thank goodness, Guy Hardwick, who we had hoped would be lieutenant governor, and had urged people to support, had won in the first primary. We were so happy that Guy Hardwick was elected lieutenant governor, because I had worked with him in the senate, and he and I had developed a close relationship. I felt sure the administration could work with him as lieutenant governor.

There were a lot of accusations that we stole a lot of votes, but the Folsom people did not steal any votes. Some of our friends stole votes in two different counties, but it was not for the Folsom campaign. It was for the sheriff's race in those two counties, and in one of those counties we came in third. One of our strongest enemies stole some votes and got indicted for stealing them. In order to win himself, he stole 1600 for us, but we didn't need them. And we didn't need the 2500 hundred votes in another big county or the 1500 votes in a medium sized county that turned out to be stolen. But nobody got indicted except our strongest enemy.

As I said we had six strong opponents. Several of them had statewide recognition. Some had done a good job for the state of Alabama in the legislature, but as it turned out we had a clear majority in forty-three counties. We led the ticket in all but five counties. Of course, that left us without a run-off.

SEVENTEEN

FOLSOM'S ADMINISTRATION BEGINS — I REALLY WENT TO WORK

Soon after the campaign started, we found the atmosphere all over the state was very good. Instead of fighting Governor Folsom and his administration as they did at first, the newspapers were afraid that the harder the press fought him the better it would be for him. He had gained so much popularity it appeared he was going to succeed. He called them the those "lying dailies." As Hugh Sparrow, the most bitter enemy of Folsom's and mine in the first administration, put it, "It looks like Folsom will go back to Montgomery with more power than has ever been possible in a governor's administration before." That turned out to be true. So the newspapers became less and less critical, but still not all that favorable, and in a quiet way withdrew much of their criticism.

During the campaign, I was careful in a quiet way to check out and help legislative candidates whom I knew would vote with us and support the Folsom program. As it turned out, an overwhelming majority were elected in the House, and I could select committee members who would vote to bring the administration's bills out of the committee immediately and place them on the calendar.

I was a member of the Fayette City Council, and was so pleased with the turnout of voters in Fayette County. We got a big majority of Fayette County's votes. Ironically, some of the counties like Calhoun, Cullman, and Marshall that went the strongest for Folsom in the 1954 election went Republican two years ago, in 1998, when "Little Jim" was running for re-election.

The people in Marshall County elected Representative Olin Hearn, who voted with the administration at all times. Haygood Patterson, the commissioner of agriculture during Folsom's first administration, was nominated in the first primary. But almost immediately after his nomination, he took sick, and after a short time it was apparent that he would not be able to serve because of his illness. After the May 30 primary, every person we had supported was elected. Albert Patterson, who was nominated as attorney general, did have a runoff. But June 18, following the May 30, primary runoff, he was shot and killed. The Democratic Executive Committee was still waiting and had not tried to do anything in regard to the commissioner of agriculture vacancy, so that made two vacancies to be filled somehow or other.

I was elected to the Democratic Executive Committee by a clear majority without a run-off. So was Judge Roy Mayhall of Walker County, who had been a very close personal friend for a long while. When I was in the senate we developed a closeness. I talked to Governor Folsom, and he suggested that I go see Ben Ray, who was chairman of the State Democratic Executive Committee, in regard to the two vacancies. I did, and we worked out to call the committee together. Haygood Patterson's two sons sent letters to Mr. Ray declaring, according to his doctor, he would not be able to recover and serve, so that confirmed the two vacancies.

In order to keep things smooth, the committee decided to throw the two offices open and give people thirty days to qualify. Before they called the committee, Senator Rankin Fite and Emmett Odom called to see if I was going to be in the Cullman office. They went by and picked up A. W. Todd, and came to Cullman, and we met with Governor Folsom and decided to support A. W. Todd for commissioner of agriculture. He had served in the senate during Gordon Persons' administration before then. There was no doubt that John Patterson, the son of Albert Patterson, would be the nominee for attorney general. I watched very carefully and made sure nobody qualified. Actually, nobody tried to qualify for commissioner of agriculture, but three very close friends of mine wanted to qualify for attorney general against John Patterson.

In the meantime, before this happened, all hell broke loose in Phenix City, Alabama. I was so afraid a run-off campaign would be jeopardized, since John Patterson was from Phenix City and his father was an attorney in Phenix City. Both of them lived there at that time. Phenix City was very, very corrupt at that time according to all the records. Governor Persons had sent in the National Guard to clean it out, and judging from the books I've read it was quite a job.

The three friends kept calling, and I told them, "I'm telling you not to run. I'm saying you better not run." It wasn't that I thought they wouldn't be a good attorney general as much as I was so afraid the Folsom's upcoming administration would get involved in the Phenix City situation. That would have a great effect on our ability to get the program through the legislature that Governor Folsom had explained to the people as he went through the state campaigning.

The very last day, I called A. W. Todd and John Patterson. A. W. Todd and I went to see Mr. Ben Ray and sat in his living room until twelve o'clock midnight. At 12:05 Ben Ray said, "I haven't had a telephone call or a telegram; the deadline for qualifying is over." A. W. Todd and I went back to the hotel and spent the night. When we got back to the hotel, John Patterson and Charlie Merriweather were in the room. Merriweather was to be John Patterson's administrative assistant, and would manage his campaign four years later when he ran a successful campaign for governor. Merriweather would also serve as John Patterson's finance director. Anyway, we had avoided the expense of another election, and Patterson was the nominee.

I went to John Patterson's room and told him I had just dared these folks to run, and he said, "I've been hearing about it, I know about it." I never heard anymore regarding it, and he worked really well with us until he decided to run for governor. Then he begin to find some way to make headlines and did pretty good.

Although I was instrumental in getting John Patterson elected attorney general without opposition—and he knew about it— he had his sights set on being governor of Alabama, and he had to make headlines some way or other. About a year after we had been in office and the administration's rating was high, we were doing so well, but Patterson had to try to get the spotlight. Along about that time Bill Drinkard decided to renovate Elks Lodge, a small lodge owned by the state. If I remember right, there were eleven small apartments at Elks River, west of Athens, Alabama. He got Jerry Gwin, a general contractor, who was also a road builder, to do the work. Of course, we took no bids on it. In fact, I did not know about it until Patterson filed a law suit and got an injunction in Judge Walter Jones' court. Judge Jones was not much in favor of the Folsom administration, so he issued an injunction to stop all state repairs without a bid. The only company he named was Glencoe Paving Company's asphalt plant, located in Gadsden, owned by Cecil Folsom, the Governor's brother, and Rex Edwards. But it included the Elks Lodge and affected every asphalt plant in Alabama. They were completely shut down. The order affected all asphalt re-surfacing of highways, but it did not affect the purchase of steel. It did alter the buying crushed stone, cement, liquid asphalt and similar products for repairs. Judge Jones ruled like Attorney General Patterson wanted him to.

We hired John Blue Hill, who was an attorney. Of course, to file the suit against Glencoe Paving Company and Bill Drinkard, he had to include the finance director, because all purchases came through the Finance Department. We hired John Blue Hill for $25,000, and I paid my one-third of it, and Jerry Gwin paid his one-third. Walter Jones ruled in favor of Attorney General Patterson, but we took it on to the Supreme Court, and they ruled in our favor—that Patterson couldn't shut down state road repairs. You had to have bids for building roads, but that was not building roads. Repairing roads was classified as maintenance, and you didn't have to have bids for maintenance. The Supreme Court ruled in our favor, and we were back in business.

Quite a few vendors had invoices, and I did not dare pay those, but I remember some of them — Couch Construction Company had $30,000; J. P. McKee in Dothan, Alabama had $38,000; Glencoe Paving Company was larger than either of those, though I don't remember the exact figure on it. The court usually ruled on Thursday afternoon, and I got the ruling immediately. The next morning, before these folks got out of bed, I called and told them to come get their checks. We had it cleared, and I wanted to get them out before any other action was taken.

It was right funny, when I called Rex Edwards to tell him about Cecil Folsom's check, he said, "You take my check down to the bank and cash it so I can have the cash when I get there." Frank Plummer, president of First National Bank in Montgomery, and I were pretty good friends at that time. We would have a drink occasionally in the afternoon, and we had some other business together. Anyway, I took the check to the bank, and he looked at me funny and asked, "You going to endorse it?"

"Yes, I got the authority by telephone," I answered.

"Okay," Frank said. He sent it down by one of the cashiers who brought a packet containing the money back up. By the time I got back to my office at the State Capitol the other vendors were waiting at my door for their checks, and we gave them their money.

One of the things I did, which I should not have had to do, was necessary because Drinkard had never paid his one-third of John Blue Hill's attorney fee. In 1959, after I had been home about a year, John Blue Hill called and said, "Fuller, I don't like to do this, but under the law, if I sue Bill Drinkard for his one-third of my fee, I'll have to sue you and Jerry Gwin."

I said, "Don't do that. I'll send you a check." I sent him a check for Drinkard's one-third of the attorney fee, which amounted to a little over $8000. I paid two-thirds of the fee, which was not right. But I did it because I did not want to be in the limelight anymore. I was back home doing pretty good in business. I had lots of friends all over the state and didn't want anything to happen that might have an adverse effect on the relationships I had with my many friends in the state of Alabama.

Afterwards, it was time to talk about the program and organization and decide who was going to be in the governor's cabinet. Murray Battle, Bill Drinkard, and Myra Hammond said they needed to be paid if they continued to work full time. We kept two of the original four girls working in the office and decided to pay each of the two girls $150 a month and pay Battle, Drinkard, and Hammond $500 each a month.

Governor Folsom wanted Myra Hammond's husband, Ralph Hammond, to come work because he had been the speech writer part of the time in the first administration and also executive secretary part of the time. Governor Folsom wanted him back as speech writer again. Hammond was working for American Red Cross in North Carolina making $600 a month and would not come for $500, so we paid him $600 a month. One person I failed to mention that worked in the campaign full time was O. H. Finney, who was executive secretary in the first administration, and had worked most all the time in the campaign. It was time to bring him in because he would be handling the correspondence for the governor. We had to pay him $500 a month. He was a bookkeeper in a clothing store in Albertville. I never took any salary or any money for my personal use. I used my own car, paid for my own gas, and took care of all my expenses all during the campaign.

People could not understand why we wanted to keep that many people on the payroll, and it wasn't easy to get money. I talked to O. H. Finney, and he called Governor Folsom in North Carolina where he was spending a week or two. He asked Governor Folsom to go ahead and appoint me finance director. On my birthday, June 22, Governor Folsom wrote a letter appointing me acting finance director. After that, I was able to raise money to take care of the above transition team. Of course, he was very careful to see that we didn't raise any more money than was needed, although you didn't have to account for it or report it.

It cost a lot more from the time he was nominated until we got down to Montgomery on January 15, 1955 than it did to run the campaign, because he needed money for traveling expenses. For instance, we went to the National Democrat Leadership meeting in New Orleans and stayed several days, and he vacationed at Gulf Shores quite often. And salaries amounted to much more, which I was able to handle easily enough. But we never accumulated much surplus, as it was his philosophy not to have any more money than you just had to have.

In the meantime, we began to think of who was going to fill certain cabinet offices. It was decided almost immediately that Bill Drinkard would be conservation director. Herman Nelson, who was the district one division engineer in the highway department located in Huntsville, and had been assistant highway director part time in the first administration, would be highway director. O. H. Finney would be executive secretary. Ralph Hammond would work in the governor's office to help write speeches and handle correspondence. Frank Long, who had been a Young Democrat, was still in law school. But he came every Sunday afternoon, and I gave him $500, which he would hand out among the young law students who would work for the campaign at the University of Alabama. So we had a big young folks vote. For several weeks, I gave Frank Long $500 from the campaign fund every week during the campaign. After that I gave him $100 or $150 a week, so he came down as legal adviser to the governor for a while. It was decided that Ed Pepper, who had been the governor's chauffeur and body guard in the first administration, would be my assistant as finance director. LaRue Horn from south Alabama, who was a very close personal friend of Governor Folsom's, would be the Revenue Commissioner. Pleas Looney, who had worked in Montgomery County, was going to have a cabinet post. Little by little it was put together who was going to be in various cabinet positions.

Two Baptist preachers, one, Reverend Swearington, a long time friend of Governor Folsom's, the other, Reverend Clay Kimbrell, my brother, would come by almost every Monday, and I gave each of them $200 or $300 from the campaign fund to go out and campaign for Folsom, and they divided it with other preachers to campaign. They felt very strongly about the Folsom program because it would help the people who needed help so badly. One of the first things I did after I became finance director was get Frank Lee, the prison commissioner, to appoint them as prison chaplains; one at Kilby and one at Speigner. It turned out really well, and to this day we still have chaplains at all the prisons, which we didn't have before.

I tried to come up with an indirect way to have influence in who was going to be in the cabinet. For instance, I wanted Frank Long to be legal adviser, and I said, "Governor, you got this made. You have four years and you want to skip four years and be governor again. I'll tell you what; we will pick out a young lawyer, someone with a statewide name, to be your legal adviser. What we will do is take a young lawyer like that; there is big talk of revising and rewriting the Code of Alabama, to do that."

Governor Folsom said, "Yes, we need to do that. We sure do. How about Frank Long? He worked a lot in the campaign."

"Yes, I kind of depended on him to handle the University, particularly in law school," I said.

"That will be good. We will get him," he said.

While Governor Folsom was at the horse races in Louisville, he developed a friendship with Happy Chandler, the governor of Kentucky. When we went to the national convention in 1956, one of our campaign leaders in Montgomery, Pitt Tyson Manor, nominated Governor Chandler for vice-president on the Democratic ticket. Governor Folsom picked Pitt Tyson Manor to be a member of his cabinet. Manor was a cabinet member in the first Folsom administration, as well as a cabinet member in Governor Bibb Graves' administration.

The State Centennial celebrations had started in many Alabama towns. Many Alabama men, including me, had grown a beard, which I kept until my friends started calling me "Gabby Hayes," so I shaved it off. Governor Folsom was invited to the centennial celebration in Opelika. He asked me to drive him. While we were driving down we got to talking: Billy Partlow had stood by me in the 1952 Convention, trying to help Kefauver get nominated for president and later vice president, so I wanted him to be adjutant general. We got to talking about the campaign again, and I said, "Of course, you know we talked about young lawyers to rewrite the Code, but it would be good to appoint to the Cabinet younger fellows with statewide names." Folsom had recognized Frank Long because his daddy had been a revenue commissioner under Governor Bibb Graves and was a Walker County native. He felt more close to people from north Alabama and from down in the Wire Grass section than to those from other parts of the state. We kept talking, and I said, "We need to find some statewide political names."

"Yes, you are right. You know Billy Partlow wants to be adjutant general," he said.

I said, "The Partlow name is known all over the state. Most everybody either knows somebody or has somebody at Bryce Hospital, and they know who Dr. Partlow is. That's a statewide name, and that's what I'm talking about."

"Billy put me off the train one time when we were going to a ball game or somewhere. I was just a buck private, and he was a Captain in the R.O.T.C. at the University. But that's been a long time ago. We'll just name him adjutant general," Folsom said.

One thing I got a good laugh about: on the way back from Opelika we stopped at a country grocery store and bought a carton of buttermilk. We had a bottle of Early Times in the car. The Governor poured a small paper cup full of buttermilk, put a little bourbon in it, and handed it to me. But he never offered me any more all the way back to Cullman. He drank the rest of the buttermilk and Early Times from the milk carton.

After August, it was time to look toward the November election; although, no one had qualified for governor or lieutenant governor or any major offices on the Republican ticket. In one or two counties there might have been someone running as a Republican for representative. In Winston County, one man was running for representative. on the Republican ticket, but he did not have a Democrat opponent, and none of the candidates running for statewide offices had an opponent.

It was before the upcoming election and time to talk with candidates who were nominated to serve in the legislature and get their views on how they felt about the governor's program. We had gotten our lesson up really well. The governor didn't meet with us much, but O. H. Finney and I would take minutes about what each legislator said and give them to him. Back then I had a remarkable memory. I could remember almost word for word what each legislator said. I had Rankin Fite to sit in on most meetings, and a few times — especially in Montgomery — I asked Lieutenant Governor Guy Hardwick to sit in when we interviewed senators. He was very helpful and very congenial about it. I would make notes, and Rankin would, also, as to who to appoint on the various committees. The legislature did not have as many committees as they have now. Of course, the press did not follow each individual legislator as close as they do now.

One day, John Drinkard came in and said, "Fuller, it's decided. George Hawkins will be the Speaker of the House."

I said, "No way." Who decided?" I asked.

"I just talked to them, and the labor leaders and all of us are for it," John Drinkard said.

"There is no way. George has statewide ambition. There is no way. Rankin Fite is going to be Speaker of the House. We will just call Governor Folsom," I said.

We were at the Redmont Hotel and we called him on a pay phone. I said, "Listen, George Hawkins has statewide ambition. Rankin Fite will be just as loyal and never look back and there has never been any doubt in my mind but what you were expecting Rankin to be Speaker."

"That's right, but I don't want any looking back," Folsom said.

After the call, I called Rankin Fite and told him what had happened, and I called George Hawkins. It was a bad incident, because George Hawkins never forgave us for it. He did run for governor later on and came in fourth. I think it was out of about five. If John Drinkard had stayed out of it and never brought it up, we would not have had that problem. George Hawkins stayed mad at me all the time, and the first thing he tried to do was to pass a bid law. But I wasn't ready for it to be passed then, and fortunately it never got out of the committee for a long time. Democracy!

Guy Hardwick came to me with a list of people he was going to appoint on committees and said, "I owe $18,000 on my campaign. I can get the Business Council to give me that money if I will let them name five people to be on three different committees. Or if you want to give it to me, I'll let you appoint them."

"Show me who they will ask for," I said. He just handed me the list. "Will it be easy for you to get the money from them?" I asked.

"Yes, they are ready to give it to me," he said.

"You know what, they are exactly who I would ask you to appoint," I said.

"That's wonderful! We will just take their money," he said. I never heard any more about it, but he really did the job. I'll have some interesting things to tell about my association with the Lieutenant Governor later.

The general election was the first Tuesday in November, and we had no problems with it. We felt good. The governor began to call all the legislators to Cullman to meet again, and I was sitting in on it. We had a perfect thing. After the November election, Charlie Pinkston, George Wallace, and I stayed in Montgomery a good bit, and we began to get bills drawn up. The folks in the Legislative Referencing Service were really good to work with us, and we put forth the program as Governor

Folsom presented it. Rankin would look over everything really well, and so would Lieutenant Governor Guy Hardwick. We explained to Governor Folsom in detail what the bills said and never had to change them. They went through the House with all ease, but had some opposition in the senate when they came up. Some of them we didn't get through exactly like we wanted, but we had a very successful first two years. Back then the legislature only met twice every four years, instead of meeting every year like they do now.

When we were making the final selection of the members of the committees in the house and the senate, Rankin Fite was in the old Exchange Hotel, and I was in the Jeff Davis. We met in Rankin's room, and we called Eddy Reed, who was a very strong supporter during the campaign. He was the executive secretary to the League of Municipalities and was well liked by all the members of the league, city council members, mayors, and members of the legislature. He was one of the finest story tellers Alabama has ever had. He had a pretty good expense account and would buy those 45 cent drinks at the Jeff Davis for the legislators quite often when they were in Montgomery. We called him, and he came. Guy Hardwick was in town, so we called him, and he came to Rankin's room. We sat around a big table after the November election and decided who would be the members on all the committees, and very few changes were ever made after that. I was the only member of Folsom's cabinet who really had anything to do with selecting who would serve on each committee.

EIGHTEEN

THE ADMINISTRATION CONTINUES

After the election in the first primary of May 1954, when the votes were tallied there was no question that Folsom led the tickets in sixty-two counties with a clear majority in forty-three counties. Several of the counties came in above seventy percent, two counties were up in the ninety percent range, and Folsom carried one county by ninety-three percent of the votes. It was certainly an unheard of event in Alabama. Hugh Sparrow, a political reporter for The Birmingham News, was very outspoken against Folsom's first administration. He wrote that never in the history of Alabama had so much power been granted to one incoming administration. That was true because it was obvious that most of the county officials, city mayors, councilmen, and small businesses had supported Folsom. It became more apparent when the time came to plan for the inauguration. A special planning committee was appointed; every county contacted the committee, either by writing or calling, and asked if it could have a float in the parade and wanted to know what it could do to help with the event.

Raising money for inauguration expenses was no problem.

Several lumber companies that donated lumber said, "Just tell us what you need. We will send it." There were contractors who sent their carpenters to Montgomery to build the stands. Everybody was ready to help, and it looked like the grandest time Alabama had ever known. Everybody was on the same track as far as progress was concerned and pushing Alabama ahead. It made me feel very proud.

Almost every county in the state sent a float for the parade. Fayette County sent a float down that was decorated with flowers on each side. The flowers were arranged to read: "Fayette County gives you Jamelle Folsom and Fuller Kimbrell." Governor Folsom and his administration had much to be proud of because the floats were so beautiful. The sun was shining, and there were so many floats, and high school bands marching in the parade, that it took more than three hours to pass the governor's stand.

The inaugural committee made big plans. Someone asked if it would be possible to have a big dance at the Montgomery Coliseum. I contacted a lumber man in Cullman. He came to Montgomery; we went to the coliseum and measured it. I had worked with Dee Hodo, the director of finance under Governor Person, who was always very nice to me and cooperated fully. I told Dee that I wanted to buy the materials and put in a floor in the Coliseum. He said, "You go ahead and buy it, and you can issue the purchase order after you become the director of finance." I bought the materials for the floor, and told them to lay it so it could be taken up after the dance. I remember that it cost $39,000, but it would probably cost $300,000 today.

It was one of the grandest inauguration parties that had ever been in Montgomery, surpassed only by descriptions of the party thrown for LaFayette when he visited Montgomery in 1825. The Corn Grinders, the band that played for Folsom during the campaign, led the music, and people came from all sections of Alabama to the party. Of course, there were special parties for the legislators and other elected officials, but this one was open to the public at no charge to anyone for anything. The soft drink companies set up free soft drink stands. Everybody was happy, friendly, sociable, and elated. "Big Jim" Folsom was the Governor! It was an unbelievable, successful celebration.

Work I had done before the governor's second term helped make a successful transition. Governor Person had set up a prison board meeting for the purpose of appointing the prison commissioners. There was one board member from each congressional district. Although Governor Person appointed the commissioners, some members would be replaced by each governor, staggered every two years. The chairman of the prison board called me and said, "Mr. Kimbrell, if there is somebody you want to be a prison commissioner let me know. The board appoints two. We are going to meet in December. If you have someone you want appointed, bring them to the meeting." I already had in mind Frank Lee, the sheriff of Greene County. Doc Martin, the representative of Greene County, who was in the legislature during the first administration had supported Folsom in the House in most incidents and could be depended on to be supportive, contacted me and told me Frank Lee wanted to be prison commissioner. I called Doc Martin and Frank Lee and asked them to meet me in Montgomery. We went before the prison board, and they appointed Frank Lee prison commissioner. Ralph Hammond, who was going to be the governor's speech writer and press secretary, had picked out Lawrence Seaborn, the former sheriff of Jackson County. The board didn't appoint him at that meeting, but at the very next meeting they appointed him.

Also at that meeting, Mr. J. M. McCollough, the chairman of the prison board told me that it was time to renew the contract to sell the cloth the prisoners produced. At Wetumpka they had a big textile plant, and they made a very nice print and other kinds of cloth. Under Alabama and federal law you could not sell anything made by prisoners except to other institutions. A lot of the other institutions also produced cloth. Although it wasn't quite time, Mr. Hodo, who was the finance director I would replace when Governor Folsom took office, said that I needed to go ahead and handle the contract. He said, "I don't want to fool with it. It is your job now. You go handle it."

At that time Alabama had a contract with Libya. The representatives from Libya had made arrangements to meet us in New York at the Waldorf Astoria Hotel. They got us train tickets, made our hotel reservations, and took care of all expenses.

I took Reba, Charlie Pinkston and his wife, two members of the prison board, J. M. McCollough, the chairman of the board, and his wife, Nell, as well as John Britton and his wife, Evelyn, who later became real close personal friends of mine and Reba's. I met with the two representatives from Libya. We reviewed and worked out the contract and ended up getting an increase of eight percent on the cloth. We all had a grand time. The people from Libya had never been to the South. They were really interested in our conversation and amused by our southern accent. I had developed into a pretty good story teller so I entertained them quite well with amusing stories. They laughed so hard one of the elderly ladies said, "Oh, Mr. Kimbrell, please don't tell another story, I can't stand it."

Everything, almost, was in favor of the incoming administration. We were invited to several events and meetings. For instance, the governor, Jamelle, Reba, and I were invited to New Orleans to a two-day National Democratic Executive Committee meeting. This was the meeting where the top members of the National Democrat Party would pick the next presidential candidate.

We went down to New Orleans, and stayed at the Roosevelt Hotel. There must have been at least a dozen in our party. It happened to be Reba's birthday, the 4th day of December, so I decided to give a dinner party in her honor in the main dining room of the Roosevelt hotel. I had invited three other couples, the governor and Jamelle, Ed Pepper and his wife, Ann, and Guy Hardwick and his wife, which would have made eight of us, but I kept adding to the guest list until we had sixteen for dinner that night; Governor Folsom and Jamelle, the Governor of Louisiana and his wife, U. S. Senator John Sparkman from Alabama and his wife, U. S. Senator and presidential candidate Estes Kefauver and his wife, Lieutenant Governor Guy Hardwick and his wife, the Lieutenant Governor of Louisiana and his wife, the Mayor of New Orleans and his wife, and Ed Pepper and his wife. I don't know why I don't have a picture of the group at the party, but the press did come in and they made a lot of pictures. The next day there was a write-up of the party in the New Orleans newspaper, The Times Picayune, but I didn't even save the newspaper.

One other thing of interest, Ward McFarland was the highway director during the first administration, and Governor Folsom wanted him to be the docks director in the second administration. It was getting close to inauguration time, and we were down at Gulf Shores. One of the high officials of Brown and Bigelow liked to be around Governor Folsom. When he came to Montgomery to visit, Governor Folsom would invite him to stay at the Mansion. The official was in Gulf Shores with us. We had gone to the Canal Cafe in Gulf Shores and were standing outside talking. It came up that Ward McFarland had just been indicted about income tax. Of course, he couldn't serve in the cabinet as long as he was under indictment, and the CEO from Brown and Bigelow asked, "Governor do you want him pardoned?"

"Yes, I want him to be docks director, but I can't appoint him while he is under indictment," Governor Folsom answered.

The man never said a word, but walked to a pay phone close by. We didn't know what he was going to do. We were just standing there talking. He wasn't gone long when he came back and said, "I think I'll have the White House on the phone in a little bit." The phone rang and he answered and talked a good long while over long distance, but we couldn't hear him. After he hung up the phone, he came over and said, "We'll have Ward

McFarland pardoned by morning."

I don't know whether he had talked to President Truman or one of his aides, but the next morning when we came to breakfast, he said, "Ward will have his pardon by telegram today." And he did. That's politics to the fullest extent. I say politics is a vicious thing, if handled right.

After time off for the holidays, the incoming legislature usually met on the first Tuesday in January for an organization session. Then the governor comes in the second Tuesday in January. The out going Lieutenant Governor, James Allen, Sr., was very nice to newly elected Lieutenant Governor Guy Hardwick. He took Hardwick's recommendations for committee appointees. We had already decided long ago that Rankin Fite would be Speaker of the House under this administration. In the organizational session they announced all the committee assignments. We were very careful because our main program was going to be—first roads, then old age pensions, followed by education and then industrial development—in that order. We knew the governor would call special sessions first for roads and then to consider old age pensions and probably would wait until the regular session for our education program and the industrial development program. Of course, he never forgot the rewriting of the Constitution.

It was really a feeling of success to see how anxiously the incoming legislators cooperated on the program, particularly in the house and more so in the senate. Of course, in the senate you always have a few that want to be heard. They were probably planning to run for statewide office later and wanted to get their name before the public as much as possible. We didn't have television coverage. We did have radio, but not in the house or the senate. I don't remember anyone being unhappy with their committee assignments. Governor Folsom had announced from the beginning that he would call a special session for roads and old age pensions— which I will get into later.

After the organizational session, he immediately called a special session for roads, and introduced the two-cents per gallon gasoline tax, which came with a $50 million bond issue. The two-cents gas tax passed in the House with little opposition. There was a little delay, but it passed without too much objection, and the bond issue had no objection. But when it got into the senate, it was more of a problem. One group felt one-cent was enough, but when it finally got down to the committee, they said they would vote for the $50 million bond issue and one-cent or a $25 million bond issue and two-cents.

I was handling the bill for the administration, so I asked the committee to recess and put it on hold until I could check and see what that would do to the program. I called the highway director, Herman Nelson, and asked him to meet in my office with me and the budget director, Jake Jordan. So he came over immediately. I laid out the story to them, and Jake said, "Give me a little while to go figure, and I'll come back." When he came back he said, "If you take the two-cents and $25 million bond issue over the four year period you will have $13 million more to spend for your road program than if you take the one-cent and the $50 million."

I said, "Let's go tell the governor about it." We went to Governor Folsom's office and laid it out, and Jake confirmed his statement.

The Governor said, "No, I'm going to have a $50 million bond issue. I'm not going to be happy with a $25 million bond issue."

I went back and worked a little more, but I saw almost immediately that we were not going to get the two-cents. Somewhere in my scrapbook is a picture taken of me in the middle of the committee, with me trying to sell them on the two-cents and $50 million. So I compromised and settled for the one-cent and $50 million bond issue.

In early 1950 my machinery and automobile business had expanded—I had opened the store in Aliceville and bought the John Deere tractor agency, including building and land, in Columbus, Mississippi, and built a very modern building to house my tractor, implement, and automobile business in Fayette. This being true, quite often I needed to borrow above the legal limits of the Citizen Bank in Fayette. Mr. Tom Lindsey cashier of the Citizens Bank in Fayette suggested that I go to Birmingham Trust National Bank (now South Trust) and talk to Mr. Boykin Haynes, the vice-president. I did, and made an application for a $60,000 loan. Mr. Haynes talked to Mr. Smith, the president of the bank, and they agreed to come and look at my business and property in Fayette. I told Mr. Smith and Mr. Haynes when they came to bring their fishing gear. When they came, I took them to Harkins' Lake, which had not been opened to the public for fishing yet. They had on their bankers' work clothes. It was surprising that Mr. Smith had a pretty little fishing box, arranged the neatest and most orderly of any I've ever seen, including a half-pint of bourbon, but Mr. Haynes only had his tackle. Me being a country boy, I had my ole cane fishing pole which I called a catfish pole, and a can of worms. We fished about two hours; Haynes caught three fish; Mr. Smith only caught one—I must have been fishing at the right place because with my ole catfish pole, I caught seventeen trout. I dressed the fish, and Reba fried the fish and hushpuppies, made slaw, and cooked green beans, hot biscuits, and made ice tea. I helped her, which left Haynes and Smith in the living room to visit while we were in the kitchen. After the meal, which we enjoyed very much, I walked them to the car. When they got in the car they said we are going to drive down to Millport. "Will you be in your office when we come back through?" they asked.

"Yes," I answered.

About two hours later they came by the office and said, "We have decided to approve your loan. Bring to the bank at Birmingham a description of your property and your financial statement, so we may prepare the papers for your loan."

After the election in November, Governor Folsom asked me one day, "Do you know anybody in the big banks in Birmingham?"

"Yes, I do. In the Birmingham Trust National," I said.

"I want to borrow $12,000 to buy a business in Cullman," he said. Then he asked, "Do you think you could arrange that loan for me?"

"I'll be happy to try," I told him.

I went to the bank to talk to Mr. Haynes and Mr. Smith. "You are supposed to be finance director?" Mr. Smith asked.

"Yes," I said.

"We will not ask you to endorse the note, but you would give friendly assistance in collecting, if necessary?" they asked.

My answer was, "Yes." The note was paid before I left Montgomery.

When it came time to sell the bonds, there was no question that we would use the Birmingham Trust National Bank, which was the first time bonds had been handled by a bank outside of Montgomery. I drove from Montgomery to the Birmingham bank, and Mr. Haynes called in John Shores, who was the trust officer for the bank. I told them I wanted them to be the fiscal agent for the $50 million bond issue approved by the legislature for the construction of highways. We would probably want to sell $15 million worth of bonds immediately. I asked them to suggest a bond attorney. They recommended Alfred Rose with the law firm White, Bradley, Arant, and Rose. They got him on the phone for me to talk to. I told him, "I'm in Mr. Haynes' office. He and John Shores have recommended you as an attorney for the $50 million bond issue that the Folsom administration plans to sell." He came to Montgomery, we worked out the details and agreed on a fee of $30,000 for the entire legal work. We walked around to Governor Folsom's office, at which time Mr. Rose went over the full details with the governor. Folsom agreed and gave his approval. It was understood that we planned to sell $15 million of the $50 million right away. Mr. Rose said he would go to work on it immediately.

In a short period of time Mr. Rose had the $15 million issue advertised for bids. When the bids were opened, the lowest bid was 2.73 percent. I accepted with Governor Folsom's approval. No state bonds have sold for a lower rate of interest or a lower attorney fee percentage-wise, since. Even so, the newspapers took us apart, they were very critical of this price, although it proved to be an excellent bargain. Unknown to me, and it was quite some time before I found it out, two people who were really close to the governor had worked out whereby they were paid a large fee, also.

Three weeks later, John Shores, the fiscal agent, called and said the bonds were ready to be signed at the Chemical Coin Bank on Wall Street in New York. Mr. Shores made plane reservations, and bought the tickets and also made hotel reservations at one of New York's finest hotels. John Shores, Randolph Lurie, Frank Barfield, the administrative assistant to the state treasurer, Sybil Poole, I and all our wives, except Barfield's, went to New York for me to sign the bonds.

A few things I learned that I did not know before was Mr. Rose had required a $300,000 certified check with the bid, and that $300,000 earned $22,000 in interest by the time I got the bonds signed. I signed all the bonds that made up the $15 million in one day. A man from the Chemical Coin Bank stood there and checked and corrected the signatures, and since they were negotiable at   that very moment, he handed them to two Brink's representatives, and they took them to the bank vault, which meant that $14,722,000 was immediately deposited to the State of Alabama.

That night, John Shores took us to a nice seafood restaurant

I will always remember upon the wall there was a sign that read, "The seafood you eat today, slept last night in Chesapeake Bay. Our host, Mr. Shores insisted on ordering for everybody. For appetizers, he ordered escargots and fried rattlesnake, and other ungodly delicacies. Needless to say, Reba and I, coming from Berry, Alabama, were ready to skip the hors d'oeuvres. Needless to say, the entrees and meal as a whole were really delicious, and we all enjoyed it very much.

Another first for me was when I went to the bank the next morning with John Shores, Frank Barfield, and Randolph Lurie to take delivery of the money. I didn't know that the bank loaned out their deposits over night. Mr. Shores and the representative of the bank argued quite some time about when the money would be good at the Birmingham Trust Bank. They finally agreed, splitting it, which amounted to $800 for each bank.

About eight months later Herman Nelson, the highway director called and said he needed about $10 million, which meant it was time to sell some more of the bond issue. I advertised and took bids, I don't remember the interest rate on this $10 million, but it was a little higher than the previous sale. John Shores notified me when the bonds were ready to sign in New York. I went to the governor's office and told him I planned to go to New York to sign the bonds, and he said, "Tell General Partlow to get the National Guard plane ready, (which was a DC-3 World War II plane), and I plan to go with you."

By the time we were ready to leave for New York, the crowd had grown to include Bill Drinkard; Senator Allen from Cullman County; Melvin Dawkins, the ABC administrator; Murray Battle,

Folsom's legal adviser at that time; and Roy Drinkard, Bill's brother. Also, Elbert Ponder met us in New York at the Taft Hotel, where John Shores had made our reservations. We had just gotten in the room, which was a two-bedroom suite for the governor and me, when the crowd started assembling in our suite. At that time, the beverage of choice was something new to me—they had ordered up a case of sweet milk, containing twelve quarts, along with several quarts of brandy. They would take a six ounce hotel glass and fill it with milk, pour the milk out and refill the glass with brandy and pour it into the carton of milk, shake it, and drink it through a straw. After a little while, the governor said, "Fuller, why don't you go down to the dining room and make arrangements for us to have dinner?" In the meantime everyone said they would take a steak. When I got back to the suite, Melvin Dawkins had called the Schenley representative, and he was in the room. He found out I had made reservations for our party at the hotel dining room, and he said, "No, we are going to my restaurant." So I called and canceled the reservations I had made in the dining room. By that time, most everyone in the crowd was really enjoying the sweet milk mixture. We all caught a street car and headed for the restaurant, at least thirty minutes away. When we walked in, the restaurant manager, a beautiful lady about twenty-five years old, was playing the piano, and all the crowd, feeling the full energy from the sweet milk, made for the piano. Some sang bass, some sang tenor, some loud, some not so loud, and some didn't sing. Pretty soon our host saw that he may have made a mistake, so he ordered each one of us a steak and got us started eating right away, and of course served everyone Schenleys.

Elbert Ponder and I were sitting at the same table, and he and I had only about one drink. He asked me, "Fuller how about you and me getting a cab and going back to the hotel?"

"I'm ready," I said.

We returned to the hotel and looked around in the little shops and then went to our rooms, and I went to bed.

Some of the others went to a stage show, but the governor and Murray Battle rode the street car all night.

The next morning I went to Wall Street and had breakfast at the Chemical Coin Bank with John Shores. Elbert Ponder went with me. After breakfast, we went up and I began signing the bonds. I signed all the $10 million issue that day. Ponder met me back at the bank and he and I went shopping at a wholesale business where he bought a fur stole for one of his customers, and I bought a windbreaker. Incidentally, he and his brother owned the building where Folsom's campaign headquarters were on the second floor, and operated Ponders Department Store on the first floor.

We never heard from the rest of our group until about 4:00 the next morning. The governor had left word for the house detective to wake everyone at an early hour so we could get to the airport ahead of the morning rush traffic. The first sound I heard was a loud noise and confusion, the house detective was trying to quiet everyone, some of whom had just gotten into bed. Part of the noise was Murray Battle trying to get Bill Drinkard awake enough to get up, and Murray had poured a pitcher of ice water on him.

When everybody was dressed, we decided to go across a six-lane wide street to a small all-night cafe for breakfast. A funny thing was, on the way State Senator Allen from Cullman, had a quart of the milk mixture in his right hand, and was leading the Governor with his left hand. He held the carton of milk up over his head and stopped traffic and said, "Stop, wait right there, let the Governor of Alabama pass."

When I walked into the restaurant, I heard a terrible noise, and here comes the cook with a meat cleaver in his hand chasing Roy Drinkard and loudly saying, "I don't let anybody come in my kitchen." I ran up and stopped him and told him I would take care of it, while Roy went around the bar and right back into the kitchen on the other side. Of course the noise started all over again. But Drinkard came on out and had his breakfast. From then on everything was peaceful.

After breakfast, we checked out of the hotel, went to the airport, and took off immediately in the Gully Jumper. We had to fuel the plane in Richmond, Virginia. Needless to say, that many people with their luggage was a pretty good load for the old DC-3, and I was really scared when we barely cleared the pine trees at the end of runway on take off. The rest of the flight from there to Montgomery went well, but believe you me, I was really happy get home to Reba and Cynthia that night.

Another thing that came up during the session that was talked about some during the campaign was a toll road. I had a resolution drawn setting up a toll road committee. The resolution gave the committee authority to go to Oklahoma and study its toll road, because we felt Oklahoma's situation was more similar to Alabama's than the Florida toll road which was in existence at that time. I had a bill drawn up creating the toll road authority in Alabama, called the Turnpike Authority, and presented it to the legislature. It passed. The Authority is still in use today, and they have used it some. Incidentally, we do not have any toll roads in Alabama, but there was a toll bridge opened November 1, 1998 across the Warrior river south of the city of Tuscaloosa, and two toll bridges in Montgomery earlier.

I also got a resolution passed giving me the authority to hire a consultant to work with the highway director to do a feasibility test between the Tennessee line and Montgomery and from Montgomery to Mobile. But it turned out that after the test the only road in Alabama that would support a bond issue at that time was the highway from Athens to Huntsville. This being true, since roads were about the only thing other than local bills that were in the call for this special session, the legislature adjourned with the understanding that the governor would call them back immediately to consider old age pensions.

Indeed, he called them back asking them to appropriate extra money for old age pensions, known before then as welfare. The governor had included in the call, of course, local bills and local bills with general application. The session only lasted about ten legislative days, but it was one of the most interesting and colorful special sessions I've ever seen in my whole political career.

A special joint hearing of the house and senate was called for Governor Folsom's program concerning the old age pension, and was advertised all over Alabama inviting concerned people to come to the hearing. People came from all over Alabama. They came in buggies and on horseback. School bus loads of old folks came. It was the biggest crowd I've ever seen at a public hearing about legislation in Montgomery. It lasted all day. People kept coming. Of course, the old folks thought Jim Folsom was their governor, and they felt right at home around him because he was that kind of person, down-to-earth with everybody. I remember, I had gone to the governor's office, which was right around the hall from my office. When I was leaving the governor's office, I met this elderly fellow, all stooped over with a walking stick. He stopped me and asked, "Mister, can you tell me where Big Jim's room is?" I took him into the governor's office. It was just amazing the impression it made on the legislators. They did the maximum for the governor's program as far as the old age pension was concerned. Even the opposition in the legislature didn't fight. I don't remember any figures, but I know that we were able to more than double their pension. Later during the four year term, as the economy got better and the revenue started coming in, I was able to raise the pension again. I wish I could remember the numbers, but I'm sure that we went from about seven dollars a month, originally, up to $30 something a month. It does not compare to what they get now, but it was certainly a lot more than they had ever expected before.

As I stated before, it was decided from the beginning that we would wait for the regular session to try to legislate the governor's education program. With the second special session over, the governor's office was busy talking to his leaders and campaign managers, and appointing people to fill the various vacancies, such as the Board of Registrars, the Milk Board, and the vacancies which may have occurred in county and city offices. As I remember, all total there were about 156 different appointments, such as members of committees and boards, for the governor to fill. The governor was really good about talking to the people who made his campaign such a success. Being a campaign manager, I sat in on almost all of the meetings when he made his appointments to the various committees and boards.

The regular session in May came quickly. We were into it right away. I had the budget, which was worked on in public hearings and hearings before the legislative committees on all the departments, including education, agriculture, and judiciary, which were all part of the finance director's responsibility. Also, the finance director had to schedule the committee hearings and see that each department had its requests for its appropriations ready to present to the budget committee and respective committees. All of this had to be put together. After hearings before the committees, it was the finance director's and budget officer's duty to boil it all down, because almost every department asked for twice as much as they expected to get. We got all the figures and information ready by the time the legislature was ready for it.

We didn't have all that much trouble with the budget. We got it passed almost exactly as we hoped to pass it. I remember that the senate had added so much to the general fund budget that the senate had added so much to it, and—since the house did not agree to it, and we did not try to get them to—we had to call for a confrere committee. So I got Speaker Rankin Fite and Lieutenant Governor Guy Hardwick to appoint the members of the confrere committee I had selected, and they only appointed one member of the opposition. When we got into the confrere committee meeting back in a side room, I just took my budget exactly as I had originally given to the House without changing a word and said, "This is the way we want it."

The opposition on the committee was Senator Albert Boutwell from Jefferson County, and he asked, "What is that Fuller?"

I said, "That's exactly what I gave to the house the day it was introduced." He sputtered and stuttered around an awful lot, and I said, "Well, this is what we want. We cannot live with the things the senate added to it and the house added to it, and it is so that I don't think it will work. And the budget officer says it won't. We won't have enough money to pay for it, and I don't want be in proration later."

Senator Broughton Lamberth was on the committee and he said, "Albert, just go on and shut up. We have five votes here for it. Go on and vote for it."

Albert said, "Well, I just can't agree to it. I'm going to talk against it." When it got over to the senate, he did talk against it, but nobody listened to him. So we passed it. That's the only time I've ever known that a budget was passed exactly as it was recommended to the legislature. With one exception — I had put in it a $500,000 conditional appropriation for the old age pension. When the budget director, Jake Jordan, brought me the bill, he had failed to include this, and I didn't know it until the next day, which was too late to attach it to another bill and get it passed. I called Governor Folsom and told him about it and he asked, "Aren't you happy with the amount you have?"

"Yes, but I had hoped for a little something special for the part of the program you stressed so strongly in your campaign," I said.

About an hour later, the governor called me from the mansion and said, "Senator, if you want to fire Jake Jordan, I'll back you up."

I thought about it and realized to do so would create a lot of dissension that we did not need.

One time Dr. Austin Meadows, the state superintendent of education, was in the governor's office wanting to declare proration. He kept making statements to the press about proration. Finally I told him to quit barking about it, we were not going to have proration. I knew it was very close, so since the last day of September was on Saturday, I asked Frank Barfield, the administrative assistant to Sybil Poole, the state treasurer, to pick up the mail and open it so it would go in September's increase. It was close. We had $226 extra.

During Governor Wallace's first administration, the last day of the legislative session they were having the same problem as we did passing the budget. I had Governor Wallace's private line number, so I called him from home in Fayette, and told him what I had done in working with the confrere committee. He said, "I wish you had been here, but it is too late now. I'll just have to call a special session to pass the budget."

During the regular session we had numerous bills passed.

The senate passed a resolution asking that the Auburn-Alabama football game be televised. When I was in the senate during the first Folsom Administration, a resolution was introduced — and somebody wanted to make the resolution binding — that Auburn and Alabama Universities' appropriation would not become effective until they agreed to play football again. They had not played each other for years. They didn't make it quite that binding, but they did pass a resolution resolving that Auburn and Alabama start playing each other again, and it became effective a year or two later.

They passed a bill through the legislature to appoint a building commission to set up a corporation to build the State Office Building, now known as the James E. Folsom Building. Also they passed a resolution that Fort Morgan would be renovated and made an historical site.

In setting up the old age pension, we got the legislature to create the Alabama Department of Pensions and Securities, and its director was appointed to the cabinet and drew the same salary the other cabinet members received at that time, which was $10,000. The governor's salary was only $12,000. Gordon Person sent me a note by one of his friends asking that I increase the governor's salary, because he was planning to run again. So I got the legislature to raise the salary from $12,000 a year to $25,000 a year. Governor Person did run again, but his campaign didn't turn out to be successful. John Patterson, who was then the attorney general, followed Folsom into office.

NINETEEN

ADMINISTRATION'S ACCOMPLISHMENTS

I n order to show the results of the legislature's first session, as I've discussed already, we met and the lieutenant governor announced the committees assignments, and Rankin Fite was selected Speaker of the House.

Governor Folsom's administration was made up of strong personalities and his leaders were willing to help put his platform into action. For instance, the very first thing we were concerned with was the Constitutional Convention. In his first administration, every time the legislature met—all special sessions and regular sessions—Folsom's leaders introduced a resolution calling for a Constitutional Convention. It never got out of committee in his second administration, much to the sorrow now of the people who stopped it then.

Number two was his mailbox roads, which Folsom really did an outstanding job promoting in his first administration. More than 100 miles were paved, and the majority were in rural sections, which was just what he called for—mailbox roads. But in his second administration, he called a special session the very first thing after the organizational session for the purpose of trying to pass a $50 million bond issue, to be paid for by a gasoline tax. We had no problem passing it in the house, but did have problems in the senate. I think I have explained about the problems in the senate already.

Number three was the old age pension; which he had promised to try to arrange for every person sixty-five years or older to have a pension of fifty dollars or more a month. We didn't quite accomplish that, but it was in the upper thirty dollars a month, which was more than four times what it was when he took office in his first administration in 1947.

Number four in his platform was health and welfare. In his first administration he had set out to build a hospital in every county under the Hill-Burton Act. He didn't quite accomplish it, but that was part of his platform and something we in the administration worked hard to get done in his second administration. We didn't get one in every county, but in almost every county. In the welfare department, we worked it out for people who were not able to pay their doctor bills to have free testing for tuberculosis and various other diseases that were troubling the South at that time.

To improve the hospitals and Mental Health Department was another top priority. As I remember, I increased the budget that I recommended to the legislature. I raised that from $3.50 to $7.50 per day for every person in a mental health facility, including Mt. Vernon, which at that time was a 100 percent black.

During the first administration, Governor Folsom had built and repaired many school buildings, which were just as good for the blacks as they were for the whites. It was in his speeches everywhere he went that he would not force the blacks to go to school with the whites, but would build equal facilities for them. And he repeated it in every speech in every county in the state. One of the things about education was—at that time the governor and Mrs. Folsom had six children—as he said, "Now when it comes to my educational program, I have six young'uns and the Lord willing, I'll have six more." That would bring the house down, but that was his way of saying everybody should have an equal opportunity for a better education.

In the second administration we appropriated additional money for school buildings. Of course, I don't think we had a bond issue, but we did more than double the educational appropriation. By comparison though, as I remember at that time the legislature met every two years and a duty of the legislature was to pass the budgets for each of two years. I recommended to the legislature and they passed the educational budget for the last two years—1958 and 1959. It was for $196 million and that included universities, four-year colleges, and the two-year colleges. This was before we had the big two-year college program. The second biennium the education budget was $212 million, a great improvement, but much less than the modern-day $4 billion educational program. I don't remember the exact figure, but it more than doubled the teachers' salaries and increased the qualifications and requirements for teachers. I think one of the things we required was that teachers have a college education before they could teach in high school. Another thing, most importantly, was to encourage hiring of better personnel and more qualified teachers, to strengthen the retirement system, and also to give tenure. Back then, politics in schools was stronger, and it was not uncommon for a teacher to get crossed up with the superintendent of education or the county board of education and get fired for political reasons. It was our goal to establish a tenure system so teachers were kept because they were qualified and not because of their political beliefs.

Labor was another plank in the platform. Governor Folsom and his administration had an extremely good relationship with labor, because one of his strongest votes came from small farmers and laborers throughout Alabama, from Mobile to Muscle Shoals. Mobile particularly and the Tri-Cities were very strong for him, also Etowah and Walker Counties. In Jefferson County, labor was not quite as strong, because back then, the high minority population in Jefferson County had as much effect on the outcome of the election as anything. At that time the blacks would work cheaper than the whites and that meant that the whites didn't exactly cooperate with the overall labor requirements because of that. But Governor Folsom's idea was to improve those situations as much as possible, and he did a lot to improve them. He appointed labor leaders who would work to promote effective labor policies.

The Governor was very sympathetic to veterans of military service. As I remember, we changed it so that veterans could get an automobile tag and license for one dollar. We passed the law that any veteran who wanted to go into business could have a favorable business license, and in some instances it was free or cost a dollar.

Governor Folsom, having been raised in a small farming area, was most anxious to create favorable situations for small farmers and for farmers in general. Luckily, we had A. W. Todd as commissioner of agriculture, and he understood this as well as any member of Folsom's administration. In fact, this was the beginning of the poultry industry in Alabama, and by the end of that time, if I remember right, Alabama was number three in the nation in the broiler production and ranked high in egg production.

Our administration—working with A. W. Todd—made it possible for us to promote farmers' markets. We built a lot of farmers' markets, particularly in Birmingham, and added a big addition to the coliseum. We built a farmers' market adjoining the Cow Coliseum in Montgomery, which is still used very, very much. In fact, it is used now as a wholesale market. Farmers with watermelons and other produce bring it in by the truckloads to sell to small stores. Sometimes before watermelons get to the consumers' table they have changed vendors two or three times from the field. The old railroad car shops in Birmingham were changed over to what is probably the biggest farmers' market in the South today. Any kind of produce can be found there. They handle peaches from Chilton County, Dothan, and even from the state of Georgia. Peaches are brought in on large trucks to be divided, loaded into small pickup trucks, and transferred to the various markets in Alabama. The big, previously abandoned, railroad car shop on the left of Finley Avenue as you go into Birmingham is now a hugh farmers' market.

As stated earlier, one of the planks in the platform I had insisted on was balancing industry and agriculture as did our neighboring state, Mississippi. This had just begun to come into its own. I think research will show that over a billion dollars of new industry came into Alabama during that four years as a result of industrial development.

I asked the Legislative Reference Service to draw up a bill to create the Industrial Development Board. I got Representative Emmett Odom from Franklin County to introduce it. It passed exactly as I had it drawn up all the way through. The Board was set up with a board member from each congressional district, which made it work well statewide, and we hired a person to represent Alabama in Washington for a while. The Board is still in existence today under another name, Alabama Development Office (ADO). Although the Board has changed some, it is much more effective than it was in the beginning, having expanded and improved with age. This turned out to be a wonderful program, and one of the greatest departments in Alabama.

One of the first new industries to come to Alabama was the 3M Plant at Guin. Among its products are scotch tape and reflective road striping paint. It cost several million dollars, I don't remember the figure, but it really put a feather in the Folsom's administration's cap. Senator Rankin Fite was Speaker of the House then, and it was located in his district, twenty miles south of his hometown, and thirty miles north of my hometown. The president of Minnesota Mining and Manufacturing Company came down for the dedication. I was there with Senator Fite, who was the principal speaker. It was a great day for Alabama. The 3M company has expanded several times through the years and is still one of the finest industries that has come to Alabama. After they came to Guin, they built a plant in

Monroeville, Alabama and a huge plant in Decatur, Alabama. All the plants are successfully operating today. It just goes to show that a little seed planted can grow and develop into something really worthwhile for the whole state.

Some of the ADO's most recent accomplishments have been to land the Mercedes plant in Tuscaloosa, the Tuscaloosa Steel plant, the big steel plant in Decatur, the Boeing Engine Plant in Huntsville, the Honda Plant in Lincoln, and many others. Each governor since 1955 has bragged about breaking the record for getting industries to locate in Alabama. The ADO in the last few years has created thousands of high-paying jobs and added over a billion dollars a year to the Alabama economy. Tuscaloosa and Jefferson Counties have really received a great deal of industrial benefits due to the fact that Mercedes and Honda wanted their suppliers and satellite plants to be located within one hour of the main plants. When the Honda plant starts operating, and with the proposed expansion of the Mercedes plant, the state of Alabama will be receiving enormous benefits.

Governor Folsom's administration was outstanding for its cooperation with local government — cities and counties. As I've said earlier, when I first accepted the responsibility of managing his campaign in north Alabama, I had really made outstanding friendships and connections with the mayors, city councilmen, commissioners, judges, and small bankers. I told them that we would set up a platform for roads, bridges, schools, welfare, education, and agriculture. The leaders were well-pleased with what we told them. This really was proof to them that the Folsom administration was determined to go forward with the program put forth in his first administration.

In the first administration, Folsom had promoted and developed the state docks by issuing $4 million of revenue bonds to improve the docks. Folsom sent Ward McFarland, who was the former highway director in his first administration and an outstanding business man as well as professional financier, to Mobile as the state docks director. The state docks did extra well at that time. The coal industry was just beginning to progress, and McFarland came up with the idea of building coal loading docks in Mobile, which have been used very extensively in the last 10 years. In the second administration we also issued a $10 million bond issue to build inland docks in places such as Birmingham Port, Decatur, Demopolis, Eufaula, Florence, Huntsville, Phenix City, and Tuscaloosa.

Conservation was the last thing in the platform. Working with the Auburn Extension Service, we improved forests and promoted terracing, which improved the land an almost untold amount during those last four years. We had a much better relationship with the Extension Service in the second administration than we did in the first.

One thing of concern was a conservation program that has touched more people in Alabama by now than anything we did the entire four years. Bill Drinkard, the conservation director, came to me one day and said, "Fuller, if you can transfer $25,000 to the Conservation Department, I can get $175,000 federal money to match, and we can use it to distribute deer and turkey throughout the state. I think the $200,000 would let us do a fairly good job of distributing deer and turkey all over Alabama, possibly every county in Alabama. You are probably aware that there only five counties in Alabama that have deer and maybe less that have wild turkeys. We will have to use a little of the money to start oyster beds in Gulf Shores, Orange Beach, and that area, but the rest can be used to stock deer and turkey."

I told him to give me a few minutes, and I called Jake Jordan, the Budget Officer, to come down. I had Bill tell him the same story he told me. I asked, "Jake, do we have $25,000 we can transfer to the Conservation Department, and if so, can I transfer it?"

"I know you can transfer it, but let me see where you can take the money from," Jake said. He was gone a few minutes, then returned and said, "Yes, we have a place we can get $25,000 that won't disturb the budget in any way."

"What do I have to do to transfer it?" I asked.

"I'll fix the papers right now, and you sign your name," Jordan said.

As I said earlier, I sold Sumter Farm and Stock Company in Sumter County most of its farm machinery for that big plantation and had developed a good relationship with Mr. Ted Bish, who was the farm manager at that time. Every year around the first of the year, Mr. Bish invited me and several neighbors down for a hunt and barbecue. The last time I went deer hunting I remember him telling me he had too many does and needed to thin them out. I told Bill I could get a hold of Mr. Bish, and they might even redistribute the deer for him. Bill told me to do it. I called Mr. Bish, and he said he would work with Bill, and if Mr. Drinkard would send one of his men over there to talk about it and see what the situation was they would work with him. Mr. Bish furnished a lot of the deer. I don't know where Drinkard got other deer to go around over the state, but he did stock some in almost every county. One thing I said was, "Bill, I'm doing this now, but I want to be sure you stock some deer in between Fayette and Tuscaloosa, south of Berry, and between Berry and Carbon Hill."

"Don't worry, I'll take care of your area good enough," Bill said. It is amazing now, the number of deer in this area. One fellow told me last week the recommended number was fourteen does to each buck, but now the count is twenty-two does to each buck. Next season they plan to have open season on does for at least thirty days to get the population more balanced. That one act has given as much or more pleasure to the hunters of Alabama than anything that has happened in sometime.

I didn't say anything about the turkey, but I go from Tuscaloosa to Fayette quite often, and almost every time I make the trip I see some turkeys. This very morning coming to Fayette, I saw three out in a field. I was driving about sixty-five miles per hour and could not tell if they were gobblers or hens, but they were not too far away. With a high powered rifle I could have shot them. There has been just as much pleasure for the turkey hunters out of this act as there has been for deer hunters. The only thing is, there are many more deer and deer hunters than turkey hunters, because you have to get up too early to hunt turkeys.

One of the things I thought of and discussed with Governor

Folsom and the highway director was the need for more asphalt plants stationed around various places in Alabama. If you haul hot asphalt too far it cools down and it is harder to make a good smooth surface than it is if you roll it while it is hot. I picked out several supporters and people sympathetic to the administration and Folsom's program, particularly in districts where the legislators had been supportive of the programs we were trying to put in force. Since this was before the bid law, in Jackson County I picked J. P. McKee and told him if he would buy an asphalt plant, I would give him enough business to pay for it. Which I did. In Dothan, where we had legislators that were favorable, I told Quinn Flowers of Couch Construction Company if they would buy an asphalt plant, I would give them enough business to pay for it.

Of course, one of the things that got in the limelight was that Rex Edwards went in with Cecil Folsom, the Governor's brother, and bought an asphalt plant in Gadsden. There was not an asphalt plant in Gadsden, so we went ahead and gave them enough business to pay for it. And then there was Blue and Roberts in Tuscumbia. Roberts was a good friend of mine, and I told him the same thing. I don't remember, but we had about two plants in Jefferson County. One was Warren Brothers, which later became APEC. They had an asphalt plant there and one in Tuscaloosa. Because we did not have a bid law, I could carry through on my promises. So I was going right along and buying asphalt and making people happy in carrying out our platform and keeping our promise to the people of Alabama in building roads. We were building better roads than had ever been built in Alabama before. Of course, the political opposition just could not stand the praise, compliments, and notoriety we were gaining by carrying out the promises Governor Folsom made when he spoke in most of the counties in Alabama.

Another thing we did: I came up with an idea when the contractors who were building bridges could not get steel. I went to Herman Nelson, the highway director, and told him if he would give me a list — if there is such a thing — of the standard length and size of steel to go in bridges and bridge trusses, I would go and talk to U. S. Steel in Birmingham, since the Highway Department had some money just laying in the bank. As director of finance, those figures were available to me. I would go and see if I could buy the steel we needed to put in the Highway Department inventory, some in Birmingham, some in Huntsville, some in Mobile, and some in Montgomery. Then, we would sell it to the contractors and take their money and put the steel back. That way they wouldn't have to wait three to four months to get steel in order to build a bridge. Up until that time they would just pour the abutment and wait for steel before they could make the trusses or piling to build the bridges.

I went to Birmingham and had lunch with Art Weable, who was the President of U. S. Steel in Birmingham at that time, and who was later moved up to the main office in Pittsburgh as president. We had lunch in his suite at the U.S. Steel office, and I told him about it my idea. He said, "Well, we are not promising delivery for less than three months." I told him the story, and he called in Mr. White, the sales manager, and told him the story.

"We are not trying to do anything except move Alabama forward as fast as we possibly can, and I've come up with this idea and the highway director has approved it. The governor knows about it," I said.

"Give me a little time," Mr. Weable said. Mr. Weable had lunch served to us as we waited. Mr. White came back in about twenty minutes and said, "Mr. Weable we can deliver about half of that in less than thirty days. We can deliver the other half in ninety days."

Mr. Weable said, "You go back and write a purchase order for the steel you want, and we will start delivering immediately. Maybe we can even move that thirty days up a little bit from what Mr. White whispered in my ear while you weren't looking."

I went back and called the Bethlehem Steel Company in Baltimore, Maryland, which was the only other company in the United States that produced that kind of steel, and they would not even quote me a price. That turned out to be good because I used it later on. I took Mr. Weable the purchase order, and it really moved up the bridge building a lot in Alabama.

After John Patterson brought the suit against us, the opposition was pleased because it slowed down the administration's program. It gave the opposition a lot of steam in the legislature in trying to get a bid law passed, which we still did not have. Of course, we had the majority so far, and I had done well by all the supporters and most of the people I felt were helpful in getting Governor Folsom elected and getting his program into effect. It was one of the finest programs any governor had put forth and came as near, or more so, to being carried out and completed than that of any governor in my lifetime, and I have followed politics pretty closely.

One bill concerning the bid law was introduced by Senator Joe Calvin of Morgan County, who was a very smart senator and very likeable. He never ran for re-election. I think he did run for lieutenant governor, but he got very little support statewide. Anyway, he had several people join with him, and in the bill he introduced to take all the power away from the Finance Department and put some of the power in the Revenue Department, and Examiners of Public Accounts Department. Several people in the cabinet had a voice in approving the purchases.

I went before the committee and thought I had the Calvin Bill killed by a majority vote. I told them that I was not going to be finance director always, and Governor Folsom was not going to be governor always. Some of their friends might be governor sometimes, and they would look at it a little differently. They took a vote on it, and it lacked one vote having enough to bring it out. I left, and somehow they got it up again and brought it out by voice vote, but I arranged for it not to be brought up again in the senate. Lieutenant Governor Hardwick and I were good friends, not that he would do anything unethical. He did things that were fair, and he knew the bill was not good for Alabama.

Another Bid Bill was introduced in the house by Representative Charles McKay of Talladega County. He ran later for attorney general, but did not get too many votes. His bill was similar to the bill that Senator Joe Calvin had introduced, but was changed around somehow. I arranged so it would not be brought up in the house. I figured the thing was getting pretty hot, so I had the Legislative Reference Service draw up a bill and gave it to Emmett Odom, a friend of the administration, as well as mine, and a good friend of Speaker Fite's. I got Joe Dawkins, Emmett Odom, and Rankin together, and we went over it. They liked it and approved it. I got Emmett Odom to introduce it and had Rankin to put it in the committee that I wanted it put in. I don't remember the committee. Anyway, I went before the committee and asked them to approve it. Then Rankin and I talked about it, and he put it on the calendar so it could be handled according to his wishes, which would be my wishes. We let it lay there for several legislative days.

About two and a half or three years after Folsom had been in office, one morning at five o'clock, just as I was getting out of bed, Governor Folsom called and asked, "Fuller, didn't I promise on the campaign stump I would pass a bid bill?"

"Governor, maybe you did. I don't remember. I wasn't at all your meetings," I said.

"I want it passed and you are not letting it pass," he said.

"Governor, do you really want it?" I asked.

"Yes, I want it," Folsom answered.

"Do you want it passed today?" I asked.

"Yes," he answered.

"You come to the house after a little while, and we will pass it today," I said.

"You promise?" He asked.

"Yes. We will pass it in the house today," I said.

Of course, Senator Fite and Emmett Odom and three or four others would usually come to my office first on legislative days and we would talk about what we wanted to do and what we wanted to bring up that day, and it was working most effectively. So when they came in that morning, I told Rankin without the other people hearing it what the governor had said about passing the bid bill. I told him that I had promised to get it passed. Rankin looked at me and asked, "Do you mean it?"

"I made a promise," I replied.

"We'll bring it up the minute after the prayer," Rankin said. He didn't bring it up quite that fast. We followed the rules of the journal, but we brought it up out of order before any other bill, including local bills, and passed it. Governor Folsom had come to the house to watch it. I was sitting with the Rankin at that time, and Folsom walked up to us and said, "You damn boys know how to work democracy, don't you."

The Bid Bill went right on over to the senate. There were a few senators trying to take the power away from the finance director. Of course, in the committee they tried to amend it, and Joe Calvin had another shot at it. In the house, George Hawkins tried to amend it and take the power of the finance director out of it. Well, I wasn't going to be finance director always, certainly not but about another year and a half, and he was not able to get any kind of amendments on it. I had gotten Lieutenant Governor Hardwick to put it in another committee so those folks would not have a shot at it. When it got on the floor, they kept trying to amend it, but were never able to because I got Lieutenant Governor Hardwick and some of the people in the senate favorable to the administration together, and we were able to defeat all the amendments. It passed just as I had asked the Legislative Reference Service to draft it, and Emmett Odom had introduced it in the house. Governor Folsom signed the Bid Bill into law, which fulfilled his campaign promise.

The governor, seeing what we had done in the house about the Bid Law, felt like it was time for us to try for reapportionment. Of course, Speaker Rankin Fite and I knew we did not have the votes to pass the reapportionment bills that were on the calendar. The leadership was discussing it while other members of the administration were trying to get some extra votes. The opposition was pushing to bring it up for a vote, but Speaker Fite knew it would fail. This was on a Thursday when the legislature usually adjourned for the weekend. One of the supporters made a motion to recess until the following Tuesday. Speaker Fite knew that the opposition would not support the motion, because they felt sure they could kill the bill. With a voice vote, he declared the ayes have it, gaveled the recess motion, and got up and left the speaker's stand. He knew immediately he had made a bad mistake.

He came to my office very much disturbed, and said, "I made a bad mistake. I adjourned the house by the voice vote motion. "The problem is that the house did not accept the adjournment which I had announced. They are still in the house now reorganizing and have elected Paul Meeks from Jefferson County as Speaker of the House to replace me."

We talked it over and decided the best thing to do was to get lost until the following Tuesday. I called Bill Lyerly, the chief of the highway patrol and asked him to have a highway patrolman pick up Rankin's wife, Aline, and Buddy, their son in Hamilton and bring them to my house in Montgomery. Then I asked my secretary to make reservations for Rankin, Aline and Buddy, and Reba, Cynthia, and me at the Grand Hotel in Point Clear. We drove down to Point Clear in my personal car.

The whole weekend we discussed the problem. Carl Harrison, the representative from Columbiana, was a very conservative representative who had only voted with the administration part of time, but certainly had the respect of the representatives who were so offended by Rankin dismissing the house. Late Monday afternoon we called Carl Harrison and Rankin told him he would come to the legislature Tuesday morning and apologize to the whole body. Rankin asked him if he would be willing to come and take the lead in this endeavor. He agreed.

Tuesday morning, Speaker Fite took his seat, and asked me to come sit with him, which I did. He did a wonderful job apologizing to the whole house. One of the things that pleased the house so much was the fact he agreed there would be a roll call vote on every issue for the remainder of his term. This brought loud cheers from the whole house. I have a framed picture of Speaker Fite and me taken during this unusual occurrence.

Emmett Odom, the representative from Franklin County was always up to some trick. About a week later, he got up an introduced a resolution to repeal a resolution that had passed earlier, which raised the legislators' per diem from ten dollars per day to twenty dollars per day. Of course this vote would put each representative on record as voting to lower their per diem. A great roar came from the floor. After the noise quieted down, Odom got up and withdrew his resolution with unanimous consent. The Speaker said, "Without objection, the resolution is withdrawn."

About the many problems in the Folsom's administration: a funny thing happened in the first administration in 1947-1951. The legislature, particularly the senate, was doing everything it could to take power away from the governor's office. In line with this intent, they passed a bill they called the "Self Starter." That was a bill where the legislature, by a majority signing a petition, could call themselves into session. Governor Folsom decided that would give him a good reason to go back to the people, because he was paving mailbox roads all over the state in the first administration. Back then you could do it so much cheaper, and you didn't have to build the quality of roads that they do now because they only had two and a half ton trucks and not nearly as much traffic on the roads. Governor Folsom would make appointments and ride all over the state, and that would give him a chance to go back and report to the people what he was doing. He had surveys made as to what he had done about the roads and if he had started a hospital. For instance, in my district in Fayette they had started building a hospital and a National Guard Armory and were doing some work on the existing armory in Jasper. So when he came to

Fayette to speak he would bring it up and did so in almost every county.

His chauffeur was Winston Craig, a fine, educated black gentleman, and Governor Folsom would tell this on the speaker's stand almost everywhere he went, "We were driving down the road and Winston ran over a rooster. I could see when he did it, and I asked, 'Winston, what did we do to that chicken?' Winston said, 'Governor, we killed it dead just like we gonna do for that Self Starter Bill.' That story went over big and always brought a big laugh. He never failed to work it into his speeches to the people.

One of the things that happened almost immediately after Governor Folsom took office in the second administration in 1955 was about Jamelle, the governor's wife and first lady. She and I came from the same town of Berry, Alabama, and she was my secretary when I was in the senate in the 1947-1949 administration. Someone came up with the idea that they could start a cosmetic business and sell cosmetics called "Jamelle's Cosmetics. She'd have her picture in the ads. She was and is a beautiful lady.

She had no idea and I had no idea how to market cosmetics. They hired two ladies in their early thirties to represent them and go out to try to sell their products. Of course, they had them packaged in a nice attractive package, and they sold to stores. They were not selling too much, because Governor Folsom was still not all that popular with the business clientele. They came to me and said, "We've run out of money." I got in touch with Senator Fite and Lieutenant Governor Hardwick and asked them to come to my office. I got them to put the two girls on the payroll. They put one in the senate and one in the house as clerks, and they did just about as much work as several of the clerks that the senators and representatives had on the payroll at that time. Things were handled very liberally in those days, but their clerk positions gave them freedom and a paycheck every two weeks.

They still were not selling the cosmetics, so I talked to Ed Pepper about it. He and Representative Pete Matthews from Clay County were very close friends and thought if they could go into Chicago, they might find some wholesaler or a sponsor that would take it over. They carried Jamelle's pictures, some cosmetic samples, and were gone about four or five days. They had a nice little expense account claim when they got back, but I don't think it improved the sales. I just did not have time to give to anything like that, so I never did. It went on while the legislature was in session, but afterwards it kind of died away. Needless to say, the Folsom's cosmetic business was unsuccessful. Since this was promoting private enterprise, I felt justified in putting the two ladies on as clerks in the house and senate.

My mother's youngest brother, Otto Kemp was a member of the city council in Fairfield, Alabama. He called me one night and said, "Fuller, I'm in a run-off in Fairfield, and I didn't get the black vote. If I don't get it, I might not win." Reckon you can do anything for me?" he asked.

"Maybe I can. Let me see what I can do," I said. The next morning I called Winston Craig, Governor Folsom's chauffeur in his first and second administration. He came around, and I told him what happened, and that Uncle Otto Kemp had a barbershop in Fairfield and had been there a good many years. He had served on the city council two terms before, but for some reason or other the black vote did not come out and he was a little uneasy about it. "Would you go down there and help him?" I asked him.

"Yes sir, Mr. Kimbrell, if you want me to," Winston said. I gave him two $100 bills, and asked him to go see what he could find out and what he could do. He went to O. H. Finney, Governor Folsom's executive secretary, and told him that he needed the limousine for the day—the governor happened to be out of town. "I got to do something for Mr. Fuller," Craig said.

O. H. Finney was my friend and told him, "Go ahead and take it. Nobody is going to know it but us." I didn't see him any more that day, but the next morning he came in and said, "Mr. Kimbrell, I think your Uncle is going to be all right. He is going to get the vote."

"Can you tell me about it?" I asked.

He said, "I went to O. H. Finney and told him I needed the limousine." At that time it was a big black Packard and one of the most outstanding automobiles, classified with Cadillacs and Lincolns.

"I put on my chauffeur's uniform and cap, drove to Fairfield and down into the Quarters. I stopped the car and folks saw the

Number One tag. When I stepped out they saw my uniform, and they came to see what was going on. I told them, 'Now listen, Mr. Otto Kemp is Senator Kimbrell's uncle, and he could do a lot for y'all here. He's our friend and we've got to put him back in office. I want y'all to go to the polls, and vote for him.' I visited with folks, passed the time of day, drove around the block and stopped at three or four places. Every place I stopped, hundreds of blacks came to the car, and I made the same talk. I believe your uncle will be all right this time." Uncle Otto went in with a big vote.

TWENTY

HEADACHES

Pretty soon after the May primary, Governor Folsom's two brothers, Fred and Cecil Folsom, and his brother-in-law, Ross Clark, were indicted pertaining to their income tax. Governor Folsom called me in and said, "Fuller, you have developed good relationships with Claude Vardeman, the chairman of the Republican Party, and Cooper Green, the public relations director with the power company, who is also the mayor of the city of Birmingham. Why don't you go talk to them and see if you can work out something for Fred, Cecil, and Ross regarding their income tax?"

I did go talk to Claude Vardeman and Cooper Green, and they said, "Give us a few days." Later they called me, and I went back to see them. They both had offices in the Alabama Power Company building. They had worked out for Fred, Cecil, and Ross to plead nolo contendere and each pay $2500. Governor Folsom was awfully unhappy about the decision, and he told me, "Raise the money and pay it." I didn't tell him that if I had not been able to work that out, all three were in for a big attorney fee and maybe serving some time. By my doing this, it limited the publicity and had little effect on the upcoming administration.

I called two of our strongest supporters from Russellville, Alabama—Tom Formby, who was in the cotton business, and Emmett Miller, the Chevrolet dealer—and asked them to bring me $7500 to pay it. They did. That didn't satisfy Cecil Folsom because he came to see me with George Hawkins his attorney, and said, "I've got to give him $2500." I don't remember where I got that $2500, but I raised it some place and paid George Hawkins his attorney fee. That settled it. Everything was all over, I thought.

After I came back home to Fayette, the tax folks started checking me. It went on for ten—almost eleven—years, and they didn't find anything wrong. I had the John Deere Tractor Dealership in Tuscaloosa and Aliceville. At the time, John Deere paid a volume discount based on the amount of business you did. My volume discount for that year was about $25,000. The managers of my dealerships were not making money at all, and I felt I didn't want that money to be mailed to those dealerships and go right into the business, because they were careless enough with their operation already. So I called Mr. Hassell, the assistant branch manager in Atlanta, and told him I wanted to pick up the check myself. Since I thought it was not prudent to send a check of that size through the mail I drove to Atlanta. Everybody was always watching the director of finance, so I thought the best thing for me to do was to cash the check in Atlanta. I got Mr. Hassell to call the bank and tell them who I was, and I went to the bank and cashed the $25,000 check. I knew it was taxable income, so I came up with the idea to make fictitious invoices, over a period of time, for used equipment to which sales tax did not apply.

To put the money into two different agencies, the one in Columbus and the one in Aliceville, we would write up sales for used equipment that had no sales tax until I put in more than the $25,000. However, in the John Deere Plow Company Atlanta Finance Department they had fired a young fellow, Mr. Taylor, and he called the IRS in Atlanta and told them I had cashed the check. Almost immediately they started the checking that went on for almost eleven years.

They knew about a corporation that Formby and Miller had formed that represented Minnesota Mining and Manufacturing Company. Minnesota Mining and Manufacturing Company produced a special paint for striping highways. The paint contained little beads that reflected at night and was used almost exclusively all over the United States. I did buy the paint from the corporation.

When my tax case was brought to trial, they had summoned twenty-eight people to testify. I don't know how, but they knew about me buying the paint from Minnesota Mining and Manufacturing Company through the Formby and Miller Corporation, and the judge said, "Although we haven't proven anything, we have you charged with $33,000 plus interest and penalty. We are going to make you pay it, because even though we've checked and all the taxes have been paid on the corporation that belonged to Formby and Miller, you ought to have to pay it because you made the money for them."

I was stunned. I took an appeal. Unfortunately, two of the three judges selected to serve on the appeal were judges I had asked Senators John Sparkman and Lister Hill to recommend to the President that he nominate them to the court of appeals, so they had to recuse themselves. The other judge knew I was connected with the Folsom administration, and he had no love for the Folsom administration and hated Governor Folsom with a passion. He ruled almost immediately that I had to pay. The total amounted to $33,000 plus interest and penalty. Since it had been almost eleven years, the total was $53,820. I had to pay the money out of my own pocket.

Before the deadline came I could have paid it off. They had it figured to be $103,000. Of course, there was no way I could have paid that much. If I had been able to pay it, I could have sued for the $103,000 plus interest and had a jury trial. My attorney said there was no question I could have won. I had to let the deadline go by. Of course it went to the grand jury, but one of the people checking and auditing my books went to Bill Drinkard and told him they were going to indict me. Bill Drinkard called me at two o'clock in the morning and told me an IRS man had called him and told him I was going to get indicted that week. He said he had told Governor Folsom and Folsom said, "Don't tell him." My records and everything were before a federal grand jury in Birmingham. Although I knew only one person on the jury, I would not have tried to do anything about it, but maybe some of my friends might have. I called my tax lawyer, Walter Mims, and he said, "Maybe if you went to Washington — with your connection with the two senators — you might get it brought back, and we could do some more work on it."

I got up that very Monday morning and flew to Washington and stayed three or four days. I went to Senator John Sparkman first, and he said, "You have the wrong lawyer." I didn't pick my lawyer, but Senator Fite, my very close friend, and James Money, who was doing my tax work at that time, suggested I go to Walter Mims. Mims was really the best tax lawyer in Alabama at that time and was for a long time. But Sparkman was real close to an attorney in Tuscaloosa who had always managed his campaigns and he had excellent luck with him. I might have had excellent luck if I had asked him to take my case, but I didn't.

I went to see Senator Lister Hill, whose office was next to John Sparkmans' in the Rayburn Building in Washington. When I told his secretary I wanted to see Senator Hill, she went into his office and came back and told me to be there at 1:30 that afternoon. When I got back at 1:30, a young fellow, Louis Ogledorf, came in and he recognized me. I didn't recognize him but I had heard of his father. Lister Hill came out and with his usual great hale and hearty greeting and said, "Imagine these two great Alabamians in my office at the same time." He visited with both of us a minute then turned and said, "Louis, let me talk to Fuller awhile first, because you and I want to talk a good bit." Louis Ogledorf's name was going to come up before the senate for confirmation. He had been nominated by Senator Hill to be assistant district attorney. I'm not sure of that, but what he really wanted to do, I learned later, was to get my story.

When Senator Hill and I finished talking I came back home, and three days later, I got a letter from a Mr. Folsom in the Tax Department in Washington stating that my tax records were being brought back to Washington for further review. Eight months later, both my lawyer, Walter Mims, and I got a letter to come for a hearing in Washington.

We went to the designated place in a great big conference room. They sat us down with me sitting on the side of the table where I was looking into another big conference room and on the other side was an office. Shortly, Louis Ogledorf walked by the office door and asked, "Oh, is that you Senator Kimbrell?"

"Yes," I said. He came in; he didn't know Walter Mims, but his father was good friends with Mims, so he visited a little while. Then the IRS man came in with his pad, and we talked and visited around awhile. Six or eight months later they sent it back to Birmingham for a trial.

Walter Mims did not summon or ask for any witnesses except my accountant, Raymond Gordon, who lived in Fayette, and kept my books and made out my tax returns. I would have been better off if Mims had not summoned him, because Gordon got so excited he didn't know what he was saying. The government had summoned twenty-eight people and we were there all day long with witnesses. Finally Mr. Mitchell, the prosecuting attorney, who got promoted after that, turned to the lady judge and said, "I rest my case." She worked him over good.

"Where are all the other witnesses?" she asked. And she made other negative remarks. She asked about two or three other witnesses, who had been summoned, but had not testified.

"Your Honor. I've interviewed everyone, and I know Mr. Kimbrell has not talked to a single one. You've seen what has happened here with fourteen witnesses. We are getting nowhere, and after talking to the others, I see no way we are going to get any further," Mr. Mitchell said.

"Well, you better get in here and try to compromise," she said.

I went in, and after looking at it, there was about $8000 that might have had taxes due on it the year before. So I offered to pay the tax and interest on the $8000, and she just blew her top. She said, "Well, we will take the $8000 from the $33,000 and settle for the other."

I talked to Walter and felt if I took an appeal with no better case than they had, that they would throw the whole thing out because I really didn't owe a nickel of it. So we took an appeal.

I've said a lot of times if that lady judge had held a gun on me and told me I had to pay it, I would have felt just as good toward her as I did with that. I truly had tried to be honest with everybody and did not owe that money. I had hired someone else to pay my taxes and count my money, even so, it was the most unjust thing that could have happened to a poor farm boy.

For instance, the year before I became finance director I paid taxes on income that was more than my total income from the state while I was serving as finance director. Let me say again, never in my life have I tried to be more honest and sincere in doing what I thought was right in trying to serve the needs of the good people of Alabama.

In Governor Folsom's first administration, the opposition that I have spoken about before in the senate, had worked with the press in trying every way possible to keep the Folsom administration from having any favorable publicity. For instance, any thing they could make look bad, they did. Of course, any thing that the administration did, that was really fine for the people of Alabama, the press dealt with it most conservatively.

As director of finance, I'd hoped that I could work with the press in a way that the good people of Alabama would know about it and understand that we were trying to fulfill the platform, which was roads, old age pensions, education, and industrial development.

I am proud that I was able to do this by calling in the political reporters from the daily papers and the Associated Press, and keeping them advised of the things that we planned to bring up in the legislature next, as well as any major projects that might be up and coming. This way the reporters did a wonderful job in conveying to the people of Alabama the facts.

An incident with two of Folsom's brothers had me really upset. I thought if I couldn't get the situation stopped, I was going to resign. I called Rankin Fite, the Speaker of the House, and told him about it. He asked, "You want me to come down?"

I think it is time because I can't go on like this any longer," I said.

"I'll be there in the morning at eight o'clock," he said. He was there at eight o'clock.

We went to see the governor. I just sat there while Rankin talked. He said, "Governor, Fuller has told me about what is happening in regards to the finance department. You cannot circumvent the law by word of mouth or by executive order. You are sure asking for trouble. This situation must stop, because

I cannot defend you. You have a man here that is as loyal to you as he knows how to be and has the good will and support of all your supporters that I know about."

Governor Folsom said, "I'll call and have the situation stopped immediately." That was the end of it.

The incident with Governor Folsom's brothers was not the end of things similar to what I just discussed. I can think of others. For instance, one incident involved Knox McRae from north Alabama, who was in Folsom's cabinet in his first administration and continued to be close to the governor. We were selling scrap iron to Sabel Steel Company in Montgomery, and getting a really good price for it. Nobody was getting a commission or anything out of it. But I knew Governor Folsom was hoping to run again in four years, and this connection would give him a strong supporter. If I may be a little more specific, Sabel Steel Company had a close alliance with the First National Bank, which later became the First Alabama Bank in Montgomery with branches in most Alabama cities. They probably would have been a great asset in his next campaign.

Knox McRae came to the governor's office, and the governor called me to come to his office. He asked, "Where you selling the scrap iron?"

"Sabel Steel Company, and I have a reason. It will help later on," I answered.

"Well, they ain't my friend. I want to sell it to this fellow in Decatur," Governor Folsom said. I checked it out later, and that friend of the governor's was going to get eight dollars a month out of it. Folsom lost the support of the First Alabama Bank four years later in order to help a fellow that didn't care about anything but himself. A fellow who only wanted to make eight dollars a month.

TWENTY-ONE

PRISON FARMING, FIRE ANTS, AND FAYCO

I met with the Prison Board and asked them to appoint Frank Lee, the Sheriff of Greene County, as prison commissioner. Soon after I became finance director, I had a great ambition to change the prison farm system completely to power equipment for cultivating, planting, and harvesting. I called Frank Lee and asked him to come see me. I wanted to talk to him. We discussed buying power equipment, selling the mules, and developing the cattle ranch in Hale County. The first time I was involved in politics, somebody was trying to buy the 4,000 acre cattle ranch in Hale County all the time. I don't know how many people tried to buy it when I was in the Senate, knowing that I was close to administration, but Governor Folsom would not talk about it. Of course, Governor Persons who followed Folsom's first administration would not talk about it. When Frank Lee came in we also discussed hiring someone who was schooled in beef cattle and cattle raising and making him manager of the State Cattle Ranch in Hale County. He agreed with it immediately.

I asked Charlie Hassell, the assistant manager of John Deere Atlanta Branch, to come to Montgomery and told him what we wanted to do. He brought an experienced farm and equipment man with him. We got together and had lunch at the Elite Cafe — the most popular restaurant in Montgomery — and discussed it. Frank Lee took the John Deere salesman — not Mr. Hassell, but Mr. Hassell did go with them part of the time — to look at the farm, particularly the part at Atmore. We decided to buy six John Deere Model A's and two larger tractors from John Deere Plow Company. As I remember, Frank Lee sold 400 mules and horses they were using on the farms at Speigner and Atmore. I'm not sure they were doing any farming in Montgomery at Kilby Prison, but we immediately switched over to power equipment. I had told him of my relationship with Sumter Farm which I've talked about already. Mr. Charles Farquhar, the manager of the beef cattle at Sumter Farm, had a son who had just finished agricultural school, I think in Tennessee, so Frank Lee had him come over and talk about it. Charles Farquhar, Jr. agreed to come immediately. We got busy and built him a nice little house, and he moved in. Frank put the trust worthy prisoners over with Charlie Farquhar to operate the farm. He had his home and a kind of dormitory for the prisoners. Later he said about eighty-five prison trustys were living there.

Many years later in 1984, after I had moved to Tuscaloosa, I went to see Charlie several times at the cattle ranch. He always appreciated the fact that I was involved in getting him the job. By then, the catfish farming in Hale County had begun to be profitable, so he took me and showed me the catfish ponds. At that time, I believe he had twenty-nine small ponds, which amounted to a little over 300 acres in catfish lakes. I think the largest pond was only about 30 acres, but they ran anywhere from five to 30 acres. He worked out with the Amish people to come in and build them. They had big John Deere four-wheel drive tractors with dual wheels, and Charlie told me they would come in at daylight, and they didn't stop until they got a dam built and everything completed. Of course, they took advantage of quite a few artesian wells located on the state farm, which later became known as the State Cattle Ranch. The time I was down there, they were harvesting one ten-acre pond. What they would do was have the prisoners get in the pond and pull a wire around to make a small pen. Then they would lower a lift on a truck, and would lift up the catfish, drop them in big tanks, and take them to Greensboro to the processing plant.

While I was talking I told Charlie I was a member of a coffee club in Tuscaloosa and he said, "Why don't you bring them down here and we will cook catfish and give them a little tour." I came back and told the men at the coffee club, and that went over big. I called him and made arrangements for a certain day. We went down and had the finest catfish, slaw, hush puppies, and fresh corn on the cob. He had two vans, and anybody that wanted to could take a tour. I think when we went down he had 400 registered cattle, and I don't remember exactly, but he had several hundred feeder cattle. It was really a highlight. Of course, that wasn't the only trip. Every now and then someone would call me and say, "Fuller, let's go down to the ranch and eat catfish." For two or three years, we went down two or three times a year and ate catfish.

The story came to a very sad and tragic ending, though. One

of the prison trustees murdered Charlie Farquhar, his wife, and two guards, and burned their home.

Power equipment turned out to be a wonderful change for the prison system altogether. The only thing was it didn't leave enough work for all the prisoners. So some were transferred to work at the highway department. At that time, they had guard houses or prison housing in several counties in the state. Prisoners were transferred to those counties to work on state highway rights-of-way.

The prisoners had been growing Irish potatoes, not just a few, but thousands of bags. The first year in 1955 after we switched to power equipment we grew 9,900 bags of Irish potatoes on the farm at Atmore. Of course, we got a potato digger since we had power equipment to pull it. That cut down on the amount of help we needed, except for the bagging and sewing.

Another interesting thing was a fellow who owned a wholesale produce business came from Mobile and wanted to buy the radishes. So I shopped around and got a little idea of the price to ask. He said, "I'll give you $100,000 for the radishes in the field."

"The state has a digger. We can use the potato digger and shake the radishes out," I said. But the potato digger didn't work on radishes. "Lets just trade at $125,000 for the radishes," I said.

"All right," he said. I sold him the whole crop of radishes off the Atmore farm.

Since we had cut back the number of prisoners on the Atmore farm — with power equipment and that fine flat land, we planted corn, and then we got two-row corn pickers. The second year we got two-row corn pickers that would shell the corn and put it in a wagon. It was a wonderful thing for the state that we switched from mules to machinery. Of course, we got rubber tired wagons to pull behind the tractors.

It was the talk of the country that Alabama prisons had switched from mules to power equipment. No question but what it was a good change financially. Just selling the corn, potatoes, and vegetables, created an enormous income. Of course, labor was supplied by prisoners. The only cost was feeding and housing the prisoners. This change in the method of farming increased the yield of the above farm crops, plus the fact, we had no mules to feed. The entire year the amount of corn we grew was amazing.

The second year we started growing oats and wheat, and feeding hogs and cattle. When I became the director of finance the requisition every three months for meat for the prison system was 20,000 pounds of what I call white meat, and 20,000 pounds of backbones and neckbones. Then they began to sell beef cattle and hogs to the stockyard, and buy from the packing house pork shoulders, backbones and neckbones, and front quarters of beef to make stew meat, roasts, and hamburger, since the prisoners didn't want steak. The prison system became self supporting almost immediately. We paid for the equipment in a minimum length of time with savings from selling beef and farm products.

Earlier I told about Kenneth Griffith, the governor's legal adviser, bringing up a bill to establish the Department of Examiners of Public Accounts and telling us the governor wanted it. I thought it was funny, Senator Jimmy Colburn, from Greene and Hale Counties who later became a Supreme Court judge, was standing there looking at it and he said, "Yes, I looked at that. It's a good bill." Bob Kendall was also standing there. He voted with the administration some, but not a majority of the time. They each looked at it like they had never seen it before and said, "Yes, I'll sign it." They laid it on my desk.

Rankin Fite was sitting at his desk next to mine and he looked up and asked, "Kenneth, are you sure the governor wants this?"

"Yes, I talked it over with him and he wants it," Kenneth. replied.

"Okay," Rankin said. I signed it, and then Rankin signed it. Then Bob Kendall signed it, and Senator Jimmy Coleman signed it. The bill passed without a dissenting vote and went to the House and passed immediately. It went down to the governor's office, and he vetoed it.

Rankin and I were talking about it, and Rankin said, "Fuller, I can't vote to sustain the veto on my own bill. I'm going out in the hall. I'm going to "cabbage patch."

I said, "It doesn't make that much difference to me. I'm not a lawyer. I'm going to vote to sustain the veto." This happened in the first administration, but in the second administration Ralph Eagerton, who was the Director of the Department, established by the bill, was no friend of Governor Jim Folsom. The bill set up the Department of Examiners of Public Accounts, with the head of the department selected by four members of the senate and four members of the house. Of course, if he already had tenure he was okay, but if he didn't he could work three years and have tenure. Ralph Eagerton had been appointed to head the department. He decided he wanted to audit the governor's office, because the newspapers really took Folsom apart in the first administration and later began to get hold of him again. I kept the reporters off of him as much as I could, but you couldn't keep them off 100 percent of the time. Eagerton threatened to go to the courts and get a ruling to audit the governor's books, and I knew he would win if he did. So one day Lieutenant Governor Guy Hardwick came in and asked, "Fuller, you want to get Ralph Eagerton off the governor's books?"

"I sure do," I said.

"I'll be back in a minute," he said. He came back and said, "You go down Highway 100 toward Monroeville into Lowndes County to this place and Shorty Millsap, the probate judge of Monroe County, will meet you there, and you talk to him. Shorty said for you to come by yourself." I knew Shorty really well; he was a friend of the administration.

I went by myself. I met him right at the place Lieutenant Governor Guy Hardwick described. Judge Millsap had a black man driving for him. I heard him tell the driver when he got out of the car, "Now you drive up the road and you be gone exactly fifteen minutes."

Shorty came over and said, "Senator pull out that road right there." We pulled out a side road and he asked, "Say you want Eagerton off the governor's books?"

I said, "I sure do. It's just giving me a headache. The governor is so upset, not because there is anything in the books he is worried about, he just doesn't want the papers to have that much to write about."

He said, "I'll tell you what. I have a road I want straightened out and paved." "Reckon we can get it done?" he asked.

"Yes, I think we can," I said.

"When?" he asked.

"You want to meet me at the governor's office at 8:00 in the morning?" I asked him.

"Yes, I'll be there at 8:00," he said.

I called Governor Folsom at the mansion that night and told him Judge Shorty Millsap would be there at 8:00 the next morning, and we had something important to work out with him. I told him I had met Judge Shorty Millsap that afternoon, and we had worked out a deal to get the Department of Examiners of Public Accounts off of his records and stop all the headlines in the newspapers and the worry over it.

The next morning at exactly 8:00 we met with the governor, and he asked, "How you going to do that?" Shorty said, "I have a road in an awful red muddy place in a certain area, it will probably cost a few thousand dollars to fix. I want it straightened, fixed, and paved, and you won't hear from Ralph Eagerton again." Governor Folsom picked up the phone. Herman Nelson was the Highway Director then, and Folsom said, "Herman, Judge Millsap is a good fellow, one of our very best friends from Monroe County. He has a road I think is a must. I think we ought to fix and pave that road for him. He's coming over there right away. See what you can do about it. I don't know what Shorty had on him, but we never heard from Ralph Eagerton again.

To finish the story, during George Wallace's administration eight years later, Rankin Fite was a representative then instead of senator, and the floor leader for Wallace. He stopped by my office in Fayette. He asked, "Fuller, how did you get Ralph Eagerton off the governor's books?"

"Aw, Ralph Eagerton turned to liking me all of a sudden," I said.

"Tell a lie. You're joking. Governor Wallace wanted me to ask you how you did it—because we know you did it, and Wallace is worrying to death about it," Rankin said.

I told him the story, and he said, "That's fine." Rankin had gotten the State Highway Department to put a whiteway with lights on each side of the highway through Winfield, Guin, Hamilton, and Hackleburg, and the state was even paying the electric bill. "Shorty wants a whiteway in Monroeville like I have in Marion County. I think we can work that out." Monroeville got its whiteway, and they never heard from Ralph Eagerton any more.

Once during the second administration, I was having a lot of problems getting a bill through that the governor wanted pretty bad, but I could not get it through the senate after it passed the house. We usually had better luck in the house than we did in the senate. There were a few people in the senate who still couldn't stand for Folsom to be a winner, because they were worried about the here-after. If they had tried to do something about it instead of trying to stop it, they would be better off today than they are. A senator from east Alabama was one of the strongest fighters and filibusterers of the bill.

At that time, there was an awful lot of discussion about the fire ants. They were just beginning to get into Alabama and all over the South. People didn't know how to get rid of them, particularly down in the cattle raising section of Alabama and across the middle section called the Black Belt. If a calf was born close to an ant hill the ants would cover it, and there was no way it could survive. The legislature and people were willing to try anything, so I came up with the idea to send the senator from east Alabama to Argentina to study the fire ants. I called Emory Solomon, the representative from Headland, Alabama, who was a very close friend of mine. He didn't always vote with the administration, but I could get him to when I really needed him. He would come for a soda water or something. I called him in and said, "I need to get the Senator from east Alabama out for a few days. He will kill one of the bills the administration is pushing. If we had him out of the way we can pass it easy enough."

"What do you have in mind?" Emory asked.

"How would you like to have a state, all-expenses-paid trip to Argentina?" I asked.

"Fine, that sounds like a winner to me," he answered. I let him go down the hall, and I called the senator to come to my office and he came. About that time Solomon came back. So I told them we were having so much discussion about the fire ants in Alabama. The governor wanted to do something about them, but Auburn Agriculture Department and even the U. S. Agriculture Department had not been able to come up with anything to control them. I said, "I understand the fire ants came from Argentina, and they have done a lot of research, and developed a system that is working fairly well to get rid of them. I would like to send you two to Argentina. The state will pay for you to go to study the problem and come back and report to the legislature if there is anything we can do to get rid of them."

"Argentina?" the senator asked.

"Yes, I don't know any other way for us to get the information. I can't call down there, because I can't speak Spanish," I said.

"You know that sounds like a wonderful idea," the senator said.

Emory said, "If you want to go Senator, Senator Kimbrell, the director of finance will work it out for the state to pay our expenses.

"I'll have the secretary of my department make your reservations. We'll pay your expenses. You take a week or ten days, whatever you think best. Go down and look around and see what you can find out," I said.

We were off to the races. The next day was a legislative day. We passed the bill.

The Senator and Solomon came back from Argentina, They each stood up in front of the legislature and reported what the Argentineans were doing about the fire ants in their country. Representative Solomon went before the house, and the Senator went before the senate. It made the headlines. What a wonderful idea it was. It ended there, but it did get the Auburn Agriculture and Extension Department to give more thought to trying to discover something to control the ants. But they are still not conquered. If you notice today, the ant problem is worse than it has ever been.

Other benefits for east and southeast Alabama included road improvements. Lieutenant Governor Guy Hardwick wanted a by-pass around Dothan. Lewis Opry, a campaign manager, wanted one on the east side, and Guy Hardwick wanted one on the west side. Governor Folsom called Herman Nelson, the highway director, and told him to build a bypass on both sides. Governor Folsom was really popular in Dothan. He carried Houston County by a big vote. One of the leaders in the senate was Richmond Flowers who became attorney general and ran for governor, but wasn't successful. After the by-pass was finished, it made a complete circle around Dothan. They came up with the idea to name it the Ross Clark Circle. Ross Clark was Folsom's brother-in-law.

Another thing we were able to do involved Representative Jimmy Branyon from Fayette and the Alabama Extension Service. Fayette wanted an auditorium at the Experiment Station at Winfield which was in Fayette County and served three or four counties in that district. We've talked about it before, but he had a bill, and he just couldn't move it. He came to me and said, "Fuller, I wonder if you can help me move it."

"Yes," I said. I went and told Rankin Fite to go on and pass it. When it got over to the senate, I got hold of Lieutenant Governor Hardwick, and he got it out. They built the auditorium at Winfield, which is still there and has been used quite often as a meeting place for farmers to go and discuss the agricultural experiments and progress in that section of the state.

A funny thing that happened in the legislature: I've talked about Emmett Odom, the representative from Franklin County. He came across an act breaking off a part of Franklin County and making it Colbert County. He introduced a bill in the house to undo this act, and sent it over to the senate. Senator Lynchmore Cantrell, who represented the same senatorial district that Rankin Fite represented, which was Colbert, Franklin, and Marion County, never thought anything about it. He just thought it was one of Emmett Odom's pet projects, so he passed it. But before the governor signed it, Odom went over and took two or three folks with him to get a good laugh at Cantrell's expense.

He said, "Senator, you know the bill you just passed did away with Colbert County. This resolution you just passed killed the bill that broke Colbert County away from Franklin County." The senator got so mad and upset he pulled his knife out and was fixing to jump on Odom right there. Emmett Odom said, "It hasn't gone that far. The governor hasn't signed it. We'll just let it die right here."

The very first political donation I remember making was to R. C. (Red) Bamberg, a very fine gentleman who lived in Marengo County. He was running for commissioner of agriculture and was elected. When Governor Folsom was elected the second time, Red was defeated as commissioner of agriculture by

Haygood Patterson. I don't believe there was a run-off. Haygood Patterson had served as commissioner of agriculture before and was running for re-election, and was elected. But he got sick and was not able to serve, and the committee nominated A. W. Todd at the request of the Folsom administration. Afterwards, Red came to me and said, "Fuller, there is a vacancy in my district on the Auburn Board of Trustees, and I sure would like to have it."

"Well, I feel we did wrong. You ran for Commissioner of Agriculture, and we didn't put you in. We put in Todd. We all wanted someone from north Alabama. I think you understand," I said.

"I understand perfectly, and I hold no ill will. But I sure would like to serve on the Auburn Board of Trustees," Red said.

"Come on," I said. We went to the governor's office and he was appointed right then. He served until he died. The last few years he was superannuate trustee, but he was chairman of the Auburn Board for several years.

Bob Gwin was a partner in the Bedlow Law Firm. At that time, it was one of Alabama's most outstanding law firms, located in Birmingham. Gwin had been very helpful and active in the campaign, particularly in Jefferson County. Gwin's father was clerk of the Senate, as I've told before. Bob Gwin was one of Kefauver's delegates when I managed Kefauver's campaign and went to the 1952 convention in Chicago. We had a big Folsom rally in Centerville and Mr. Green, owner of Twix and Tween Restaurant—known all over the state for his really good barbecue and steaks — brought all the campaign head people into the back dining room and served us steaks. Bob Gwin came in with two airline hostesses. I think he had recently gotten one a divorce, and maybe he had said something like, "I'm going down to Centerville to a Folsom rally. Come on and go with me." Of course, I invited them in to have steaks with us, which they did. Governor Folsom, Jamelle, Reba, Bully Moon and his wife, and three or four other campaign workers and their wives were there.

We went on to Mobile, and on the way back, Jamelle and Governor Folsom, instead of riding with Bully Moon and his wife, rode with Reba and me. About half way back, Governor Folsom had a bottle of Early Times in the floor, which he was taking care of pretty regularly. He asked, "Fuller, why in the hell did that Bob Gwin bring those two old whores from Birmingham down to eat with us and our wives?"

"I think he just got one of them a divorce, and maybe he just brought them," I said.

Folsom said, "Aw hell no. He knew better." "What did he do that for?" he asked.

Nothing else was said about the incident then, but after we got in Montgomery there came a vacancy for a judgeship in Jefferson County. I went to the Governor and told him Bob Gwin had worked in his campaign, and he would like to be the judge.

Governor Folsom said, "There is no way I'm going to appoint a fellow who would bring two old whores down to a rally to eat with us and our wives. So you just forget it. He isn't going to get no appointment."

Later there came a vacancy for a judgeship when John

Patterson was governor, and I went to him and told the story. He understood the situation, so he asked, "You want him appointed for that vacancy?"

"I sure would appreciate it," I said.

"I'm going to appoint him," Governor Patterson said. Judge Bob Gwin served as judge for at least twenty years, and then he became superannuate. He did a lot of lobbying for the Judges Association before the legislature in Montgomery until he got to the point he just couldn't go anymore. He passed away about two years ago.

While I was serving in the senate, I was appointed by Lieutenant Governor Inzer to serve on the Eleemosynary Institution Committee (institutions such as Bryce and Mt. Vernon), along with Representative Skelton from Tuscaloosa, and others. One individual, a lady from north Alabama, was in the insurance business. Our job was to go through the boys' and girls' industrial schools and the blacks' industrial school over at Shorter and in Macon County, at Mt. Vernon. We visited almost all of them. Skelton was chairman, and he would make arrangements for us to eat lunch at each of the places. They didn't know in advance the committee had planned to eat with them, but they had good food and the area was clean and orderly. I felt a little uncomfortable eating at some of the institutions, but I enjoyed it.

One thing that was most painful was that when we went to Bryce Hospital, I did not know the lady serving on the committee with us had a child at Partlow. When we were touring we went into a great big room that must have been 20' X 20'. In the room there were about seven or eight children who looked to be five or six years old. As it turned out, her son was fifteen years old, but he had the mentality of a six year old. All of a sudden, the lady began screaming, squalling, and carrying on. Come to find out, one of the children playing on the concrete floor was her son. She was quite a successful insurance agent in north Alabama. We got the supervisor to talk to her and try to calm her, but as my brother, Wyman, who was a retired naval officer says, "It sure put a feeling on you" for a while.

One of my very best friends when I was director of finance was Jimmy Thrower, who married into the Flowers family in Dothan. In fact, after I got into the pipe business, I sold him pipe for a big shopping mall he built in Dothan and helped him get a bank charter. To show you how a slip of the tongue can get you into trouble: under Governor Person's administration, Thrower had a liquor account, which was quite profitable. Back then, they had liquor agents in Alabama, and the "spirits" people were paying money to a fellow whose name I've called before. He was handing over part of it to Jimmy Thrower. They were in Chattanooga at the Hamilton Hotel eating and talking around the table about how it was handled. Sitting at the table next to them were Internal Revenue men, and they overheard it. That slip of the tongue led to a thorough investigation. Jimmy Thrower told me later it cost him $25,000 in taxes to settle it.

Another thing we learned about, I can't say I absolutely knew about it, but it came from reliable sources, was that one of

Persons' ABC men said he had a little house built behind his home where he had stowed 200 cases of prime spirits. I understand our people were following it all the way through, and it was sold in Colbert County. I could not call any names of people involved. I was advised of it, but I wasn't there to look into things of that nature. I was there pledged to try to get Governor Folsom's program through. So I never got involved and tried not to know any more about it than what I heard.

When I was director of finance, I decided to join the Masons go through the Blue Lodge and Shrine. I had to start with the Blue Lodge first. I had so much on my mind, I almost never memorized all the things required because it isn't written down and you are forbidden to write it down. An old fellow, Mr. Sharp, was teaching me. Every time I felt I could go for a session I would call him and say, "Brother Sharp, I think I can come see you."

"Come on," he would say.

I would go sit with him at night and finally got enough to struggle through.

Jimmy Lawson, one of the bitterest enemies of the administration, was assistant to P. O. Davis, the director of Agricultural Extension Service, and they had really been a "fly in the ointment" during the first administration. When he found out I was going through the Blue Lodge, he came to me and said, "Fuller, I really want to be the man who takes you through." To back up: I think I've told about when I was President of the Fayette Chamber of Commerce and I tried to get an assistant county agent. P. O. Davis and Jimmy Lawson in cooperation with Judge McGough, refused this appointment. Later, P. O. Davis and Jimmy Lawson met me at the airport and told me they were ready to work with me. They said they would send an assistant county agent and also replace the present county agent immediately. They would move the present county agent to Auburn. So I guess one good deed will take care of another good deed. Lawson came to Fayette to officiate in raising me in the Blue Lodge.

The fun really started when I decided to go through the Shrine in Montgomery. The Montgomery district attorney and I were going through at the same time, along with eight or ten others, and he and I were the top politicians. They put vertical striped breeches on us and sent us all over town selling chewing gum. I was on the Board of Guaranty Savings Life Insurance Company, and went down there and tried to get five dollars a pack for the gum. We had Doublemint, Spearmint, Dentyne, etc. Leroy Ursery, the president of Guaranty Savings Life Insurance was there. I pulled out a pack of Dentyne and told him, "I'm going to charge you twenty-five dollars for a pack because I'm selling you the burny kind."

Afterwards every time he would see me he would tell me he was saving that "burny kind." He gave me twenty-five dollars and Bob Engelhardt, the secretary-treasurer of Guaranty Savings, gave me five dollars for a pack. The district attorney and I worked together all day selling gum, and I think we brought in over $300. Back then, you could buy a pack of chewing gum for five cents. We made the headlines that night.

When we went for initiation, the district attorney and I were put into cages with iron bars wired with electricity so when we touched the bars we would get a shock. They would tell us to sing. I said, "I can't sing." About that time they would turn the juice on. "Just listen. I'm singing now," I said.

The district attorney couldn't sing either. They kept us in the cages about thirty minutes. They all laughed at us, but it turned out good.

One thing which was a most enjoyable occasion was the Southern Governor's Conference. It was held at the Grand Hotel in Point Clear, Alabama. As director of finance I was invited to attend, along with my wife. General Motors had furnished transportation—Cadillacs for the governors and "four hole" Buicks (as they were called back then) for lieutenant governors and finance directors, and for the other cabinet members they had "three hole" Buicks, and some Chevrolets. They had arranged with the highway patrolmen to be chauffeurs for all the top officials—governors, lieutenant governors, and finance directors. Reba and I were chauffeured around in our own "four-hole" Buick for the three-day Governor's Conference at Point Clear, and it was quite an event. One of the highlights of the Conference was golfing, but since I did not play golf, Reba and I went with a group to Gulf Shores for dinner one night. And one night, there was a big banquet and dance at the Grand Hotel.

Pretty soon after I became director of finance, my very good friend, E. A. Bagwell—called Cage Bagwell—who lived in

Fayette and owned the Fayette Concrete Pipe plant, and his son-in-law, Garen Williams, who operated the concrete pipe plant in Tullahoma, Tennessee, and came back home to Fayette to visit on the weekend, called and asked if they could come see me. They came up to my house and Garen said that for $30,000 we could go into the metal pipe business. That would buy two riveters and a roller, and we could get started in it. There was a big market for metal pipe, and Armco were the only people selling metal pipe in the state at that time. Although, I found out later that Choctaw, Inc. located in Memphis, was in the pipe business at the same time. But they were not doing all that much business in Alabama. Armco was doing most of it.

"What do you want me to do?" I asked.

"See if you can organize it," Garen said. Jimmy Hinton and Henry Waugh from Tuscaloosa were two of the strongest supporters in Folsom's campaign, so I called Jimmy and Henry to come see me. I wanted to talk to them. They flew up in a little plane, and we met them at that airport. I had Garen tell them what it was about, and Jimmy Hinton asked, "What do you want us to do Fuller?"

I said, "You all put me in, and we will make it a four way deal. You put in $6000 each—Jimmy, you and Henry put in $6000, Garen you put in $6000—and the state will buy the metal pipe from the company. They agreed to it right away and each pulled out a check and wrote it. We voted unanimously right then to call it Tennessee Valley Metal Culvert. Garen went back and put in the pipe machine right away.

We didn't have a bid law, so I called Mr. Z. O. Riddles, who was the Armco state manager. He was a friend of Jim Folsom's who had put some in the campaign, not much though. I said, "I'm going to divide the state. Everything south of Clanton, in pipe Armco sells. North of Clanton, I'm going to buy from Tennessee Valley Metal Culvert. A friend of mine from Fayette owns it. He is the son-in-law of some folks that worked in the campaign."

Riddles said, "That's fair enough. Of course, that lets Armco sell the metal buildings and such which has developed into a pretty good business." The National Guard and highway department were buying storage buildings and other similar items, and it just turned into a wonderful business for Armco. This led to a smooth and successful arrangement. I had a price list in the office and had some Tennessee Valley stationary, and if the pipe was in north Alabama, my secretary would type a quotation and send it to the purchasing department, which issued a purchase order and sent it to Tennessee Valley. They didn't know they had sold it until they got a purchase order for it. That went on until we got the bid law.

I resigned as finance director in March 1958 before the four year term was out. I came back home and ran for the senate, but I lost the race. I still had the house in Montgomery, and Reba and Cynthia still lived there until after the May primary.

I found out half of Fayette Concrete Pipe Company was for sale. Mr. Cage Bagwell had passed away, and his oldest son, Howard, who was killed in an airplane crash, had owned half of it. Now it belonged to Howard's widow, Mac, who married

Frank Myers, a druggist. They were living in Aliceville, so I called and asked her if she wanted to sell her share, and she said she wanted to sell it. I bought it and had money enough to pay for it because I had sold something else. She had fifty-one percent so that gave me fifty-one percent of the business. The other forty-nine percent belonged to E. A. Bagwell's youngest son, Ectalane, who was a dentist practicing in Fayette. Ectalane thought the business would make him a living while he played golf, and of course, that wasn't my way of doing business.

I made myself president of the company right away because I owned fifty-one percent. Ectalane rarely showed up at the office. He wanted to build a building on some land he owned for the Jitney Jungle store of which I owned a third interest, but he wanted to build the building and own a fourth interest in Jitney Jungle. I didn't want to go in debt for the building and didn't want to give up any of my interest in Jitney Jungle, because he had not proven himself to be a good partner. He came to my office at the plant and said, "I own the building where you are. I'm going to move you out."

I said, "Throw it out in the street. I can stand it if Mrs. Freeman, who owns the drugstore on what is now Columbus Street, and Mr. Wiggins, who is manager of the Jitney Jungle on South Columbus Street, can." I studied about it a while. Mr. Wiggins came down and we talked about it, and I asked, "Why don't I swap my interest in Jitney Jungle to Ectalane for his interest in Fayette Concrete Pipe Company?" Mr. Wiggins left. He and Ectalane came back right away, and I traded my interest in Jitney Jungle for $38,000. I had put $7000 in Jitney Jungle, and had been drawing about $150 a month for quite some time. That deal made me the sole owner of Fayette Concrete Pipe Company.

I called Garen Williams, Jimmy Hinton, and Henry Waugh to meet me at the Stafford Hotel in Tuscaloosa and arranged that for $45,000 each they could buy a fourth interest in Fayette Concrete Pipe Company. By that time Fayette Concrete Pipe Company started producing metal pipe and we changed the name to Fayco, and it operated as Fayco until we sold it.

We decided to put a concrete pipe plant in Huntsville, so we bought thirty acres of land from Cecil Ashburn on the south side right close to the bridge over the Tennessee River, and built a new concrete pipe plant. Garen was supposed to manage it, but he could never do anything with it. He wanted me to take it over — which I did for a little while. But I just had so much to do I told them I wasn't going to do it any longer. The company never made any money. Jack Brown, a competitor, was sitting right in a limestone plant so he was buying limestone from fifty cents to a dollar cheaper than we were, and that gave him a big advantage selling pipe. We sold it to a concrete pipe company based in Atlanta.

We closed out the metal pipe and finally sold the asphalt part to the Bunn brothers, Terry and Sonny, who owned S T Bunn Construction Company in Tuscaloosa.

Caine Butler and I owned the Independent Construction Company, and he had been operating it since 1956. It became apparent that Fayco and Independent Construction Company were using each other's equipment on a continued basis. I decided to merge Independent Construction Company and

Fayco. Garen made such a fuss about Caine's drinking that I bought out Caine.

During that time, I sold Garen Williams my part of Tennessee Valley Metal Culvert and bought back his share of Fayco. I got a little more for my part than I paid for his. He was such a source of complaint all the time. If he made more profit one month than I did, he was really ugly about it. But if I made more profit than he did in a month, he didn't say a word. He was buried a few years ago. That left Jimmy Hinton, Henry Waugh, and me, as owners of Fayco.

I decided I wanted Jimmy Hinton and Henry Waugh out of Fayco. I worked out to give them $200,000 each for their part. In return for the $55,000 they put in Fayco, they got $337,000 in all, and did nothing. I couldn't even get them to come to a board meeting. Naturally, they were happy I bought them out. Henry Waugh passed away several years ago, and Jimmy Hinton and I are still the best of friends to this day.

During that same time, Henry Waugh owned Tuscaloosa Pre-Mix. He had a partner, Gaston Hocutt, who owned a little less than one-fourth interest and operated it. They were not getting any state business to speak of, and Henry asked me to help him. I started helping them get business, and he asked, "Why don't you buy Hocutt out?" Hocutt owned twenty-two percent. I gave him $80,000 for it, paid over a three year period. I was able to get enough business so it paid itself off. Later, when Henry took over the management of it, he decided he could get the state business as good as I could. But it turned out that he wasn't getting it, and he got into some tax trouble by getting a senator from South Alabama to represent him. The senator got into trouble also, and I ended up having to help them both.

Henry would not keep up his asphalt plant, and I was not getting him any business because he didn't want me to. He finally closed down and let the plant rust. He had a rock crusher that I needed, so he let me have it. It is still at the plant now.

After I moved to Tuscaloosa in 1984, he passed away. I settled with his family for $27,000 for my interest. All in all I guess I made enough and more than got my money back out of the deal. Henry asked for it to be changed to Sub Chapter S, and I paid tax on some money I didn't get. It really was not a fair settlement. He had five daughters, and I didn't want to get into a fuss with them. It has all been behind me for several years.

My nephew, Bailey Thomson, moved back to Tuscaloosa a few years ago. He retired from the Mobile Register, one of three or four top daily papers, which he served as an associate editor. Now he is teaching journalism at the University of Alabama. he is the principal speaker for the Alabama Citizens for the Constitution Reform committee. He moved from Orlando to Mobile and has a good friend in Florida who sponsors boys and girls similar to the Boys Ranches, particularly those who drop out of school, and he tries to find sponsors for them. I didn't try to learn that much about it, but enough to realize it would be a good thing. He talked me into trying to help get something promoted. I thought of the old Kimbrell family farm I once owned and later gave to Arthur, my oldest brother, Part of the state lake they are talking about building will be known as the Tom Bevill Lake if it is ever finished—and I don't know any reason why it won't be—backs up to the old farm about half way across on Caine Creek.

I thought if I could buy 100 acres that Arthur sold to Denver Clark on the southeast side of Caine Creek, maybe I could get the state to raise the dam. Highway 63 from Berry to Carbon Hill goes across about three quarters of a mile down from where the Kimbrell road crosses through the Kimbrell farm. Since they are going to have to do something about the road or change it, I believe I could get the Highway Department to build that road up higher, make a spillway, and back the lake up another quarter of a mile and cover the bottoms where it is backing up in the creek beds so far. That 100 acres would be an ideal place to build housing and training facilities for these teen-agers.

I went to see Denver Clark, who still owns the land, and asked him if he would sell me that 100 acres. I didn't know who he had married, but his father used to come visit my older brothers when I was a small boy. Of course, I've known the Clark boys for a good long while. They are all fine people and very successful in life. We got to talking about his wife, and I asked him who he married and he said, "I married a Bozeman, but my mother was Preacher Jess Pendley's daughter."

"Well, you know when I worked at Theron Cannon's we had four Jess Pendleys on the book—we had Long Jess, Stove Jess, Hoss Jess, and Preacher Jess," I said.

"Preacher Jess was my grandfather," he said.

"Preacher Jess was a Church of Christ preacher. We had a Primitive Baptist preacher named Harris at Boley Beat, in the east part of Fayette County. Folks came to Cannon's to trade and usually met most Saturdays right by the loading door, and they would discuss the Bible," I said.

"Yes, that's grandfather," Clark said.

I said, "I'll tell you another funny thing about a Jess Pendley. One of the other Jess Pendleys was Long Jess. When I worked at Cannon's I handled the sales of sugar, shorts, and malts to make wildcat whiskey, and I had several customers. They were all good customers. They would come up front, and pay cash for what they bought. When they were ready to load, I would go to the back door in the warehouse and load them. Most of the time they would put it in the trunk of their car and put the lid down, or else they would have a pickup with a tarpaulin to cover it. A few years ago, I still owned the old farm before I gave it to my brother, and somebody called and told me there was a fire on the Madison place adjoining us. I didn't know then that Weyhauser had bought it. I went over there and asked about it and was told Weyhauser owns the Madison place, and Weyhauser's people have come and put the fire out.

I wanted to go to Jasper, so I decided I would go the back way through the Pendley's settlement and come back into what is now Highway 18 in Corona by Wolf Creek. I was driving through there and here comes a tall slim fellow, and I knew it was Jess Pendley. I rolled the window down and I said, "Hey Jess."

He asked, "Is that you Fuller? That you Fuller? Yes sir, sure is. That's you, Fuller." We visited and he talked about not seeing me in a long time. I had a good relationship with him.

I said, "Jess, you know, I haven't tasted any good wildcat whiskey in a long time. I would like to have little just to have in my pantry at home."

Jess said, "Fuller, you know I haven't made any wildcat whiskey since I started drawing my Social Security!"

Denver Clark said he had already promised that 100 acres to his daughter.

TWENTY-TWO

FOLSOM, WALLACE, WALLACE, DeGRAFFENRIED, BREWER AND JAMES

During the 1954 Folsom campaign, in which Judge George Wallace was the south Alabama campaign manager, and all during the four years of Governor Folsom's administration, it was no secret that Wallace had in mind to run for governor fours years later. Quite often he would tell me to keep Folsom from making certain statements because it was apparent that the next campaign would be a different philosophy altogether, meaning consideration of the blacks would be a political "no, no."

Wallace's first move toward his 1958 campaign, when John Patterson was his strongest opponent, was when Congressman Adam Clayton Powell, a black congressman from New York was invited to the mansion by Governor Folsom, and was served an alcoholic beverage. Of course, the press made much of it. Judge Wallace gave a press release which was very critical of this incident by Governor Folsom. This, was highlighted by the press statewide.

Speaker Rankin Fite came to my office the next morning after he read the newspapers. We were disturbed by the statement Judge Wallace had given to the press. We discussed it and decided to try to talk to Wallace. I called Wallace and made arrangements for Rankin and me to meet him the next morning for breakfast at a little restaurant in Clio, his home town. We met there and after breakfast we sat and talked from about seven o'clock until eleven. Finally, Wallace said, "Fellows, you can say all you want to, but I'm going to the governor's office with this philosophy."

"George, you are crazy. You will never make it," I said.

Wallace capitalized on two things that turned out to be very effective politically statewide. One was that there would be nor entertaining of blacks in the mansion, the other was that there would be no alcoholic beverages served in the mansion.

I was wrong. In 1962 he was elected governor. A funny thing, after he was elected governor, Speaker Fite and I were invited to Clio for a George Wallace Day. As we passed this same little restaurant, Speaker Fite asked, "Well, you want to have breakfast there again, Fuller?"

"Maybe not," I answered.

In 1958 and 1962 I had much encouragement to run for governor, but I knew my philosophy would never let me run a winning campaign.

In 1958 Attorney General John Patterson ran for governor, and won over his strongest opponent, George Wallace, who was still the circuit judge in Barbour County. My political activity during the Patterson administration was minimal. However, I was operating the Fayco Pipe Plant and one asphalt plant with the combine. Of course, my children and I also had the Glen Allen Materials asphalt plant, but we didn't enjoy a lot of business during those four years.

In 1962, Governor Folsom decided to run again for governor. Had he been elected it would have been his third term. His opponents were Judge George Wallace, from Barbour County, Senator Albert Boutwell from Jefferson County, and Representative Ryan DeGraffenried, from Tuscaloosa County. It was Judge Wallace's second time to run for governor.

I was not active at all in Governor Folsom's campaign. He had selected Herman Nelson, the former highway director, as his campaign manager statewide, and Bill Drinkard and Murray Battles were in the office again. Both of them had been in the other campaigns. Ralph Hammond and Myra Leak Porter were not active any more and did not take any part in the campaign.

About two or three weeks after the campaign started, Bill Drinkard called me at my house one Sunday morning about two o'clock. He asked, "Fuller, what's wrong with the campaign?"

I said, "Bill, two or three things. Number one, Folsom is slipping in and out. After the Corn Grinders play, he comes in and makes a little speech. He is not making himself available to go around and speak to all the people. Then he leaves and gets out of the way instead of shaking hands and talking to the people at the rallies. He isn't gaining any votes. In fact, he may be losing some. Another thing is that after the intermission the band plays a little, and he gets up and makes his second little talk. He tells what he has done, but doesn't tell what he plans to do. He doesn't explain his platform or tell what he plans to do to make the state better. What he needs to do is to call Ralph Hammond and get him to make a list of the things he wants to accomplish and maybe have him outline a platform. He needs to get Ralph to write him a speech." Folsom was pouting at Ralph at the time, and Ralph was glad of it. I think he was pouting at me, too, but I never knew why.

"Will you come tell him that?" Bill asked.

"I'll be happy to. Actually, I've promised his brother, Cecil, that I will come to the Gadsden courthouse this afternoon at two o'clock and make a little talk to the campaign leaders. I'll come back by Cullman and talk to Jim," I said.

"I'll set it up, and you come by and talk to the Governor about it," Bill said. I did go by, and Folsom, Bill Drinkard and I sat on the front porch. I told him what I thought about it and told him he needed to generate more enthusiasm himself, develop what he was going to do, and work out a platform.

"Will you come to work and help us straighten it out?" asked Folsom.

"I'll be happy to, Governor. I really would like to see you as governor again. Alabama needs what you stand for," I said.

"When can you come?" he asked.

"I'll come in the morning," I said.

The next morning when I got there, Frank Long, who had driven up from Montgomery, was there, as well as Bill Drinkard. Bill came out and said, "Just come and sit on the porch and wait for him to come. Frank and Bill went into the house. After a little while, Bill Drinkard came out and said, "Fuller, go on home. I can't tell you anything right now. I'll tell you later."

I couldn't imagine what had happened. I went back by the campaign office, and Frank Long came to me and said, "Fuller,

Bill wouldn't tell you, but I'm going to tell you. Herman Nelson found out you were invited to help with the campaign, and he said he was resigning and went back home. Of course, we can't have that happen."

"No, you can't have that happen. I didn't think I was coming to be campaign manager. I just thought I was coming in as an adviser or worker. But it is all right with me," I said.

It rocked on and, finally, Governor Folsom called me again. When he spoke at Hamilton he asked Rankin Fite and me to ride back to Winfield with him. He said, "Fuller, the word is out that George Wallace has bought Senator Albert Boutwell." Boutwell had served in the senate and also as lieutenant governor.

"Albert has withdrawn, and Wallace has raised $90,000 to refund him his campaign expense. Will you come into Birmingham to the Bankhead Hotel? We have rooms set up with Watt lines. Will you come in and see if you can salvage the Boutwell votes and support?"

"I will be happy to if you want me to, but it will be tomorrow afternoon or maybe Friday morning before I can come. Tomorrow afternoon I have promised to speak to the Music Study Club in Fayette, and I'll come after it is over, but I will probably wait until Friday," I told him. I went in early Friday morning and called a few of my friends and political leaders, and folks I thought had been supporting Albert Boutwell. From the first they said, "Fuller, if you had been here earlier and asked us we would have been glad to have gone with you and Folsom. But we have already promised to go with Wallace. In fact, we helped raise the money. Had we known you were connected with Folsom and would be included in his administration for the next four years, we would have been glad to come in and help do it."

I worked on it Friday, spent the night, and called people all day Saturday. I came home Sunday and went back Monday and started calling again, but just had no encouragement. Fred Huey, from Bessemer, who managed the campaign office in the Bankhead Hotel in Birmingham, came up to my room about two o'clock that afternoon and said, "Fuller, Governor Folsom and Jerry Gwin have come in and are asleep in a room on the second floor. They told me to be sure and not let you go down there." I didn't try to go.

That night when I got home, I told Reba, "Folsom is not even going to be in the run-off, because with Wallace and DeGraffenried running, DeGraffenried will get more votes than Folsom."

Friday night before that, both Harlan Prater and Richard Arthur, who lived in Fayette and were supporters of Folsom, even in his first and second administrations, had gone with me to Florence to a rally at the cattle coliseum. Bill Drinkard was there, and I asked, "Bill do you have the video tape edited and ready to play?"

"Yes, we've got it all ready. We are going to televise it over Birmingham's Channel 6 and Montgomery's WSFA television stations," Bill said. Both television stations used union labor.

Monday afternoon, about an hour before I was ready to leave—which would have been about four o'clock—he asked, "Fuller, you going to Montgomery tonight?"

"No, but I can if you want me to," I said.

"No, no need to at all. But I wanted to tell you there has been a little change in the plans. You asked me about the tape in Florence Monday night, but we have decided we will put the Governor on live and have Jamelle and all the children on, and Johnny Steifelmeyer and I'll be on with him," Bill told me.

"You sure that's all right?" I asked.

"Yes, its all settled, and everything is worked out," he said.

"Do you want me to go?" I asked.

"No, no it is not necessary at all for you to go," he replied. I didn't go and went on home, but I felt bad about it.

That night, Monday night before the election on Tuesday, Folsom came on television. He had a full hour. He looked fine, but when he got up, he called his son Jack the name of another son, Jim, and he called Jim, Jack. He ran his hands through Jamelle's hair and other things like that. I did not get excited that night about Jim's appearance on television because I knew how much he admired President Roosevelt's style and manner of campaigning, particularly his fireside chats. I thought he was just having a fireside chat. It looked like that to me, and somebody wanted it to look that way, and it did.

The next morning when I went to the post office to get my mail, Docia Forsyth, a lady who worked in the County Superintendent of Education's office, got out of her car the same time that I was going into the post office. She said, "Fuller, your old buddy was drunk last night."

"No, I didn't think so," I said.

She asked, "How come he didn't know his own young'uns'

names?" I thought, right then, thousands of people all over Alabama felt the same way.

He lost by a little over 1100 votes. Jamelle called me from Mobile that night and said, "Fuller, Jim should have been in the run-off."

"He certainly should have been in the runoff. The campaign could have been managed more effectively. His record of what he had done for the people in his previous administrations, and the program that he planned for the next administration could have been presented much clearer, as he was capable of doing," I told her.

The run-off was between Wallace and DeGraffenried, and Wallace won easily enough. Ryan DeGraffenried had served two terms in the House of Representatives and had the support of the middle class, and especially upper class people — lawyers, doctors, and larger businesses. There was no question that he could be elected four years later. Later I was involved in the DeGraffenried race, though he was unable to continue his campaign.

Wallace was elected by a fairly large majority over DeGraffenried in the run-off. Back then if you won in the May Democratic primary or run-off, it meant you were elected, because you would rarely have an opponent in the November general election. Shortly after the general election in November, Wallace called and said he wanted to see me, and asked me to come down the next Wednesday. As I have said before, Senator Rankin Fite and I talked on the telephone every day. Most of the time we talked early in the morning before we went to work.

I told Rankin about Wallace's call, that he had asked me to come to Montgomery on Wednesday. Rankin said, "Let me go with you."

"Okay. That will be good," I said. Rankin came to my house in Fayette, and we drove to Montgomery. Governor-elect Wallace had told me to come to the Jeff Davis Hotel and give him a ring. He would meet me there or tell me where to meet him. When I called him, he said, "Fuller, there has been a little change in my plans. I'm invited to go to Columbus, Georgia to speak to a joint meeting of the civic clubs." "Can you ride with me?" he asked.

"Yes, I'll be happy to. Rankin Fite is with me," I said.

"That's good. Bring him too," Wallace said.

In a little while they picked us up. Oscar Harper, George's right hand man was driving, and in the car was a Mr. Smith, who was kind of a bodyguard to George. He stayed with him most of the time and went everywhere Wallace went. Smith sat in front with Harper. Wallace always wanted to sit on the right side in the back seat. On the way over, I found out why he wanted to sit there. He would pretend he had to use the bathroom every time we came to a clean looking service station. But really what he did was get out of the car and shake hands with people standing around. One time we stopped at a place and Wallace was looking around, and Oscar said, "Look at him, he's looking for somebody to shake hands with."

We got to Columbus, Georgia a little early. The meeting was going to be at a hotel. They gave us a key, and we went to the room, freshened up, and sat down. I said, "Governor, you know

I have two asphalt plants, and a metal pipe and concrete plant, and sand and gravel operation. My biggest interest is who is going to be highway director."

"Not at first, but Herman Nelson has known for quite a long time he is going to be highway director. We are going to start out with someone different." Finally, he said, "It is going to be Ed Rodgers, the head of the Roadbuilders. He has served as highway director once before. He continued talking, "What I want with you, Fuller, is to be my adviser. I'm going to have Seymour Trammell, Richard Stone, Cecil Jackson from Selma, and a young attorney, who will be my legal adviser. Seymour Trammell will be finance director. Richard Stone will be his assistant. You managed the asphalt business, road building, and prison department so well during the Folsom administration, I want you to be my adviser in those areas."

"I'll be happy to do that," I said. It was putting me in the front seat.

Before Rankin could say anything, Wallace said, "Rankin, quite a long while ago I promised Albert Brewer he would be Speaker of the House, but you, Tom Bevill, and Pete Matthews will be my floor leaders in the house. I figure you can handle it. You have done such a good job as Speaker of the House during the second Folsom administration." Rankin agree to. We listened to his speech, then went back to Montgomery, and Rankin and I came home.

The next day, I read in the paper about Lawrence Seaborn's desire to be prison commissioner. Lawrence Seaborn was the former sheriff of Jackson County and assistant to Frank Lee, who was one of the two prison commissioners. Seaborn had not been very active with the prison system, but he was a close friend of Ralph Hammond's, who was Governor Folsom's speech writer. He reported to Ralph Hammond everything he could think of that was not pleasing, particularly about the prison system. I found out that he was trying to replace Frank Lee as prison commissioner, and that he gotten John Kone, an old time prominent lawyer who was real close to Wallace, to join in with him. I read all this in the paper.

Seymour Trammell called and asked me to come down; he wanted to talk. I went down. Originally, Wallace had told me they had set up four rooms in the Jeff Davis hotel, and I would have one any time I wanted it. But they set up separate rooms for George's brother, Gerald, Richard Stone, Cecil Jackson, and Seymour Trammell—Seymour, who was going to be finance director. The first thing I said was, "The person you are thinking about putting out there (Seaborn) does not have the ability to handle the prisoners and the people. They probably have 6000 inmates. Every one of them have five, six, eight, or ten people back home that think they shouldn't be locked up, and every one of them have eight or ten people back home who think they should be locked up for life. There is no way to win." About that time Governor Wallace walked in, and I said, "Governor, I want to repeat to you what I've just told Seymour and Cecil."

He studied a minute and said, "Fuller is right, Seymour, we'd better nip that in the bud now. Tell our lawyer friend that we don't want to fool with that anymore." That was the end of that, and Frank Lee stayed as prison commissioner in a couple of other administrations after that.

When Wallace knew he was going to be elected before the end of the run-off, he had his campaign manager, Seymour Trammell, call me to come down. As I've said before, my friend, Ed Pepper, who was my assistant when I was finance director, had served out my term as finance director when I resigned to come back home and run for the senate in the 12th Senatorial District. When Seymour called and asked me to come down, he said, "Fuller, we are reasonably sure George Wallace is going to win, and he wants Ed to serve on the Public Service Commission."

Ed Pepper had made a race for Public Service Commissioner and was in a run off with Senator Joe Foster from Huntsville. There wasn't that many votes difference, but with Wallace backing Ed Pepper, Foster was reasonably sure he was going to lose. They had somebody talk to Foster about withdrawing so Ed would not have to spend his money and run the slight risk of not winning. Senator Foster said he would take $27,500 to withdraw, which was the amount of money he had in his campaign.

"The only friend you all have that I know about that I would take the money from is Fuller Kimbrell," Foster told them.

After Seymour told me all that, he said, "Here's a check for $5000 you can hand him. Two fellows are waiting downstairs. I'm going to call them up. They think they can have the other money for you by daylight in the morning. Tomorrow is the last day you have to withdraw." One of the fellows was Rex Moore and the other was Oscar Hyde. They were in the small loan business. I say small loan, but back then they called them short-term loans. Seymour told them I had a $5000 check and they needed to come in with $22,500. They said they would be back before daylight.

About four o'clock the next morning there was a knock on the door. When I opened it, there stood Rex Moore and Oscar Hyde. They said, "Fuller, we are ready to count out the money." I sat there in a chair with my pajamas on. Rex got on one side of the bed, and Oscar got on the other side. They opened their attache cases and pulled out long envelopes one at a time. They'd pull out one envelope, count out $500, lay it aside, pull out another one, count out $500, and lay it aside. They did that until they had counted out $22,500. One of them took out of his satchel a six pound brown paper grocery bag. They put $22,500 cash and the $5000 check in that brown paper bag and went out the door and left the bag with me.

I went on and got my bath and listened to the radio. Back then they didn't have televisions in the hotel rooms. About six o'clock I went downstairs to the restaurant, set the bag of money on the floor by my chair, ordered, and ate breakfast. When I got through, I picked up the paper bag of money, went back to my room, and called Joe Foster. He was at the Walter Bragg apartments. I asked, "Are you up?"

"Yes," he answered.

"I'm coming to talk to you," I said.

"Come ahead," he said.

I went into his room and handed him the brown paper bag, and said, "Here is your money."

"Did you count it?" Foster asked.

"No, but I watched them count out the cash on the bed in my room. I feel sure it's all there," I said.

"If you think so. I'll take your word," he said. He picked up the phone, called the Associated Press, read his withdrawal statement, and withdrew from the race. That was the highlight of that trip to Montgomery.

Wallace stayed busy the rest of the year and had a big inauguration. There were several parties. Reba and I were invited to the inauguration, so we took a big crowd from Fayette and spent a couple of nights.

One of the first things Governor Wallace did after his inauguration was to call a special session for roads. He put in the special session to propose a $25 million bond issue. I went to him and said, "Don't put in a certain amount. Just put in a bond issue for highways." He did.

I went to see him again and said, "Governor Wallace, you know the one-cent gasoline tax passed during the Folsom administration when I was finance director. We obligated a $50 million bond issue, but there is enough left of that one-cent gasoline tax money to do a $100 million bond issue. For what you need or what Alabama needs $25 million is not anywhere near enough."

"Say that again," Wallace said.

"Yes, Governor. It will retire a $100 million bond issue with all ease," I said.

"Who did you use for fiscal agent?" Wallace asked.

"Hendricks and Mays in Birmingham," I answered.

"You get Rankin Fite and Joe Dawkins, who is going to be active in my administration, and Pete Matthews, and you all go to Birmingham. Talk to the folks at Hendricks and Mays. If they tell you that it will take care of a $100 million bond issue, we will make it $100 million instead of $25 million," Wallace said.

I called the three fellows, and we all went to Birmingham to see Jimmy Hendricks, a real fine fellow in the security business with offices in the First National Bank building. I told him my story. Mr. Hendricks said, "It's almost noon. Go have lunch. Give me about an hour and a half. Come back about two o'clock or a little before. Let me do a little research on it."

At two o'clock we were back, and the secretary told him we were there. He called us in, "Yes, I've done a survey, and it will handle a $100 million bond issue with all ease," he said.

Wallace changed from a $25 million to $100 million bond issue immediately. That was when he decided it was time to bring in Herman Nelson as his highway director.

Another thing Governor Wallace wanted me to do was to handle the asphalt paving. As I've said earlier, I told several people if they would buy an asphalt plant, I would give them enough asphalt business to pay for their plant. That was before the bid law. I had told him about that, and he said, "If you can keep them all happy and keep them from cutting each other's throats, do it." That I did. Since Herman had become highway director, it was very easy to handle and place orders around to keep everybody happy. That worked fine during the first Wallace administration.

Another thing I was able to work out for the city of Fayette as I've said before, when I was senator during Governor Folsom's first administration, I was able to obtain for Fayette a National Guard Unit. The city had bought about two good-sized blocks for the National Guard armory, adjoining what is now the middle school. Where the middle school is located, in order to expand and make it larger and have more playground, the County Board of Education needed more land, and the only way they could get additional land was to get some of the National Guard's.

I headed a group and went to call on Governor Wallace. I was trying to swap West Highland, a school for blacks that was to be closed because of integration, for the National Guard land, which would give twice as much land at the campus where the middle school is now. The adjutant general, who was from Jasper, objected very seriously to this. But we kept talking, and finally, the next day after we got back, he called me on the phone and asked, "Fuller, could we work out to give you half of that land?"

"Yes, I think that will satisfy them," I said.

He said, "In fact, we will give them a little more. We will give them to where the fence is." It was about two thirds of the property they owned at that time. We worked it out, but still the Board of Education was not willing. Things had gotten so tight they could not continue to have separate but equal schools. They had to be integrated, but they continued to keep West Highland open for a while. The Bagwell estate had a pretty good sized lot between the National Guard land, and Alabama

Highway 18 and U. S. Highway 43. I insisted on the Board of Education buying that property — which they did.

What Fayette had at that time, they had begun to call a storage and training center instead of an armory. The city bought forty acres of land on the north side of town, and Congressman Bevill had worked out with Congress to give us enough money to build a new National Guard armory. Now, Fayette has a very nice National Guard armory, and the middle school has quite a large tract of land. They are not using all of it, but it is still available if the town of Fayette grows to it.

In Governor Wallace's first administration, he wanted to continue his popularity and keep his name before the people. He got the legislature to pass a constitutional amendment where a governor could succeed himself, which meant it had to go to the people for a vote. As it was, a governor had to skip a term before he could run again. The people voted against it. Governor Wallace was really upset, because he had made some speeches in various places which made quite a name for him at the Democrat National Convention.

Congressman Carl Elliott was one of the delegates who didn't walk out of the Democrat Convention held in Philadelphia in 1948. Carl Elliott had been defeated as congressman because he had been eliminated by the "Nine-Eight Law," which eliminated one of the nine elected congressmen, because Alabama has lost one seat in the U. S. House of Representatives, and had not reapportioned. In 1966 Elliott decided to run for governor, as he still had ambition to follow his philosophy, which would have been a wonderful thing for Alabama had it been carried further. The masses of Alabama would have certainly benefited. It was such a bad thing for the South, that the good works he was doing in Congress had to be stopped by his own people.

Frank Long was really close to Carl Elliott, and he had insisted that Carl have me active in his campaign as his finance man. Carl was close to a fellow who had a Top Dollar store. The warehouse for the Top Dollar stores was in Jasper. This man had married the daughter of one of the big men in Birmingham real estate companies. They were really wealthy—both he and his father-in-law. Top Dollar had quite a number of stores in Alabama, and maybe some in Mississippi, and the man's wife and her father had financial interest in them. I saw right quick that they were the kind of people who would let me do all the work. They wanted to make certain they would get credit for everything. It was not going all that well, plus the fact that one of the Bankheads, John Bankhead, Jr., was in on the management, too. He was close to Carl Elliott. The Bankhead family in Alabama was worth quite a few votes without a doubt, but I saw right away he thought he was smarter than I was, and he made that opinion very clear. As it went along, it became more apparent that I could not work with him.

In 1966, during the time I was having all the tax trouble, I went to them and told them that one of my best friends had come and told me I'd better not fool with the finance of the campaign. I felt as though the IRS was watching every move I made, which might not be the fact, but I told Carl, "If that be true, then I cannot effectively do the job you want me to Congressman. You can rest assured I'm your best friend, but I think I'd better withdraw and just do a 'little word of mouth' all around for you." Which I did, because I felt he would have really been a wonderful governor for Alabama.

I furnished a driver and kept him on the payroll for him, and gave him an Amoco credit card to buy gas during the entire campaign. He and his campaign workers liked to stay and meet at the Albert Pick Motels. They found out the Amoco credit card was accepted at the Albert Pick Motels, so they arranged to have rallies in Huntsville, Mobile, and Montgomery and the surrounding areas, and they would stay at the Albert Pick Motels. I ended up putting quite a large sum of money into the Carl Elliott campaign. Although I had to withdraw as his campaign finance man, I am so glad I kept my friendship with Carl Elliott. I felt that he was a very honorable statesman, and as I've said before, it was really unfortunate that he could not have been governor of Alabama. He recently passed away.

Another effective political candidate for Alabama was Lurleen Wallace. One night Seymour Trammell called me and said, " Fuller, Lurleen Wallace is going to run for governor. She will announce tomorrow." George Wallace's supporters had been secretly training her to make speeches, although they knew that she had cancer and would not live the full four years. But this was at the beginning of her illness, and she still had her vim and vigor. She was one of the finest and most gracious ladies I've ever met. Everybody knew it. They arranged for her to make her announcement in the House of Representatives' chamber, and the legislators knew from that very day she was going to win by a landslide. The thing I did earlier in Carl Elliott's campaign (resigning as finance man) turned out to be an asset and a wonderful thing for me because it still kept me close to the Wallaces, although I did not agree with all their philosophy. Seymour Trammell, Richard Stone, and Cecil Jackson were still the three top men in the Lurleen Wallace administration.

I developed a close relationship with Albert Brewer, who was elected lieutenant governor the same time Lurleen was elected governor. It kept my foot in the door in Montgomery whenever I wanted to go. But I dealt very little with Governor Lurleen Wallace. Seymour Trammell and George Wallace still ran the show about as much as they would have if George Wallace had been sitting in the governor's chair, and my connection would not have been any better if George had still been governor.

With Lurleen in the governor's office, with the same finance director and legal adviser, I continued to be adviser to the finance and highway departments, particularly with the asphalt division, building and repairing roads, and handling special favors for people who had made trades during the campaign. I was a go-between for the finance director and highway director. It worked out to where my area of the state benefited more than it has ever benefited before or since.

As time went on, George pushed more and more using Governor Lurleen's office to further his campaign for president.

He began to go to various states — Iowa, Maryland, Minnesota, North Carolina, and others — to campaign for president. President Nixon was running for re-election. There had been a lot of talk during the Wallace administration about Gerald Wallace having his "finger in the pie" so much. A lot of people suggested maybe he was profiting illegally with the asphalt producers. The federal government filed an injunction on the finance and highway departments during Lurleen's administration in regard to illegal practices. The alleged collusion in the asphalt business was a matter of "I won't get in your territory, and you won't get in mine."

When the federal government filed suit, they asked all the asphalt people to bring all their records to the federal building in Atlanta — which a lot of them did. A funny thing was, when I took my papers to Atlanta, Sam Torrence of Couch Construction Company, located in Dothan, and Mike McCartney of McCartney Construction, located in Gadsden, were there. Torrence said, "I've brought a whole pickup load of records. I have to find out where to unload them."

"I have three large boxes," McCartney said. "How about you, Fuller?" he asked.

"These three legal folders under my arm is what I brought," I answered.

The hearing was set up in Montgomery regarding the entire thing. The first asphalt dealer they called in was Nimrod Long, the manager of the company formerly known as Warren Brothers. Warren Brothers had asphalt plants in Birmingham, Huntsville, Tuscaloosa, and maybe Mobile. They had asphalt plants in several other states. Then they summoned me. I had two asphalt plants, but they knew at that time that I was working with the asphalt people, keeping everybody happy. After they pulled me in, I asked, "Can I talk a little?"

"Yes," they answered.

"I want it on record," I said.

"It will be on record. Everything you say," they said.

I started talking, "I have a concrete business. I have an asphalt business. I have a metal pipe business. When we order steel from U. S. Steel, they won't ship unless you give them an order for several hundred tons at a time. They will book it to you for a certain price, but then they will wire you one morning, say at eleven o'clock and tell you that the price is going up, and if you pick up your order after eleven o'clock that morning it would be at the new price." Prices were continuing to go up regularly at that time, particularly in the steel business. "Now, we buy a lot of steel from Wheeling Steel, and they will give you 30 days to pick up because they are a small steel company."

I continued, "The other thing is cement. We buy from two different cement companies. For instance, we will get a letter from one of the companies in the mail today stating cement is going up so much a ton. We will get a telegram from the other one before noon stating that their price is going up the exact same amount. The same thing is true with the steel companies. We will get word from Wheeling, then a telegram from Republic, stating that their prices are going up the same amount as U. S. Steel."

"The other is gasoline. In the asphalt business, we buy our

asphalt from Vulcan Asphalt Refining Company at Cordova, Alabama, which is usually a little higher than Chevron's and the other producers of liquid asphalt for producing asphalt. We will get a letter from Standard Oil in Mobile stating the price is going up half a cent today at noon, and we will get a telegram from the other companies saying they are going up the exact same amount that same day. That is no accident. There is where you need to start with collusion, instead of with little folks like us," I told them.

"I want to talk a little more. You do a much better job putting asphalt down in warm weather when the asphalt is still hot. The requirements are that it has to be a certain temperature when it leaves the plant. We have a plant in Fayette and try to bid Pickens County. We don't bid Tuscaloosa County. There are two asphalt plants in Tuscaloosa County, and they have the advantage because one of the biggest costs in asphalt is the freight—bringing the material in and taking the finished product out to the location on the road. If you haul it too far it gets cold, and you cannot make a really smooth surface. I don't see that you started on collusion in the right place. There are a lot of other places you could start checking. You can haul steel around the world and it is still just steel. You can haul cement around the world, and if you keep it good and dry, it is still just cement. Liquid asphalt, whether it comes from Mobile, Tuscaloosa, or Jackson, Mississippi is still the same analysis," I finished.

The government agents did not comment. They did ask me four or five questions and let me go. They questioned three or four more asphalt people and left. They had three people there from the Federal Justice Department.

It turned out that, about the same time, the revenue department started an investigation of Gerald Wallace for state income tax irregularities. It so happened we used the same tax attorney, and I was having income tax problems at that same time. Several contractors had found out who I was using, and realizing that I had the best, they used him. too. Several other contractors were investigated. One thing right interesting was that, so far as I know, the federal agents never summoned any contractor to come testify for the record in Atlanta. And I'm sure I would have heard if it had happened.

My tax attorney told me that he met with the federal judge in Montgomery. He said they sat and settled Gerald Wallace's taxes without him having to pay anything. The prosecutor met with the judge and met with my and Gerald's tax attorney and said, "Whatever you do, don't tell Gerald how this was or anything about it."

The tax attorney said that when he told George Wallace he had gotten it settled, Wallace said, "Hell, you aren't kidding me. I know damn well if I hadn't been running for president, that damn Nixon wouldn't have had the income tax man down here at all."

The asphalt situation rocked on. A lot of people had contracts and purchase orders to lay asphalt, but everything was stopped. This happened a short while before Lurleen passed away. After Lieutenant Governor Albert Brewer took over as governor the weather was warm enough, and it was time to do road paving. I went to him and told him that the Supreme Court had thrown out the suit. It was all settled, and now was the time to do the best jobs on the highway. "With all the asphalt plants shut down, with many, many people out of work, and many, many roads that need paving, I believe you will do Alabama a great favor and certainly help your administration if you will release it," I told him. He called the finance director in and told him to release it.

Hugh Sparrow had been the most critical news reporter of Folsom's first administration. He was not quite so bad in the second administration for reasons I've talked about before. When Sparrow heard about the resolution of the asphalt situation, he wrote, "Well, Fuller Kimbrell, the great mediator, met with Governor Brewer, and asphalt is in business again, as usual."

One thing that happened during Lurleen's campaign and while George was running for president that I am most proud of was construction of Brewer State Junior College in Fayette. I got to thinking about the college and how its construction came about. Rankin Fite, Tom Bevill, and Governor Brewer got together (Tom Bevill said Rankin provided the financial know-how in it) and introduced a $300 million bond issue to build two-year junior colleges and trade schools in Alabama. To begin with there were going to be just a few. But before they got through, there were twenty-six names on the bill, which meant they had to build twenty-six junior colleges or technical colleges. I was not in the legislature, and Fayette was left out. I felt like Fayette needed one as much as any other location. Marion County, through Senator Fite's ingenuity, had gotten a trade school, and Tom Bevill, who represented Walker County, got Walker Technical College in Sumiton. One morning, on my way to Montgomery, I got to thinking about it. So I went to see Seymour Trammell. They were in the Ten High Building, which was Wallace's presidential campaign headquarters. But before I saw Seymour, I went to see John Graves, the comptroller, and I asked, "John, is there any money left in the capital account for the bond issue that was passed to build the junior colleges?"

He pulled a stack of paper out of his drawer and said, "Here are the computer printouts. You bought the first computer that Alabama had. You ought to be able to read it."

I turned to the bottom of the page and it showed $1,300,000. I went to Seymour Trammell's office and told him I wanted a junior college for Fayette. Seymour said, "There isn't any money."

"I just left John Graves' office and there is $1,300,000," I said.

"There is?" Seymour asked.

"Yes," I said.

"I tell you what. You bring me $20,000 for George Wallace's presidential campaign and you got it," Seymour said.

"Okay, you hold the money," I said. I came back to Fayette and told a few people about it. The county got busy without doing anything about the money and bought the land where the Bevill State Community College Brewer Campus is now. We met in the commissioners' office. They approved and Charles Nolen, the county's attorney at the time, was to sell the needed land. They passed a resolution to pay him $40,000 for 40 acres. He had bought the land for $7500 at a bankrupt sale.

"I need $20,000 for Wallace's campaign for president," I said.

Clyde Cargile, the probate judge said, "I don't have anything to do with that. I don't know where you are going to get $20,000."

We studied it a minute and Charles Nolen said, "I tell you what. Pay me $50,000 for the land, and I'll give him $10,000."

"Do you think you can get the school for $10,000?" Judge Cargile asked.

"I believe I can," I answered.

Clyde turned to Fleetwood Watkins and asked, "Fleetwood, (the only man still living except myself who was in the meeting), can we do that?"

"We haven't put anything on record and we can record just as easily that we paid $50,000 for the land," Fleetwood replied. All the commissioners agreed to it. Charles pulled out a check and wrote it for $10,000.

I went to see Seymour Trammell. Seymour, Richard Stone, and Cecil Jackson came down, and I handed Seymour the check for $10,000. Seymour said, "I told you $20,000."

"Seymour, there is no way I can raise $20,000," I said.

"We need the money, George is running for president," Seymour said.

"I have $2000 in cash in my pocket. I'll put that much in it," I said.

"Goddamn. Fuller will go see George and get it anyhow, so we might as well go along with it," Seymour said.

That is the way Fayette got Brewer State Junior College, which is now the Bevill State Community College Brewer Campus. We sat and visited and Seymour said something I was afraid was going to have effect. He looked over at Cecil Jackson and Richard Stone and said, "Boys, you know we have about $60,000 from the rally in North Carolina last night, and Gerald is up there helping count it. There are a lot of $100 bills that won't be there when we get back, so we have to go." They said goodbye and went back upstairs.

As stated before, in 1964 I was elected to the State Democratic Executive Committee, serving my second or maybe third term during Governor Lurleen Wallace's administration. I had worked with the committee and gotten Roy Mayhall made chairman, replacing Ben Ray, who had been a wonderful chairman of the Democratic Executive Committee. Ben was really a fine person to work with, but former Governor Folsom had wanted a man from Winston County who had more of his same philosophy about politics and the benefit the government was to the people.

So when the 1964 Committee met, former Governor George Wallace was running for president. The loyal Democrats had it fixed so that, in order to run state presidential elector, candidates had to run as either Democrats or Republicans. They could not switch over and vote for whomever they pleased. They took an oath that they would vote for the nominee of their respective parties. Wallace's people, who he thought would vote for him for president, could not run on the Democrat ticket because they took a pledge to vote for whoever the National Convention nominee was.

The Democratic Executive Committee was meeting in

Birmingham and Wallace was trying to get it worked out to where the electors could vote for whomever they thought was best for Alabama and whomever they felt would be the best for the nation. We met the day before, and Wallace lacked six votes — mine being one of the six. I was a loyal Democrat and several times had made the headlines as being a "Yellow Dog Democrat" — which I was, and still am to this day, and don't plan to change. Wallace was trying his best to make it so electors could vote for whomever they wanted to. He sent Pete Matthews to see me. Pete said, "Fuller, I told Wallace the only way he can get this worked out is to send for Fuller Kimbrell. Nobody else on the committee can do it, and if they could they would not, I don't think. I told him if you could do it, you would."

In a minute, here came Seymour Trammell and Cecil Jackson. "Wallace wants to see you," they said.

We were in the Tutwiler Hotel, and I went to his room. "Fuller, my people think you can switch enough votes so the electors can vote for me if I run for president, even though I am not nominated at the Democrat National Convention," Wallace said.

"Governor, I probably could. But I need to think about it a little bit," I said.

"I want you to do it. You and I have been close, and we fought the same battles several times. You will not be unhappy if you do this for me," George said.

"Give me twenty minutes to think about it. I'll be back," I said. I went to my room and called Rankin Fite. He was already in bed, and I told him the situation. I said, "Rankin, this sure is a hard request. You know what a loyal Democrat I am, and it will have a big effect on the Democrat Party."

There was silence. For two or three minutes I didn't say anything and Rankin didn't either. Then he said, "Fuller, I know how you feel, but I don't believe you have a choice."

"I'm afraid that is true because of the situation and our relationship, including yours, makes me just have to yield," I said.

"I would, if I was in your place," Rankin said.

I went back and told George, "I think I can do it." I called five people and all five agreed to do it.

I went to George's room about midnight. He was still up, sitting in a chair pulling on his cigar. "George," I said, "I'm ready to go to bat."

"You mean you got them?" he asked.

"Yes, you will have to tell Seymour Trammell to cooperate with me later," I said.

"Hell, he will do it," said George.

The next morning, I went down to the lobby for breakfast and ran into Roy Mayhall and George LeMaister—two of the strongest democrats in Alabama, George Lewis Bailes, who became a federal judge in Birmingham, and Bob Vance, who was a federal judge, and later was killed by a bomb sent to him through the mail; all five of us were together. I met them as we were going in, and Roy Mayhall asked, "What is it?"

"I'm ready to go to bat," I said.

"Does that mean you got the votes?" asked Roy Mayhall.

"Yes," I answered.

"We won't fuss with you," he said. When it came up, I won by two votes. I voted with them, of course. I told them I had no choice. They all understood, pretty well, and they didn't hold it against me in the Democratic Party.

My doing this for George paid off with the Wallace administration for the remainder of Governor Lurleen Wallace's administration. By that time I had worked myself in with Albert Brewer. I liked his philosophy and his gentlemanly attitude and actions. Our district in west Alabama did not suffer on account of it, and benefited by the things I was able to accomplish, but I wish I had not had to go against my own beliefs to maintain good relations with the Governor's Office.

The same year that Lurleen Wallace was elected governor, and Carl Elliott ran for governor, Ryan DeGraffenried, the runner-up in the previous election with Governor George Wallace, had been campaigning all during that four years for governor and had a really nice setup—one of the best that had ever been in Alabama up to that time. I went into the Stafford Hotel in Tuscaloosa, and just as I walked in I met Ryan DeGraffenried and Bobby Cardinal, who was his pilot at that time. Ryan said, "Fuller, come on go with us. We are going to Montgomery to the County Engineers Annual meeting. They have asked me to speak. I want to talk to you; I want you to run my campaign."

"I haven't come prepared to go," I said.

"We will be back by four o'clock this afternoon," DeGraffenried said.

I flew down with them to Montgomery. He talked on the way down and on the way back to Tuscaloosa. What he wanted was for me to be his finance chairman. I had talked to him earlier and told him about how Boss Crump in Memphis had been successful in being elected several times as mayor of Memphis and had a reputation for controlling the representatives' and senators' campaigns all over Tennessee. When Donald, my son, got married while I was director of finance, they had the after-rehearsal dinner at the Cotton Hotel. I was seated by Mr. Patterson, who had been in Crump's office several years while he was mayor of Memphis. I asked him to tell me how Crump was so successful at getting elected every time and how he could extend his power 400 miles away into east Tennessee.

Patterson said, "I will tell you how. He controls the insurance business in the state of Tennessee. He controls Memphis, Nashville, and Knoxville. What Mayor Crump does is have the people who head up the departments in those cities to go out and pick beat or block managers and give them a little insurance commission. You see the managers will have so many blocks and they will give them a little insurance all four years. When election comes around, they are obligated, and led to understand they will continue."

Ryan DeGraffenried picked up on that, and he pretty much had the State of Alabama blocked off. He didn't have the insurance, but he did have block managers in every large city all over the state. He said, "I want you to come to a meeting tomorrow."

"I can't. I have to go to my wife's family reunion. She was a Shook," I said.

"I've got people coming. I'm going to tell them you are going to be the finance man," he said. He told them that Saturday that I would be coming on board the following Monday as finance man.

Over the weekend I did not hear from him, but he flew to Fort Payne for a rally on Monday, and that night they were flying to Gadsden for a rally. He and his pilot flew into a thunder cloud, and the plane crashed into trees. Unfortunately, DeGraffenried and his pilot were both killed.

I had made up my mind, that I would be the chairman of finance for his campaign. There were no further promises, and I didn't expect any more, but I had prepared to rent an office in the First National Bank building in Tuscaloosa. Later, DeGraffenried's campaign manager came to me and said, "You are pushing Carl Elliott's campaign. For $90,000 we will sell you all of DeGraffenried's records and everything."

"We can't raise that kind of money. I don't think," I told him. I never talked to him any more about it. I don't know what they did with the records.

There was no question after DeGraffenried was killed that Lurleen would be the next governor of Alabama. When Lurleen died, Albert Brewer moved up from lieutenant governor to governor. Governor Brewer did a wonderful job, and west Alabama, where I had my plants and most of my interests lay, was greatly benefited and continued to do well, as far as roads, bridges, and culverts were concerned.

George Wallace promised he would not run against Albert Brewer in the upcoming election, but he changed his mind and did run against him when the time came for Albert to run for governor. Wallace announced at the very last minute and used the same tactics he used to win his former election — the integration issue — still a very prominent issue and a sore toe all over Alabama as far as the election was concerned. Albert led Wallace by 17,000 votes in the first primary. In the run-off Wallace's workers went all over the state saying Brewer had gotten the "Bloc" vote, but they didn't say what the "Bloc" vote was, and most people thought it was the black vote. Wallace won by 12,000 or 13,000 votes.

One of the things that cost Governor Brewer a lot of votes was the chief engineer in the highway department. As always as is the case in every department in the state, and particularly in the highway department, the people who have been there so many years can have a very strong effect on the other employees. This was especially true under Governor Brewer's administration. He had brought in Marion Wilkins, the division engineer from Mobile and Baldwin Counties as highway director. Marion Wilkins was a very easy-going fellow. At that time, in the highway department they had a chief engineer who was an Oxford graduate. He gave the impression that unless you had at least a college education, you should not hold a job in the highway department, other than maybe to cut weeds, pick up trash along the highway, or use a shovel and pick. This kind of fellow can very easily have a negative effect on the people in the highway department, until the highway director gets wise and begins to handle it.

The chief engineer had been so rough it had left a bad taste in the mouths of most of the other highway employees. That information was passed on to all the other state employees. Since Governor Brewer had only two years to serve, he was never able to smooth it out during the remainder of his term, and he didn't get a good vote from the state employees. That cost him the election.

Everybody knew I was close to Wallace. One of my best customers, Mr. Farmer from Mobile, told me over the phone when we were talking one day, "Fuller I'm going to come to Fayette and see how bloody your breeches are between the legs from straddling the fence in this governor's race."

Albert Brewer really made a good governor, and I thought the majority of the people who followed and took part in politics were pleased with his administration. He lost to Wallace when he ran for election the first time. He ran later in 1989, when Fob James ran. James was an outstanding Auburn football star, but had not been in politics. Bill Baxley, who was the attorney general at that time, also ran for governor. Albert Brewer had a banker from Childersburg to manage his campaign, and I worked quite a bit for Albert in his campaign. I went down and discussed various things with the leaders working in his campaign. I took some information I wanted Albert to start telling about, especially the highways and such. "Let's save that for the run-off," he said.

"Governor, I was hoping we might win without a run-off," I said.

"That is too much to hope for," he said. "Isn't it?" he asked.

"Not really. We can make a really hard push with this and maybe another idea or two we can come up with, and win in the first primary," I said.

He talked it over with his campaign managers and they decided to save it for the run-off. Much to the surprise of almost everybody in Alabama, he did not make the run-off. Bill Baxley and Fob James were in the run-off. Most of the folks who supported Brewer, I think, supported Bill Baxley in the run-off. But Fob James, who had been on the State Republican Committee, was elected on the Democrat ticket.

I got along good when Fob James was governor. He built a road at my request, and Judge Chandler from Lamar County had the road improved from Crossville to Vernon—about twelve miles. Governor James asked me to come down and help with the legislature in passing the one-cent gasoline tax for highway construction, which I did. When the bill passed in the legislature and he was ready to sign it, he sent for me. I have a picture in my scrapbook of him signing the bill with quite a few other supporters of the bill, including several legislators.

We had problems with the highway director, Bobby Joe Kemp about the Crossville-Vernon road. He almost didn't agree to it, because he wanted to turn the old road back to the county without repairing it. But Lamar County didn't have the money to repair it at that time. We finally got it worked out later. I also have a picture of Judge Chandler, Bobby Joe Kemp, Governor James, and me agreeing to terms for construction of the new road.

TWENTY-THREE

SOME OTHER FUNNY RECOLLECTIONS

Several things that happened along the way while I was the John Deere dealer. One thing in particular I would like to tell about had to do with Mr. J. C. Grimsley, who was one of my best customers. Mr. Grimsley had quite a large farm on the edge of Fayette, part of it was in the city limits. He and one of his brothers were in the mule business, and also sold fertilizer. He and his two brothers, E. M. and A. M., owned the First National Bank (now Regions) in Fayette. Mr. J. C. came by quite often and visited, but this particular day he came by and asked, "Kimbrell, how about riding down to Belk with me? I want to look at a horse."

We drove to Belk to the customer's house. The horse was a really fine looking one. The man got the horse out of the stable, and rode it around. He said the horse was just twelve years old. Now, Mr. Grimsley had been trading and selling mules and horses for forty or fifty years and it didn't take him but a minute to know the horse was older than twelve years. In the conversation the man went on to tell that Bilbo, a former senator for the state of Mississippi, had rode the horse in his campaign. Well, that meant that the horse had to be at least sixteen years old. On the way back home, I said, "Well, Mr. Grimsley, a fellow ought to be smart enough to know who to lie to."

"What to you mean, Kimbrell?" Mr. Grimsley asked.

I said, "Well, there's a man lying to you about the age of a horse, knowing that you had been trading horses for years. And it didn't take you but a minute to know the horse was older than he said it was."

At the time, I didn't know if Mr. Grimsley paid much attention to my comment or not. But later it became clear that he had, because quite often after that Mr. Grimsley would come by and ask, "Well, Fuller, do you still know who to lie to?"

"I try to know," I would tell him.

One of the other things was I told Carey Pollard, a man that worked for me for several years, "There are two people you don't need to lie to. One is your banker. If you go lie to him, he's sitting right there. He has a bird's eye view of your business and every business in town. It doesn't take him but a minute to know whether or not you are telling him the truth." (You'll have to wonder who the other one is!)

Carey Pollard told the banker I had said that. The banker told me, "Well, Fuller, I sure appreciate you saying that. I am glad that you have lived up to that according to my experience with you." The banker was Mr. T. L. Lindsey, Sr. He ran the Citizen's bank for the Robertsons when I started doing business in 1938, and ran it until he died in 1961.

On the subject of trading mules, Mr. Butler, who was a very fine old gentleman, farmed a good bit and also owned Allen Lumber Company. I've told about his son, Caine, and I buying the lumber company from him, and he was instrumental in my owning a half interest in the Butler Tractor and Implement Company, which later became B & K Tractor and Implement Company. Later I bought Caine Butler's interest and named it Kimbrell Tractor & Implement Company, but we traded for mules; we traded for syrup; we traded for cows; we traded for anything.

One day, we traded over in the edge of Lamar County for a real fine mare that was in foal. Mr. Butler came by and saw that fine mare and he really did like the mare. "I really do like that mare. I just need that mare. I have a place, and I could raise that colt in my pasture. I have a little pair of mules I want to trade for it," said Mr. Butler. I knew about that little pair of mules. I doubt if they weighed 600 pounds apiece. They were small. "Just let me trade you that pair of mules for that mare," Mr. Butler said.

"Mr. Butler, you know Caine and I are struggling. We just don't have any room to play. We need to make everything carry its own way. I don't know what in the world I would ever do with those little ole mules. I am not criticizing them, but they are just not big enough. They are pretty and nice looking," I said.

"Well, just make me an offer," he said.

"Mr. Butler, I'm embarrassed to tell you what I think I need to have," I said.

"Well, just say it," he said.

"I think we ought to have $150 to boot," I said.

"All right. I will trade with you. Bring the mare up there

and get the mules," he said.

The very next day, I sold that little pair of mules for $266 cash. That made nearly $400 I got for the mare and it was worth about $150 or $175. Mr. Butler pouted at me for about two or three weeks. He accused me of robbing him. It was just one of those things that happens in the course of trading.

While I worked at Cannon's, along with the horse trading and other things, I had experience in not only trading mules, but I also had quite an experience trading for oxen. That was during the WPA days when a lot of people would hook up the old bull. A lot of times they castrated the bull and made a steer out of him, and started plowing with him. Of course, they wanted to trade a steer in for a mule. A little while after I started working for Cannon's it fell my lot to do all that sort of trading. I traded mules and quite often when I would go out selling farm machinery I'd run into a fellow and he would say, "Well, Fuller, I remember when you traded for my oxen, or when I traded you a heifer for an ox." I think I've told that I also bought opossum and coon hides when I worked at Cannon's.

One of the interesting things was when I was selling John Deere tractors, I had a good customer who was sheriff and another good customer who owned a store over at Caledonia, Mississippi. They invited me to come over on a Sunday morning for breakfast. Well, it happened they were having trouble with a tractor I had sold over there. I had read that John Deere tractors were so simple to repair — they just had 260 moving parts. All you had to do was take the head off and set all the valves alike and you would be ready to go again. I did just that, but when I put it back together, it just turned around. It had no pressure, so I had to send a mechanic later. Back to the breakfast: Sheriff Harry West had the big breakfast. He had a five gallon galvanized coffee maker — not a percolator — sitting on top of the fire. They had a fire built where they cooked great big center cut slices of country cured ham, and T-bone steaks which were so large one would be all in the world you could eat, if you were really hungry. They had a black man and his wife making great big, delicious looking biscuits. And sitting over in the corner was a five gallon jug of wildcat whiskey.

That coffee was strong enough it could walk off, but when you poured a little wildcat whiskey in it you could handle that center cut ham, the T-bone steak, and those biscuits and redeye gravy. I will always remember that the other host was Levert Robertson. He had a son who was there and he said, "Just go on and eat all you want to because in thy father's pockets are many dimes." That was after he had drunk a couple or three cups of coffee flavored generously good with wildcat whiskey. So I've thought a lot of times and told a lot of times about going to the big breakfast at Caledonia. The characters involved, the food, the coffee, and especially the coffee flavoring, made an otherwise routine occasion quite memorable.

Along about that time, the government announced that they were going to build a big Air Force base at Columbus, Mississippi. It was to be a Strategic Air Command base that would take the B-52s, and it would be a jet training base. Harry West and his wife came one Sunday afternoon when I still lived down on the farm. Harry said, "Mr. Kimbrell, they have come up with the idea we can do good. We can make money. Bring over some tractors and some John Deere rubber-tired wagons. They're going to hire anything at that air base. The government is going to pay big prices and we will haul dirt; we will haul anything with that equipment. We will just do well with it."

"It sure sounds good. I'll come over and check on it," I said.

Sheriff Harry had his wife as a driver, so apparently he was still feeling the effects of the "coffee" even though it was a month or two after the breakfast. But when I went to Columbus later to check on his idea of how we could make big money, he had forgotten what he had talked about. I didn't get to furnish the tractors and rubber-tired wagons for the Columbus Air Force Base.

After the War, while cars were still scarce, you almost had to know somebody to get a new car. Woodrow Roberts, who was the Buick dealer in Fayette, came to me and said, "Fuller, I think I can use your name and get a Buick for you if you want it. I'll sell it to you. We will go to Atlanta and pick it up and I will take care of all the expenses. If you don't want it, I can sell it to somebody else. Caine Butler, your former partner, wants one. We can get at least two or three and bring them back."

"All right," I said.

We caught the train Sunday afternoon. In Alabama it was still "dry," but on the train when you crossed the Georgia line, you could start having a drink, even though it was Sunday afternoon. It happened that Woodrow Roberts had stuck a bottle of gin in his suitcase. When we got across the Georgia line, he called the porter and told him we needed some Seven-ups and cups of ice. The porter brought it, and we all started drinking gin and Seven-up. When we got to Atlanta, we went to the hotel and checked in. There wasn't much open on Sunday night, but we did find two or three places. Although there was a restaurant in the hotel, we decided to look around to see if we could find something we liked better. We found one particular place, upstairs in the building next to the hotel. We looked it over and decided it wasn't fast enough for us. Woodrow was leading the line. He had enough to drink that he knew everything and figured he could handle almost anything. He said, "Come on. I think I know another place." We went up the street and there was another building with a restaurant upstairs. You could tell Woodrow was drinking, and Caine was getting to the point he couldn't handle his. We stopped and asked a policeman who was standing nearby about the restaurant.

"Yes, go right next door and go up the stairs," the policeman told us.

"I think we can make out fine here. We will get some women to dance with us, and we will eat a good meal," Woodrow said. The waiter took us to a table and seated us.

"You all wait right here," Woodrow said. He went over to a table where two ladies were sitting and said to them, "You all come over to our table. We will buy your dinner, and dance with you. We will show you a good time."

"What makes you think we are interested in you?" one of the ladies asked.

He came back to our table and we left. We ended up back at the hotel to eat supper.

That wasn't the end of our trip to Atlanta. Woodrow had made arrangements the next day for us to pick up two cars at the Buick warehouse. So we got the two cars. While we were checking out the cars Woodrow asked, "Fuller, how much farther is it to go by Montgomery? We'll go by there and eat supper."

"I don't know how much farther it is, but the roads are not all that good," I told him.

We went by Montgomery. Of course, he and Caine were riding together, and I made them stay in front so I could see if they were staying in the road. We stopped in Montgomery and ate supper. Before we got home, the car, with them taking turns driving, was wobbling all over the road.

After that episode, I decided I didn't need another Buick. That was my only Buick. I kept it a little while and decided I didn't like it. Reba and I drove it up to North Carolina to visit Governor Folsom and Jamelle. They had gone to North Carolina for a visit. I ran out of gas. The car just barely rolled around a hill to where there was a gas station, and it was already getting dark. We had seen a couple of bears sitting in the road. Since I had a lot of bad experiences with that Buick, I kept it about two months and sold it. I lost $250 on that car. That was when you could buy a new Buick for about $2000.

One of the funny things that happened during the first Folsom administration was with the ABC Board. Dr. Snoddy was chairman of the ABC Board. Back then whiskey agents were one of the subjects newspaper reporters wrote about the most. Some whiskey agents came in one day while the Board meeting was in progress and wanted to list their "spirits" for the state to buy and put on the shelves of the ABC stores. They brought samples of what they wanted listed.

Dr. Snoddy said, "Maybe we should open up some of the samples right here and try them." The story goes that all the members of the board got tight. After the meeting Dr. Snoddy decided to go to Birmingham, but didn't get there because he had a wreck in Anniston. Now Dr. Snoddy was quite a singer in the Old Sacred Harp Song Book, and Hubert Bond wrote an article which was printed in the Alabama magazine about the wreck and about Dr. Snoddy's condition. He wrote, Dr. Snoddy had a Sacred Harp Song Book on the seat right beside him. He wrote, "Sing on Uncle Zee. Sing on Uncle Zeb – with the Sacred Harp Book laying on the seat right beside him."

A member of the cabinet closest to Jim Folsom was O. H. Finney. Bill Lyerly, the chauffeur for Governor Folsom during his first administration, came into the Governor's Office as executive secretary during the second administration, and served as chief of the highway patrol, and also as assistant to the chief of the highway patrol. Bill likes to tell the story about Governor Folsom's and Jamelle's wedding. I've told before about how Governor Folsom met Jamelle Moore at Berry, which was her home town, as well as mine. Reba and I lived north of town out in the country. When we got into office, Governor Folsom sent O. H. Finney, a member of the cabinet closest to him, to me and asked if Jamelle could be my secretary. Of course I said yes.

Governor Folsom and Jamelle were courting all along, but about the time the legislative session was over they decided to get married, and didn't tell anyone but Bill Lyerly. Lyerly took Winston Craig's place as chauffeur that day and drove them to Rockford, Alabama, the county seat of Coosa County, to get Judge Thomas, the probate judge, to perform the wedding ceremony. They had already made arrangements with Judge Thomas to marry them. Bill can really make a good story about it. He said that just as soon as Judge Thomas started the ceremony, Big Jim started kissing Jamelle, and Jamelle said, "Not now, Jim. Wait."

Judge Thomas would repeat another sentence, and Big Jim would try to kiss Jamelle again. Jim said, "Hurry up Judge." "Where's that ring?" he asked.

"I have it," Bill Lyerly said. Big Jim tried to kiss Jamelle again.

Finally, when the ceremony was over, Judge Thomas said, "Now Governor, you may kiss the bride." Bill Lyerly took them back to the mansion for their wedding night.

While campaigning for Folsom in his second term, two carloads of us were going down to a special meeting in Montgomery. Paul Guin, who was in the hardware business in Guin, Alabama, was in the group. Also, he was a member of the Alabama Farm Equipment Association. Paul was a strong supporter of Folsom and one of the campaign leaders. There were no restrooms from Tuscaloosa to Montgomery, so we stopped down the road to go out in the bushes. We were talking about folks you couldn't get to support Folsom or vote for him, and Paul Guin said, "There's another SOB up there I'm going to remember in my prayers." He was talking about a fellow he couldn't persuade to help Folsom in the campaign.

Telling funny things, there is one thing I tell quite often. When I was in the senate, there was a senator from Calhoun County, Tom Blake Howle, who was a veterinarian. He would bring with him an attache', which I always called a horse satchel, and in it he would have a wide mouth mason jar containing wildcat whiskey. All during the day he would reach down, fill a little paper cup, and drink it to keep himself going.

Sitting right next to Tom Blake was a Primitive Baptist preacher from DeKalb County, Senator Burnside. As I've said before we were in a stall all the time. There were five of us senators maneuvering any way we could to keep some of the other senators from taking all the power away from the governor, while trying to get his program through every way we could. Issues would get to going really strong. Burnside, one of the finest fellows you have ever seen, would throw his head back and work his lips. He was praying for Divine guidance. The word got around pretty good that's what he was doing. One day issues were getting pretty hot, and Tom Blake Howle had been down in his mason jar a few times already. Burnside threw his head back and began to pray for Divine guidance, and Tom Blake spoke out loud enough we heard him all over the senate, "Pray a little louder Burnside. I don't know how to vote on this one, myself." One of the secretaries passed about the time Tom

Blake was pouring a little cup full, and said, "I like that perfume. It sure smells good."

South of Montgomery lived a fellow named Joe Elijah who married a girl named Couch from Fayette. The Couchs were a very prominent family in Fayette. Joe would come in to visit me. He owned a farm with a pretty good sized lake on it. Going duck hunting was quite a treat in Montgomery County, because it was seldom cold enough to attract ducks in the winter. It had been cold for several days, so Joe Elijah came in and said, "Fuller, I want you and the governor to come duck hunting out at my place in the morning."

"Wait a minute. Let's walk around to the governor's office," I said. We walked around there—my office was just around the corner from his—and Joe asked him to come duck hunting. Governor Folsom had met Joe Elijah, and I had told him he married a girl named Couch from Fayette.

Folsom said to me, "Yes. We will go. You come by the mansion in the morning and pick me up. Call me before you leave. No, I'll just tell Jack to have me up." I went by the next morning, and sure enough he was up.

We went to Joe Elijah's house on the farm. He had made the blackest coffee you have ever tasted and had a five gallon jug of wildcat whiskey sitting upon a little cook table behind the breakfast room table. He poured some out in a small cream pitcher and then poured some in our coffee. We started drinking that strong black coffee with wildcat whiskey, and it got to tasting pretty good. Then we went out to the lake to shoot ducks.

Governor Folsom was shooting a 12 gauge shotgun, and I had brought a new 12 gauge shotgun. Ducks flew over and he shot. Smoke came out all around, all over his face and everywhere. He yelled out, "Dadgum, what in the hell is wrong with my gun?" He breached it down and saw that he had put a 20 gauge shell in a 12 gauge barrel, and of course, it backfired. We killed a few ducks and went on back to Montgomery.

EPILOGUE

TENNESSEE-TOMBIGBEE COMPACT

While I was finance director, one of the things I am proud I was able to get put in the governor's budget, through working with the legislature, was a special appropriation for the Tennessee-Tombigbee Waterway Compact. In 1956 Governor Folsom, Speaker Rankin Fite, Senators Broughton Lamberth and Neil Metcalf, and I flew down to Jackson, Mississippi to meet with Mississippi's governor, Jamie Coleman. The two governors agreed to organize the Tennessee-Tombigbee Waterway Compact between Alabama and Mississippi.

When we got back to Montgomery, the governor asked me to get a bill introduced into the legislature making the compact official, which at that time was between Alabama and Mississippi. Later Tennessee, Kentucky, and Florida were added, making it a five state compact. The bill was introduced in the house by such outstanding state representatives as Tom Bevill, Albert Brewer, Speaker Rankin Fite, and others. The bill was handled in the senate by Senators Lamberth and Metcalf. The bill carried a $100,000 appropriation for an administrative office, which was to be in Columbus, Mississippi by mutual agreement.

It passed in a limited amount of time both in the house and senate. Shortly after the bill passed, Governor Folsom asked me to bring him the $100,000, so I got the comptroller to bring me a check for the $100,000, which was in line with the appropriation.

Governor Folsom took that check and went over to the Chamber of Commerce meeting being held in Columbus, Mississippi. As soon as he walked into the meeting room he said, "Let's go! Here's my money! Here's my money!" That was the beginning of the Tennessee-Tombigbee Waterway Compact.

Each state was allowed to have five members, appointed by the respective governors, on the compact board. I served for sixteen years as a member of the board and was vice-chairman in 1984 when the first boat went from Mobile to the Tennessee River.

This could have not been more timely, the reason being that Congressman Jack Edwards, a Republican from Mobile who was one of President Nixon's floor leaders, got the project from Mobile to the Tennessee River moving in Congress. President Johnson had authorized the project, and put in a $500,000 appropriation, which meant the Corps of Engineers could start work on it immediately. Thanks to Congressman Jack Edwards, the first bid opening for the Gainesville Lock and Dam was held in 1972. By that time a team made up of Senator Stennis from Mississippi, who was one of the most powerful men in the United States Senate, Congressman Beatty Whitten from North Mississippi, who was Chairman of the Finance Committee in the house, and Alabama's Congressman Tom Bevill, who was

Chairman of the Public Works Committee, was able to get Congress to appropriate money each year at the Corps of Engineers' request when they had plans completed and were ready for another contract.

Some of the board members from each state would appear before Congressman Bevill's committee in support of the Corps of Engineers' requests. Bevill performed his duty as chairman of the Public Works Committee most professionally, and in such a way that our board members were happy. I appeared before his committee almost every year of the sixteen years I served on the board.

When I first heard of the Tennessee-Tombigbee Waterway, it was estimated that it would cost $135 million. By the time the first boat went through in 1984, after quite a long delay by the Environmental Protection Agency and railroad companies, it was completed at a cost just short of two billion dollars. The cost included several locks and dams, boat landings, and recreational parks.

About two months ago, Don Waldon, the present administrator of the Tennessee-Tombigbee Authority, which is still headquarted in Columbus, Mississippi, called and asked, "Fuller, who is Senator Neil Metcalf?"

"He was state senator and one in the original group that went with Governor Folsom to Jackson, Mississippi to call on Governor Coleman, when the Tennessee-Tombigbee Compact was agreed on. When we returned to Montgomery Metcalf drew up the document under which the compact operated," I told him.

Mr. Waldon said, "Well, I have just received and

announcement of Neil Metcalf's death from the Washington Post. It reads that he drew up the document for the Tennessee-Tombigbee Compact, which since has been used throughout the whole United States without change."

As I've said before, Governor Folsom was elected to the surprise of the majority of the people who had control of state government and politics for years. After he was elected, those people thought they could maneuver so they would dictate the key appointments to his cabinet, and still be in control of the state government. When they realized that was not going to happen, one of them, a long-term senator from the Black Belt, got busy and organized the senators to the extent they could stop any part of the governor's program that they wanted to.

Among the top priorities in Governor Folsom's program was revising the fifty-year-old Alabama constitution, which originally was designed to give control of State government to a small minority of citizens. A lot of times, the Governor spoke of it as "a fair vote," which was one of the things that the traditional power brokers objected to most. The poll tax had just been declared illegal, and they lived in fear that the poor folks, including the blacks and poor whites in northwest and west Alabama would be able to vote. Ironically, the low-population, southern "plantation" counties they were trying to keep controlled are now controlled by the people who never had an opportunity to vote before, as a result of various Supreme Court rulings.

June 22, 2001, I will be ninety-two years old. In this book, written in my own words, as I remember them, are some of the highlights in my life I wanted to share with you. I have lived and am still living a good, rich, full life. I have been and am still well blessed.

In summarizing, I am proud I have been able to contribute to my community, county, and state, numerous things that have made a positive difference. Always, in my prayers, I've asked the Lord to grant that my community, county, state, and nation may be a better place for me having lived in it.

Fuller Asbury Kimbrell
May 2000

Presentation of Honorary Doctorate of Laws from University of West Alabama
L – R: Elizabeth Kimbrell, Daphne McCabe, Rick McCabe, Donald Kimbrell,
Fuller Kimbrell, Jim & Cynthia Willingham, Kim and Tom Willingham and Sam Willingham

May 1997

Daughter Cynthia Kimbrell Willingham
March 2000

Fuller Asbury Kimbrell and
son James Donald Kimbrell
1997

Fuller Kimbrell – presentation of
"Yellow-Dog" Democrat Award
Snow Hinton Park
June 1996

Highway 171 Fuller Kimbrell
1997

Fuller and Reba Kimbrell
1995

*Fuller Kimbrell with his daughter Cynthia
and her husband Jim Willingham and their family.*

Donald and Elizabeth Kimbrell and family
June 1999

KIMBRELL'S
104 Aylette Street, Fayette, Alabama
1950
Now: Fuller Kimbrell Drive

Our First Building
1937

First Avenue, N.E.
Fayette, Alabama

Our New Building
1947

104 Aylette St.
Now: Fuller Kimbrell Drive
Fayette, Alabama

My father and mother, and all of my brothers and sisters on my father's 90th birthday –
July 1957.

L to R – Donald Kimbrell, blue ribbon steers, 1st and 2nd place and Harold Dean
Simpson (1st cousin). 1946

Fuller and Reba Kimbrell
1935 - Berry

Fuller and Reba Kimbrell
Reba's birthday party
New Orleans, December 1954

Fuller Kimbrell
1931 – LaPorte, Indiana

"Let's go hunting" – Energetic Frank Boykin tells his guests "Everything is made for love" and they're ready to go hunting. Some of those who can be identified in the picture are Gov. Jim Folsom, checking his gun; Federal Judge Sidney J. Mize, Gulfport, Miss. (center with mackinaw); Congr. Bob Sikes, Crestview, Fla. (with quilted coat); Boykin, at the extreme right, Gov. W. Averell Harriman of New York. His face half-hidden by Folsom's gun barrel is George Federer, German consular. Directly back of Sikes is Congr. Armistead Selden Jr. Directly back of Boykin is Fuller Kimbrell, state finance director. At the extreme right back of Harriman is Ambassador Heinz L. Kredeler of Germany. 1956

Fuller Kimbrell – Finance Director
February 1956

1956 Campaigner – *Tennessee Sen. Estes Kefauver, making his second try for the Democratic presidential nomination, is shown arriving at the Birmingham Airport yesterday. On hand to greet him were Mrs. Dorothy Vredenburgh, secretary of the National Democratic Committee, and State Finance Director Fuller Kimbrell. Kefauver went on to Cullman for a non-political speech last night.*

Democrats Caucas at Montgomery
L to R: Lt. Gov. Hardwick, Ben Ray, Gov. Folsom, John Horne, Roy Mathall, Fuller Kimbrell

Interested

Pictured from left to right – Seated: Lt. Col. Terrance Connell – U.S. Corps of Engineers; Congressman Tom Bevill and Alabama Representative Rankin Fite; Standing: Glover Wilkings – Tenn.-Tombigbee Waterway and Fuller Kimbrell – Tenn.-Tombigbee Waterway.

Alabama leaders and conference – Some of the Alabama state officials who are at Point Clear to help Gov. James E. Folsom entertain visiting governors are shown with their wives. From left, Lt. Gov. Guy Hardwick, Mrs. Hardwick, Mrs. Fuller Kimbrell and State Finance Director Fuller Kimbrell.

The Honorable James Elisha Folsom, Sr.
Governor, State of Alabama

Fuller Kimbrell, Chairman of The Folsom Dedicatory Committee

The Winning Team 1954
George Wallace – Circuit Judge
Senator Fuller Kimbrell, Charley Pinkston – Attorney

At Guin plant dedication – Minnesota Mining and Mfg. Co. officials greeted Alabama visitors Saturday at the dedication of their new plant in Guin. Left to right are H.P. Buetow, Minnesota Mining president; Bert S. Cross, vice president; State Finance Director Fuller Kimbrell, Seventh District Congr. Carl Elliott, House Speaker Rankin Fite and Guin Mayor Rex Wright.

September 16, 1965   Photo from Fayette County Broadcaster

FAYCO OF FAYETTE turned out its millionth foot of metal pipe Tuesday of this week and called in well-wishers to make a ceremony of it. Front row, left to right, Probate Judge Clyde Cargile, Fayco Manager Carey Pollard, Fayco employees James Ary, President Fuller Kimbrell, Mayor Guthrie Smith and Jacob Hodges. In background are Donald Meadows and Odie Maddox. The fast-growing company added metal pipe to their concrete products in October, 1957. Their millionth foot came in less than eight years.

Senator Rankin Fite, Governor James Folsom, Fuller Kimbrell – Finance Director